Tourism Art a

This book examines the relationship between art and tourism through the study of the material culture of tourism: tourist art and souvenirs. It thoroughly examines how to categorise the material culture of tourism within the discourses of contemporary art and cultural anthropology, and demonstrates that tourist art is a unique expression of place and genuine artistic style. The first investigation to consider the activity of souvenirs from both indigenous and settler tourist sites, it brings a unique addition to the existing, dated, research in the area.

Working initially from Graburn's definition of tourist art, as the art of one culture made specifically for the consumption of another, *Tourism Art and Souvenirs* sheds light on important aspects of the souvenir that have not been widely discussed. The most recent research is used to consider how the souvenir is designed and consumed, consumer expectations and influence on the character of the souvenir, how the souvenir maker is consumed by the tradition of heritage and how products become successful as souvenirs. The title also investigates the language involved in the representation of place and the recording of experience through the souvenir, developing a method that expresses the descriptive data of individual souvenir artefacts graphically so that patterns of language may be analysed.

Enhancing the understanding of material culture in tourism, and therefore adding to future tourism development, this volume will be of interest to upper level students, researchers and academics in tourism, culture, heritage and sustainability.

David L. Hume is an Art Historian and Cultural Theorist from Australia. He holds a PhD from the University of Tasmania and has taught in Australia, the UK, Africa and extensively throughout mainland China, teaching Art and Design History and Theory, Tourism Studies and research skills. David currently teaches Communication Art and Design at Burapha University International College, Chonburi, Thailand. His key research interest revolves around the nexus of Art and Tourism, with a special focus on the development and management of heritage and eco-tourist sites and the impact tourism has on traditional crafts. Additionally, David has a deep interest in, and writes regularly on, the history and development of ceramic art.

Routledge advances in tourism

Edited by Stephen Page

School for Tourism, Bournemouth University

1 **The Sociology of Tourism**
Theoretical and empirical investigations
Edited by Yiorgos Apostolopoulos, Stella Leivadi and Andrew Yiannakis

2 **Creating Island Resorts**
Brian King

3 **Destinations**
Cultural landscapes of tourism
Edited by Greg Ringer

4 **Mediterranean Tourism**
Facets of socioeconomic development and cultural change
Edited by Yiorgos Apostolopoulos, Lila Leontidou, Philippos Loukissas

5 **Outdoor Recreation Management**
John Pigram and John Jenkins

6 **Tourism Development**
Edited by Douglas G. Pearce and Richard W. Butler

7 **Tourism and Sustainable Community Development**
Edited by Greg Richards and Derek Hall

8 **Tourism and Political Boundaries**
Dallen J. Timothy

9 **Leisure and Tourism Landscapes**
Social and cultural geographies
Cara Aitchison, Nicola E. MacLeod and Stephen J. Shaw

10 **Tourism in the Age of Globalisation**
Edited by Salah Wahab and Chris Cooper

11 Tourism and Gastronomy
Edited by Anne-Mette Hjalager and Greg Richards

12 New Perspectives in Caribbean Tourism
Edited by Marcella Daye, Donna Chambers and Sherma Roberts

13 The Advanced Econometrics of Tourism Demand
Haiyan Song, Stephen F. Witt and Gang Li

14 Tourism in China
Destination, cultures and communities
Edited by Chris Ryan and Gu Huimin

15 Sustainable Tourism Futures
Perspectives on systems, restructuring and innovations
Edited by Stefan Gössling, C. Michael Hall and David B. Weaver

16 Advances in Tourism Destination Marketing
Managing networks
Edited by Metin Kozak, Juergen Gnoth and Luisa Andreu

17 Drive Tourism
Trends and emerging markets
Edited by Bruce Prideaux and Dean Carson

18 Tourist Customer Service Satisfaction
An encounter approach
Francis P. Noe, Muzzafer Uysal and Vincent P. Magnini

19 Mining Heritage Tourism
A global synthesis
Edited by Michael Conlin and Lee Jolliffe

20 Tourist Experience
Contemporary perspectives
Edited by Richard Sharpley and Phillip Stone

21 Sustainable Tourism in Rural Europe
Edited by Donald Macleod and Steven Gillespie

22 The Critical Turn in Tourism Studies
Creating an academy of hope
Edited by Nigel Morgan, Irena Atelkevic and Annette Pritchard

23 Tourism Supply Chain Management
Haiyan Song

24 Tourism and Retail
Edited by Charles McIntyre

25 International Sports Events
Impacts, experience and identities
Edited by Richard Shipway and Alan Fyall

26 Cultural Moment in Tourism
Edited by Laurajane Smith, Emma Waterton and Steve Watson

27 Contemporary Tourist Experience
Richard Sharpley and Philip Stone

28 Future Tourism
Political, social and economic challenges
James Leigh, Craig Webster and Stanislav Ivanov

29 Information Communication Technologies and Sustainable Tourism
Alisha Ali and Andrew J. Frew

30 Responsible Tourist Behaviour
Clare Weeden

31 Tourist Experience and Fulfilment
Insights from positive psychology
Sebastian Filep and Philip Pearce

32 Tourism Art and Souvenirs
The material culture of tourism
David L. Hume

Forthcoming:

Wellness Tourism
A destination perspective
Cornelia Voigt and Christof Pforr

Human Rights and Global Events
Rebecca Finkel

Dark Tourism and Crime
Derek Dalton

Knowledge Networks and Tourism
Michelle T. McLeod and Roger Vaughan

Tourism Art and Souvenirs

The material culture of tourism

David L. Hume

Routledge
Taylor & Francis Group
LONDON AND NEW YORK

First published 2014
by Routledge
2 Park Square, Milton Park, Abingdon, Oxon OX14 4RN

and by Routledge
711 Third Avenue, New York, NY 10017

First issued in paperback 2017

Routledge is an imprint of the Taylor & Francis Group, an informa business

British Library Cataloguing in Publication Data
A catalogue record for this book is available from the British Library

Library of Congress Cataloging in Publication Data
A catalog record has been requested for this book

ISBN 13: 978-1-138-08196-3 (pbk)
ISBN 13: 978-0-415-83944-0 (hbk)

Typeset in Times New Roman
by Wearset Ltd, Boldon, Tyne and Wear

This book is dedicated to Sandra A. Kent, without whose belief, faith and constant support it would never have been written.

Contents

Illustrations

Figures

Plates

Table

Preface

This project was initially prompted by an interest in why souvenirs have rarely been regarded as significant objects of visual culture by artists, art historians and anthropologists. Considering the artefacts held in anthropological and ethnographic collections, I recognised a number of similarities between museum artefacts of non-Western cultures and tourist art and souvenirs. At first glance, both types of artefact seemed to rely on unique aspects of the culture of production for their attraction. They are both collected during the process of travel, when the collector is dislocated from his or her usual surroundings. Furthermore, the souvenir is usually displayed in an eclectic group of unrelated things, a mode of display much favoured by early museums for the presentation of ethnographic artefacts.

Given these initial, common characteristics, a number of further issues arose regarding the complexity and status of souvenirs: that as an imaginative expression of place, conceived, designed and formed by someone who has come to know the site intimately, the souvenir is a work of art; that if we accept non-Western artists whose skills and expression owe more to tradition than academic training, we need also to appreciate the efforts of artists working from a traditional base within Western culture; that respected indigenous artists, such as Albert Namatjira and many others, have refined their skills through the production of tourist art, and many indigenous artists continue to do so; and that there is a small but growing number of formally trained, settler artists utilising the souvenir market as a way of refining and supporting their fine art practice.

In pursuing the initial question, I discovered that, to the conservative establishment, souvenirs rest somewhere in a void between the anthropological artefact, valued for the information it contains about the culture of origin, and the work of art, with its formalist and aesthetic priorities. The humble souvenir seemed unwanted by both or, at best, grudgingly included, and was considered unauthentic by the anthropologist, because it is made as an object for exchange between cultures and is seen as operating within the Western economic exchange system. It was also cast out of fine art circles, on the grounds that it is kitsch, mass-produced, and that aesthetic and formal standards are compromised by the desire for profit.

In this jaundiced view of such artefacts I recognised similar prejudices that, for some years, had consigned the art of other cultures to museum cabinets and precluded their appreciation as works of art.

In collections, typified by the artefacts and objects that clutter *Wunderkammern* and Cabinets of Curiosity, gathered by early modern travellers, colonial explorers, Grand Tourists, missionaries and anthropologists, I discovered the genesis of the souvenir and formed the opinion that many of the artefacts found in these collections were souvenired by the collector.

Working initially from this understanding of tourist art and souvenirs, I followed a path to discover many important aspects of the souvenir that have, so far, not been widely discussed. By investigating how the souvenir is designed and consumed, I discovered that the maker has not always produced the souvenir freely, but is guided by the traditions of his or her heritage that is, after all, central to the formulation of the tourist attraction itself. Candidly surveying the buying habits of tourists, among the aisles of souvenir outlets, I recognised that the tourist, as consumer, exerts a significant influence on the character of the souvenir through his or her selection habits.

I came to interpret this attraction as fetishistic, and discovered many other characteristics shared by the fetish object and the souvenir, which led me to recognise a need for some sort of analytical assessment of the visual language of souvenirs. In particular, I recognised that objects crafted from an indigenous medium harboured an attraction that is different from those souvenirs produced from generic material, which inturn drew me closer to these modest but complex objects.

Acknowledgements

The author would like to thank the following institutions, enterprises and artists for their contributions to this book: Austin Penney; Aboriginal Studies Press, Canberra, Australia; Berndt Museum, University of Western Australia; Chris Selby; Desart Gallery, Alice Springs, Australia; Geoff Murray; Graham Davis; Jon Rhodes; Kunstkammer, Residenz-museum, Munich, Germany; The Powerhouse Museum, Sydney, Australia; Johnny Possum Tjapaltjarri; Magic Rabbit; Mark Webb; Maruku Arts and Crafts, Australia; The Michael Riley Foundation; National Gallery of Australia; National Museum of Victoria, Australia; Nu-colour-vu; Penny Smith; the estate of Peter Dombrovskis; Queen Victoria Museum & Art Gallery, Launceston, Tasmania, Australia; Simon Rose; Staatliches Museum für Volkerkunde, Dresden, Germany; Tasmanian Museum and Art Gallery, Australia; Umbarra Cultural Centre, Narooma, New South Wales, Australia.

I would also like to to recognise the support of the Tasmanian School of Art and Emeritus Professor Jonathan Holmes for their assistance in developing this research.

Every effort has been made to contact copyright holders for their permission to reprint material in this book. The publishers would be grateful to hear from any copyright holder who is not here acknowledged and will undertake to rectify any errors or omissions in any future editions of this book.

1 Introduction

> While tourism looked squarely in the eye is less attractive, almost shameful, to the principled and actively curious, we are all addicted to it. The compulsion to travel – to look, to perceive, to absorb and perhaps even understand something that will alter one's preconceptions – is deeply ingrained in Western culture.
>
> (Lippard 1999b: 87)

Today these sentiments resound in almost every corner of the globe. Tourist towns, from the southern-most tip of Australia to the far northern outposts of the North American continent, harbour a relationship with their seasonal visitors that is shaded with, largely unspoken, resentment, shame, or, at least, ambivalence. It is resentment not so much for the tourists themselves, but for the reliance upon tourism that has replaced a former mode of existence. A way of life that once offered what is, romantically, perceived as a better way. These idylls are the grist of tourist brochures and other promotional forms. They are represented through carefully selected images of pristine and picturesque vistas that allude to a way of life that may now only be sampled in short blocks of time, in controlled and often artificial environments. Such images situate the potential tourist in a time warp, in which he or she can experience pleasures and satisfactions, promoted in such images that are now rare, unknown and even forbidden, in the tourist's daily environment. Many such idylls now survive only in the representation of heritage, large and small, and are contrived for the benefit of the tourist in formalised theme parks, eco attractions, spectacles and souvenirs.

If the images presented in glossy tourist brochures, with their idyllic view through the window, function as the opening bracket that marks off a period of unsustainable hedonism, in the form of the annual holiday, then the souvenir operates as the closing bracket that, like the holiday snap, sustains the experience and marks the end of the holiday mode. For, as an aide-memoire, the souvenir's power rests in its ability to drag the experience of the destination into the tourist's ordinary life and that activity is, moreover, the subject of this project.

Tourism is a highly organised and sophisticated activity, formed of large ephemeral social groups that come together for a fortnight or so in an unfamiliar environment. Like other social groups, tourists develop characteristics that help bind them together. This solidarity occurs through many behavioural patterns that have, at their core, the penchant for excess. While the tourist is on holiday, he or she is liberated from the daily routine of work, rest, and play. For the short period of the holiday, he or she does not have to think about where the next meal is coming from, or getting to work on time – play, in the form of leisure, is in the ascendant. As a result, tourists will spend more money in a fortnight than they would normally spend in a month at home.[1] Such is the nature of excess among a tourist society, that it constitutes the main ingredient of the glue that binds the ephemeral community together. It is the single most identifiable characteristic of tourist culture and, sometimes, not without a painful effect on the host culture.

There are many examples of destinations spoiled by their popularity, while some are indeed characterised as much by the continued presence of tourists as by their own unique features.[2] For the most part the attractions endure through careful management, while it is the attendant host society that, in some way, produced the destination that undergoes the most significant change. These alterations may be summarised as 'social and economic' (Smith, V. 1977: 4–5).[3] At worst tourism results in the 'disruption of the local economic system' (ibid.).[4] Even if less evident, however, tourism's effects on the social structure of the host community are just as far-reaching. Smith suggests that 'the effects of tourism upon the lives and worldview of an indigenous population are subtle, and usually only recognised by the people themselves and the anthropologist who was there before and after tourism' (ibid.: 7). It is these structural alterations to the host culture that most affect the art and craft of that community. For many social theorists and anthropologists, culture is the glue of social cohesion and, according to Greenwood (1977), this glue comes unstuck under the pressure of tourism.[5]

This is a rather pessimistic view of tourism, and one I intend to counter through the course of this project. It is my contention that if the intention of, say, the ritual dance or artefact is communication and social cohesion, and it has endured many generations without drastic change to its meaning and purpose, then it is likely to be robust enough to communicate between different cultures. Rather than being destroyed, as Greenwood would have it, the aim of the souvenir artefact is altered and it now communicates to and coheres the ephemeral community of tourists, and provides a path of integration between guest and guest, host and host, guest and host, or tourist and destination.[6] Indeed, as MacCannell (1976: 53), among others points out, 'In some areas, local handicrafts would have passed into extinction except for the intervention of mass tourism and the souvenir market.'

The most enduring evidence of the tourist's consumption is to be found in the art and craft directed to this ephemeral society, for like all societies, or communal groups, tourism produces a particular style of art in the form of the souvenir. As an artefact of tourism, the humble souvenir serves many purposes. From the perspective of the producer, the souvenir needs to represent the culture and heritage of the tourist destination, that is, his or her home or part thereof: the more nodes of heritage that can be tastefully invested in the souvenir by the maker, and recognised by the consumer, the better. An object made from a material indigenous to the tourist destination is a good start. If the object represents some aspect of the destination's heritage, then all the better, and, if it carries with it the mark of the maker, who happens to be a local craftsperson, then better still. In this transition, formerly utilitarian artefacts are altered through artistic imagination and may be bracketed somewhere between art work and anthropological artefact, as I will demonstrate.

For fine art objects and anthropological artefacts, some authentication is required, such as title, maker, date and medium. For the souvenir, however, authentication is differently described. The date of production is relatively unimportant, as the date of collection takes precedence. This date is locked in through the memory of the collector, and the collector's experience of the site, and the souvenir will assist in the recollection of the experience. In this respect the souvenir is a geographic artefact, rather than a historical object, in that it privileges place before time. The name of the producer is also frequently subsumed by that of the collector and, as I will show later, the object often becomes known as part of an esteemed collection that refers to the travel experiences of the collector. The individual title of the souvenir is also of minimal importance and defers in preference to a generic description that refers to the place of collection and/or culture of production. In many cases, as will become apparent, the medium of the souvenir assumes priority, especially when it is unique to the destination.

The difficulty with souvenirs rests in their selection, relying on a sort of commercial foraging activity. Unlike a conventional object of fine art, presented in a gallery, against an austere neutral background, the souvenir appears with a jumble of other such goods, vying for attention. In a gallery or museum the collector understands that the object is a work of art and that it is good, or at least accorded some value and status of aesthetic worth. The same may be said of the anthropological artefact in that the museum lends status and authenticity to the object, if not to its aesthetic quality. In this respect, the presence of the souvenir in a museum works against the museum's scholarly authentication of the anthropological artefact, but that is a complex area that I will elaborate on, and clarify, at a later stage.

In the case of the work of art, the value of the object is implied by the setting, but for the souvenir, which I might add will be shown to be at times also a work of art, the place of collection is paramount.[7] That is, while the work of art must be of value in itself, the souvenir's key value is in its ability to mark the collector's experience of the site, and that is a very different aesthetic judgement.[8]

The souvenir collector must engage in a value judgement based on his or her own knowledge and understanding of the site: what materials are endemic to the site and what skills, crafts and aesthetic values are bound historically within the culture. Then, above all, the tourist must trust his or her own aesthetic judgement and always be on guard against fraudulent imitations, such as coffee mugs emblazoned with Australian flags and emblems that are made in China, or plywood boomerangs. If art is a matter of aesthetics, then aesthetic judgement would seem to receive greater independent exercise in the markets, tourist precincts, roadside stalls and souvenir shops than in art galleries and museums, where aesthetics and taste are institutionally defined and served up to the viewer on a neutral tone plinth. In the souvenir shop, the only guide to taste is in the labels attached to the artefact, perhaps some advice from the proprietor and, most importantly, the buying habits of other tourists.

The tourist must measure the quality of the work against the souvenir's ability to record the touristic experience. In so doing, the tourist, as collector, will tend to discount the artistic merit of the object in favour of the object's ability to sustain the experience. In this, the collector is prepared to accede to the surplus value of the object, a value that is not inherent in the material or labour involved in the object's production or in artistic merit.[9] For the souvenir collector, the primary value is initially invested by the maker and enhanced by the collector's perceived value of the object as a marker of place and experience. This capacity – to mark and sustain the tourist's experience – adds significant value to the artefact, a value that has more to do with the tourist's overwhelming need to lock the experience onto a material anchor than the worth of the artefact, which can obscure aesthetic shortcomings in the souvenir artefact. But, like all art, it is the principle of exchange, the exchange of experience and information and emotional response, that is at the core of the souvenir's function.

In their selection of souvenirs, tourists tend to act as a cohesive group and seek not only an object that will serve as a mnemonic device to recall the experience, but one that also demonstrates that experience to others of the group and previous groups. In this way, the cohesiveness of tourism extends historically. The collection of similar souvenirs, travel art and the material culture of other societies by early travellers and explorers provides a starting point from which it is possible to detect the development and transition of many objects, from functional artefact within the culture of origin, to souvenirs with a more expanded language. To explore this further, it is necessary to backtrack through the long, formative history of contemporary tourism and the collection of material goods from 'Other' cultures. In glancing backwards, I will demonstrate the historical precedence of the claims I have made here with regard to touristic behaviour and souvenir collection.

Method of assessment

The aim of this book is to investigate how one might categorise the material culture of tourism within the discourses of contemporary art and cultural anthropology and, in part, to demonstrate that tourist art is a unique expression of place and genuine artistic style. Although a number of researchers have considered the objects of tourism and their place within the history of material culture, this is the first investigation to consider the activity of souvenirs from both indigenous and settler tourist sites. This book investigates the common expression and language involved in the representation of place and the recording of experience through the souvenir.

Through the course of this project I have come to recognise five key components in the language of souvenirs. I have then been able to develop a method that expresses the descriptive data of individual souvenir artefacts graphically, so that the patterns of the language may be analysed in accordance with the principles of Structural Anthropology.[10]

Until now, souvenirs have been divided into two groups: the 'Sampled' and the 'Representative' (Stewart 1984). This binary division of souvenirs was established on the grounds that Sampled souvenirs are souvenirs of individual experience that are not available as general consumer goods (ibid.: 138). These objects are collected directly by the tourist, with no intervention or mediation by the host culture. They often take the shape of sea shells or pebbles washed smooth by the tide, wild flowers, dried and pressed, or animal remains.

This type of souvenir collecting finds its history in those collections of 'Naturalia' (Pearce 1995: 32) gathered by the scientific company of early explorers and conforms to what Pearce (ibid.) calls a 'systematic mode of collection', in that the imperative was to relate the exotic samples to a known botanical system.

Stewart's (1984: 138) Representative category includes 'souvenirs of exterior sights … which most often are representations and are purchasable'. Here Stewart places all other souvenirs. They are objects that may properly be called artefacts in that they are produced from human mediation and interpretation. This category embraces, on the one hand, postcards, wilderness posters and calendars and, on the other, crafted objects, such as Stewart's own example of a miniature basket (ibid.) and other crafted souvenirs like clay pots, didgeridoos, boomerangs, lathe-turned timber trinkets, models and postcards. In short, Stewart's Representative category includes souvenirs made from both endemic and generic materials. It is clear, from this range of souvenir artefacts, that there is the need to subdivide this category.

As a result, I have established a new 'Crafted' category of souvenirs that distinguishes between those artefacts crafted from endemic materials and those produced from generic media. This is achieved by recognising the deficiencies in Stewart's division of souvenirs into two categories: the Sampled and the Representative. First, it fails to recognise the relationship, based on media, that exists between artefacts contained in the two categories and, second, it does not address the difference between a souvenir crafted from an endemic material and a souvenir produced from generic media. The new Crafted category is epitomised by artefacts that function as Sampled souvenirs, through their endemic medium yet, at the same time, operate as Representative souvenirs because the endemic medium is modified through craft, often to represent the heritage of the visited site, and presented as a purchasable commodity. The Crafted category is established on the basis that the production of this type of souvenir is developed from the traditional use of endemic materials. As a result, the revised Representative category now accounts for souvenirs made from a generic medium, such as postcards.

However, the selection of raw materials, design and manufacture of souvenir artefacts accounts for only one part of the process by which certain artefacts are framed as souvenirs. It is only when the artefact is consumed by the tourist that it functions as a souvenir. In order to fully establish the new Crafted category I examine how souvenirs from this group function differently to those from the other categories.

This is achieved by analysing the visual language of souvenirs, as artefacts of cross-cultural exchange. The visual codes of these artefacts contain information about the site and/or culture they depict. The destination is consumed by the tourist who, in turn, invests the artefact with his or her narrative for the purpose of recording the experience of that site and/or culture. Depending on the type of souvenir, the subsequent narrative is shown to develop in different ways, resulting in different patterns of expression from the three distinct groups of souvenir.

For this to happen, the artefact in question must first attract the eye of the tourist and ultimately act as a material anchor for the reiteration of the tourist's experience. The souvenir must make the tourist's holiday tales believable or, at least, enhance and sustain the experience once the holiday has finished. This is the prime responsibility of souvenirs that, in the Crafted and Representative categories, occurs through the exchange of narrative between cultures. This narrative is initiated by the maker and advanced by the collector.

In Chapter 2, I examine the cross-cultural exchange of information from a historical perspective. I show how the fascination with the artefacts of exotic cultures dates back, at least, to the Roman Empire. Then how the souveniring impulse begins to emerge with the early modern collection of the artefacts of other cultures (by colonial explorers, missionaries and early anthropologists, as the agents of colonial contact) and then was fully developed during the Romantic period through the agency of the Grand Tourist.

This latter period saw the display of exotic artefacts in *Wunderkammer* collections, which enabled the collector to demonstrate the exotic places and cultures that 'he' had experienced. From this I recognise a similar pattern of display to that of the contemporary souvenir, and I show how both collections operate to enhance what Phillips and Steiner (1999: 3) term the 'knowledge, power and wealth' of the collector. In turn, both the *Wunderkammer* and souvenir collections are shown to operate as material anchors for the collector's stories about exotic people and places, or holiday anecdotes.

My next move is to scrutinise the collecting motive of the anthropologist as the proto-tourist. Here I show that the anthropologist and the tourist have much in common: both spend prescribed periods of time away from their usual environment, immerse themselves in exotic environments and cultures, and seek to record their experiences by the collection of exotic, material goods. Moreover, it is in the collection of the art and craft of other cultures that the habits of the tourist and the anthropologist are most closely related.

It has been pointed out, during this research, that many anthropologists have disregarded tourist art as a genuine cultural artefact, specific to the subject of their inquiry. It was not until 1976 that Graburn recognised the value of tourist art as a signifier of cultural change and adaptation. In Chapter 3, I analyse Graburn's typology of tourist art and find that, while its scope is restricted to the tourist art of exotic indigenous cultures, it provides an excellent typology from which to begin to assess the language of all souvenirs.

In Chapter 4, I investigate how the language of souvenirs, as artefacts of travel, functions. To achieve this I examine the structure of the fetish in the belief that souvenirs operate in much the same manner. Here I detect five common elements.

First, in accordance with Freud's (1962) theory of the fetish, and based on the Oedipus complex, souvenirs operate as a substitute for that which is no longer available. Fetish objects, like souvenirs, are fragments of an experience from which the whole subject of the experience is imaginatively reconstructed.

Second, the projection of the whole from the fragment permits the placation and integration of a difficult memory, such as the end of the holiday period. The collection of souvenirs not only helps to sustain the holiday experience, but the holiday anecdote is made more credible if it can be anchored to a material form.

The idea that the fetish object, embodied in the souvenir, could have meaning to anyone other than the collector presented a problem for my ensuing study and called for a re-assessment of the way in which the narrative, attached to the fetish object, functions. Conventionally the fetish object's narrative is understood as being circular and restricted to the collector. With recourse to ethnographic collections, notably those of 'primitive' art and artworks from the West, I have been able to show that the fetishistic narrative has the capacity to develop beyond the closed circular system, in which meaning is restricted to the collector. This is achieved by tracking the subsequent reception of one-time fetish objects and artworks from objects of furtive and personal satisfaction to their current public display within the museogallery system.

Surplus value is the next common element that I deal with. Here I examine Marx's (1951) ideas of the way in which value is invested in material goods under the capitalist system of production. This has to do with the way the meaning of certain artefacts is communally authorised. I have shown that the souvenir not only has the ability to conjure up the entire holiday experience and, as such, is invested with a surplus value by the tourist, but also that this capacity is inherent in the price the tourist is prepared to pay for the souvenir.

The final common element, shown to exist between the fetish object and souvenir, is the serial nature of both objects. In order to represent a tourist destination, the souvenir relies on 'its conformity to 'traditional' style' (Steiner 1999: 96), which results in a canonical range of souvenirs. Tourists collect the same objects by which to record their experience of the destination, authorised and sustained, in part, by the ephemeral community of tourists. Within this research, this is interpreted as a communal fetish for the same or similar objects, which, in turn, supports the notion that the fetish object has meaning beyond the furtive and deeply personal. This interpretation of the fetish is not confined to the study of souvenirs alone, but may also be applied to the study of museogallery collections, with respect to the altered reception of artefacts, due to changing economic and social conditions.

The serial production of souvenirs is investigated, more closely, in Chapter 5 where I cite a number of examples and trace the development of traditional style and its application to tourist art and souvenirs. Through examples drawn from ethnographic collections of Australian Aboriginal and Canadian First Nations artefacts, here I show how design and style may be adapted from traditional purpose and applied to the production of canonical artefacts, made for the purpose of satisfying the tourist gaze. For instance, I argue that the monochrome linear representation of events, traditional to the Koori people of the Southeastern Australian mainland, has been applied, through the pokerwork technique, to the decoration of souvenir artefacts. I also contend that miniaturisation and the use of introduced materials is common in the production of 'traditional' souvenir artefacts and, furthermore, that this affects the visual expression of those souvenirs.

In the final chapter I analyse the language of indigenous and settler souvenirs with reference to the following: the anthropologist's priority for the object/artefact to represent the culture of the site; the need for the object/artefact, housed in the *Wunderkammer* collection, to testify to the collector's 'knowledge, power and wealth', (Phillips and Steiner 1999: 3) and the activity of the fetish embodied in such object/artefacts. From this I am able to establish a typology of the visual language of souvenirs, through which the expression of all souvenirs may be assessed.

The language of souvenirs is found to be comprised of five main components. They are:

a Medium
b Maker's mark
c Relational
d Invitational
e Iconofetish

Each of these narrative components is present, to some degree, in the expression of all souvenirs. By assessing the degree to which each narrative component exists in individual souvenirs I have been able to map the expressive patterns of numerous souvenir objects and artefacts. This results in three distinct patterns of expression, specific to the three groups of souvenir, which, in turn, has enabled me to identify three discrete categories of souvenir: Sampled, Crafted and Representative.

In the development of this typology I have, in Chapter 6, analysed a considerable number of souvenirs and other artefacts and objects to demonstrate how their expression may be read as a type of language. Like language, most, if not all, of the examples I have cited have developed organically from the heritage of the people and place that the artefacts have come to represent. Aboriginal artefacts, such as coolamons, nula-nulas, shields and boomerangs, have come to be understood as symbolic of the Aboriginal people's long engagement with the Australian continent. Likewise, the Dombrovskian school of landscape photography developed out of a sensitivity toward the Tasmanian environment that emerged in the 1970s and matured with the world-wide campaign to save the Franklin River during the early 1980s. The same may be said of other souvenirs, such as Tasmanian woodcrafts and similar artefacts cited in this project, including those from the First Nations of the Canadian West Coast.

Some, like the boomerang, are steeped in thousand-year-old traditions; others, such as the Dombrovskian style of landscape photography, are less entrenched but equally symbolic of the social system and culture of the period and place that produced the artefacts. The function of these artefacts, framed as souvenirs, is, in a way, to carry the spirit of that period into the future and, in that activity, souvenirs are, as Stewart (1984: 135) claims, 'historical objects' that look backward and museumify the people and places they represent. They are ghosts with substance, or the body of the past.

From my initial qualification of the Crafted category I show that the medium from which the souvenir is constituted is the primary criterion of this group of souvenirs. This is recognised in the assessment of the medium from which the souvenir is produced, and plotted graphically along the *Medium* axis. The emphasis of this axis favours Stewart's Sampled group of souvenirs, as the object is completely reliant upon its natural medium and form to mark the site. To that end, I have allocated a numeric value of ten (10) to a souvenir whose expression is generated solely from its raw material in its natural form. In contrast, the souvenir made from a generic medium is situated at the other end of the scale, while a souvenir crafted from an endemic material is plotted in the middle of the scale.

This criterion is also accounted for when considering the mediation of the souvenir's raw material, its interpretation and manipulation under the hand of the artist/craftsperson. The capacity of the selected raw material to represent the site and/or culture is tested by the creative pressure applied by the maker and plotted graphically along the *Maker's mark* axis.

When the substance of the souvenir is strong in its narrative, the form delineated by the maker is less important. However, an enticing form, articulated from a robust substance, is shown to produce a souvenir of enhanced narrative qualities, bearing significant invitational features. This may be extended further when utility and play are among those qualities. Through play, meaning and understanding are enhanced and made easier to appreciate; they are brought closer to the viewer and their function more easily understood and integrated. It is the meaning of the artefact, the quality of what is brought to mind, its function as a mnemonic device, that is crucial to the activity of any object/artefact as a souvenir. This interactive capacity of the souvenir is plotted along the *Invitational* axis.

I show, in Chapter three, how the souvenir's meaning is understood according to the priorities of the ethnographic artefact. Both artefacts share the same traditional base and are interpreted by both the anthropologist and the tourist as being representative of the site and/or culture from which they were collected.

Meaning is bound up in narrative and within the structures of this typology it is discussed first as inherent meaning: what or whom the artefact relates to through its substance and form. In the first instance a simple narrative is gleaned from the raw material. In the case of artefacts made from rare timbers, examined in this project, the raw material is specific to the site. Like the Sampled souvenir or the exotic flora and fauna collected by early explorers, this robust medium alone is enough to bear testament to the collector's experience of the site.

A more complex critique comes with a study of the status of that meaning and how it is propelled or sustained. Most souvenirs are born out of heritage, growing and mutating organically through human interpretation and imagination that is initiated by contact with other cultures and systems of visual communication. Over time, the successful souvenir comes to be taken as the immutable symbol of the culture and place of its origin. This is shown to restrict or confine the imaginative interpretation of the souvenir makers to a canonical range of souvenirs. While offering some economic freedom, the successful souvenir is found to place some hard and fast rules regarding the type of artefact that is understood to represent any specific site and culture. These are the iconic souvenirs, authorised as much by tourism as the culture that produces them. They have developed from the strange things, collected by early explorers and travellers, whose meaning and purpose was known only to the collector and so took on a fetishistic character, that have since expanded to become, in many cases, the symbols of peoples, states and nations.

By bringing these narrative components together, and expressing them in graphic form, it can be seen that the resultant patterns describe three basic expressions, incumbent in each souvenir category. The resultant patterns give a clear indication of the capacity of any object/artefact to represent place and/or culture.

As an analytical tool, this typology is concerned with the way art, craft and other objects function between cultures. It is flexible enough to assess the material culture and souvenirs of all cultures that come under the gaze of the tourist. It achieves this by identifying the key narrative components of the souvenired object, as set out in Chapter 6 of this book. By assessing the volume of those features it is possible to discover the souvenir potential of all artefacts and objects. Furthermore, it is at the five key narrative points that the strengths and weaknesses, the efficiency of the object/artefact, framed as a souvenir, are described, debated and assessed.

With the increasing development and formalisation of many tourist destinations, this typology provides a useful framework that illustrates the necessary features of the souvenir. It shows how one narrative component may be enhanced by another through craft, and should be consulted by those engaged in the development, production and evaluation of objects, artefacts and works of art as souvenirs, in order to achieve the best design practice.

2 The European collection of 'Other' cultures

A historical structure from which to assess tourist art and souvenirs

Introduction

This chapter presents a historical overview of the European collection of 'Other' cultures. Beginning with the pre-modern collection of curio objects, during the Roman period, I consider the reception of exotic artefacts, gathered by very early explorers, and their relationship to fine art. I then discuss early modern collections of similar goods and focus on the presentation of such collections in the form of the *Wunderkammer*. Here I examine the meaning of these collections and the way they enhance the collector's social status in the light of the developing colonial project. The final part of this chapter examines the mature colonial project and introduces the role of the anthropologist in gathering exotic artefacts. Here I present examples from anthropologists working in Australia during the first half of the last century and suggest that the relationship between anthropology and tourism is sustained in the activity of present day tourism.

Pre-modern collecting

Exchange through trade is a relative newcomer in the Western accumulation of the artefacts of 'Other' cultures. Early collections took the form of natural history samples and scraps of material booty (Impey 1977: 17) that eventually found their way into important museums. Collection through plunder and the accumulation of illicit booty haunts most museums around the world. Today, some rehabilitation is occurring, while many museums steadfastly hang on to exhibits that, by today's moral standards, were obtained by theft. I will show, in later sections, how the plundering of the natural environment remains a primary mode of souveniring. For it is a matter of scale only that separates the collection of wildflowers from the illicit harvesting of rare timbers, a child's butterfly collection from safari trophies, or my own fossil and mineral collection from the appropriation of land believed to be *terra nullius*.

The Romans displayed an appreciation for exotic goods, especially silk and also imported exotic animals, fur and wood (ibid.: 20; Pearce 1995: 7–108). In the example of wood, one can detect an appreciation for the aesthetic nature and quality of exotic timber that thrives today in the esteem afforded the rare timbers from Tasmania and many other parts of the world. Such is the enduring power of this material to mark the site of origin, that the desire to own a small sample of numerous rare timbers has spawned a profitable trade in small wooden souvenir artefacts from forested areas around the globe.

By the Middle Ages, the 'trade' in religious relics was established and occupied the display cabinets of many wealthy collectors. Among them was the Duc de Berry, who, unlike many of his contemporaries, extended his collection to include Eastern works of art and other curiosities (ibid.). In fourteenth and fifteenth century Italy, porcelain vessels were afforded a special place in most households; partly from the belief that they could reveal poisons contained within, but also for their rarity. Like exotic timber, porcelain then also bore the signature of its origin, not just in its form and decorative motif, but in the unique quality of the exquisite material, as the capacity to reproduce it in Europe was absent (ibid.). However, unlike exotic timbers, this capacity to mark its place of origin is today reduced, with many potters around the globe producing fine porcelain. Today, most ceramicists engaged in the souvenir trade need to mark the site of origin through motif, image and design.

Colonial collecting

With the discovery of the Americas and a sea route to India in the early sixteenth century, the spread and collection of Eastern goods and artefacts to Northern and Western Europe took on a different purpose. Now the importation of trade goods was accompanied by objects of natural history and curios from exotic cultures. Such was the array of exotic curios that scholars, bankers and princes from all over Europe 'scoured Lisbon for curiosities – gold jewellery from Siam, exotic woods, sea shells, parrots, textiles, drugs, amber were almost as much in demand as spice and porcelain' (ibid.: 20). This period also saw the rise of botanical gardens and menageries packed with exotic flora and fauna. The influence of these expansive collections can be seen in the work of the late fifthteenth and early sixteenth century Dutch artist, Albrecht Durer, who is known to have traded woodcuts for exotic curiosities (ibid.). Indeed, Durer's famous *Rhinoceros* print is an elegant example of an artist's impression of an exotic animal and what it might have looked like, extracted from the description of a traveller. In his anatomical misconception, the artist has produced an image of a creature from hearsay, just as many exotic creatures are abstracted by artists and crafts people for the benefit of tourists today.

It was approaching the middle of the sixteenth century that the initial formulation of the souvenir emerged in the form of an ivory chest from Sri Lanka, then Ceylon, (Plate 2.1) in which Europeans are featured in the detail (ibid.). This is, perhaps, among the earliest record of a representation of European colonials in an indigenous art form made for export. As an indigenous response to colonialism, the carved scene on the front of this chest points quite clearly to the power relationship of colonialism, the central panel depicting the feasting and leisure activity of wealthy travellers that is part and parcel of tourism today.

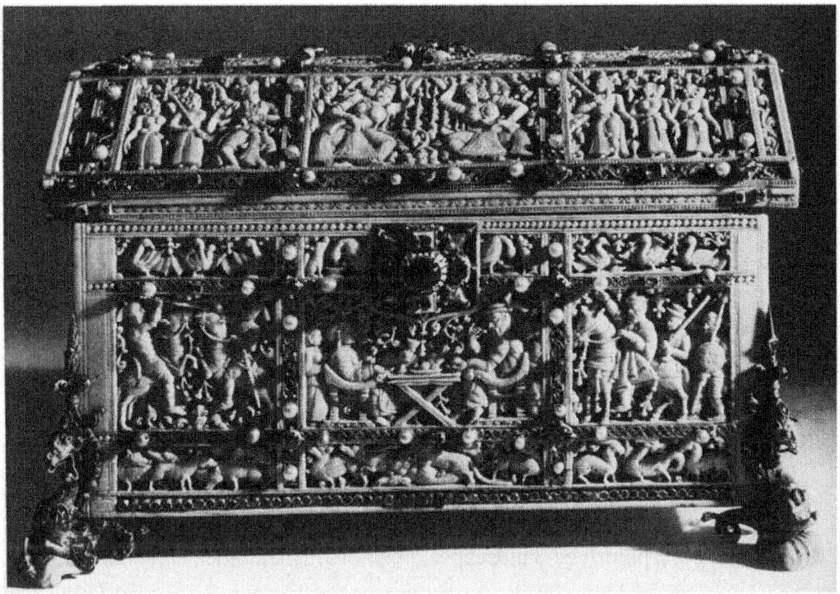

Plate 2.1 Ivory Casket with carved relief, Ceylon 1541. Collection: Kunstkammer, Residenz-museum, Munich, Germany.

Early modern collecting

During the seventeenth century, Germanic rulers began to formulate the *Wunderkammer* (wonder chamber), as a marker of their status within the familiar environment and knowledge of the expanding world. The *Wunderkammer* is conventionally defined as a square, windowless room that became the repository for private collections of curiosities (Alexander 1979). Pearce cites a number of terms that describe the space in which various collections were housed, ranging from '*studio, studiola, galleria* and *museo*' (author's italics) used in sixteenth century Italy, to the German '*Kammer*, meaning "room" or "chamber", to which would be added *Wunder* ("wonder") *Kunst* ("art") or *Schatz* ("treasure") as appropriate' (1995: 109). As for the English term 'Cabinet of Curiosities', Pearce (ibid.) informs us this might refer to 'the small room in which the whole collection was housed, or the cupboards which held it, or the collection itself'.

The keeping places in which these collections were housed may be likened to those of the inner sanctum or closet. Over time, the sheer mass of many collections reached such grand proportions that they were subsequently re-housed for the purpose of public display. This eventually led to the emergence of today's public museum and gallery systems.

One of the largest *Wunderkammer* collections at this time belonged to Archduke Albrecht of Bavaria, which was documented by Dr Samuel Quickberg and published as the 'Museum Theatrum' in 1667 (Impey 1977: 67). In this catalogue it is possible to find evidence of the seventeenth century organisation and classification of the artefacts and objects as they were developed for such vast and eclectic collections. This catalogue shows that the collection was organised around familiar and valuable objects. It further demonstrates how the division of the collection, into five separate categories, situates the collector at the centre of the collection and testifies to his knowledge and power. Radiating out from the centre, the categories are:

1 Objects pertaining directly to the collector
   a Objects of religion.
   b Objects pertaining to the owner's family
   c Views and descriptions of Bavaria – including maps
   d Local flora and fauna.

2 Sculpture, coins, medals and goldsmith's work.
3 All forms of natural history (including most exotic [Eastern] artefacts).
4 Scientific and musical instruments.
5 Works of art, paintings, landscapes, portraits, genealogies and coats of arms.

(Ibid.: 73)

This categorisation clearly privileges the collector and the home, as the point from which the curiosities of the collection are ordered. First it is demonstrated, through the collectors' own family history and immediate environment at the centre of the collection, how less familiar objects are organised. This is enhanced through the material culture of the immediate society and emplacement of the collector within that society, as witnessed through the four subdivisions of the primary category. In subcategory 1c it can be seen how descriptions of Bavaria are separated from the descriptions of other places that are contained in category 5. From this it may be understood that the sites depicted within 1c were familiar and verifiable. On the other hand, those images and artefacts within categories 3 and 5 are more clearly seen as the wondrous places from afar. The centrality of the collector is further enforced by the physical structure of the display, in which those objects contained in category 1 rest at the heart of the collection. It is interesting, too, that the exotic images and material, collected from far away places, rest on the periphery and are, as such, the most visible. In this display structure it is possible to view not just the value of the family heirlooms, resting at the secure centre but, more importantly in the context of this project, the significance of first impressions and the desire to make a display of those things collected from afar, an organisational structure of this *Wunderkammer* that sees the visible and the valuable working in opposition.

If we take Albrecht of Bavaria's collection as an example, it can be seen that it is arranged in a series of clusters that move towards the centre, where the 'inner sanctum' circle begins to reveal the most intimate details of the Duke and his family. We might look at contemporary families and their households in the same way and recognise a similar curatorial organisation in the display of exotica, artworks and souvenirs on the mantlepiece or sideboard, through to the chests of drawers, filing cabinets and jewellery boxes harbouring more personal details displayed less overtly in more private locations.

In Britain such collections were formulated as 'cabinets of curiosities' and took the form of locked cupboards or sideboards, that, in the convention of the German *Wunderkammer*, spilled out into anterooms as the collections grew. The most documented of these collections was gathered by the Tradescants and later fell into the hands of Elias Ashmole. Subsequently it formed the foundational collection of the Ashmolean Museum, the first public museum in Britain.[1] This collection was vast and eclectic and included flora and fauna samples housed in a botanical garden, a menagerie in South London and an extensive array of what was then termed artificialia, that is small works of art (Pearce 1995; Impey 1977; MacGregor 1985).

Opened on 16 May 1683, the Ashmolean Museum permitted public access from the onset and, from all accounts, bore little resemblance to today's austere institutions, characterised by glass cabinets and gilded rope. Instead, the exhibits were displayed within touching distance of the public and were, according to one German visitor, fortunate to survive the tactile inquiry of the British public, 'since the people impetuously handle everything in the usual English fashion and ... even the women are allowed up here for sixpence; they run here and there, grabbing at everything and taking no rebuff from the sub-custos' (Pearce 1995: 73). This quaint, rudimentary and, today, impractical curatorial practice may now be witnessed in souvenir shops and craft and tourist galleries around the world, where the intimate scrutiny of the artefact precedes collection.

Just as the Tradescent collection passed to Elias Ashmole and then, by deed of gift, to Oxford University, so the eighteenth century saw the waning of private curio collections in the hands of the nobility and the well-to-do. The cause of this was the burgeoning trade that went hand-in-hand with the industrial revolution and the capitalist exchange system, which rendered many curiosities no longer particularly curious through their increasing familiarity. This period also saw the emergence of contemporary tourism, through the democratisation of travel (Urry 1990; Shields 1991; Ousby 2002; Smith, V. 1977). This early form of mass tourism caused many former curiosities to fall into the hands of the growing middle classes and onto the mantles and walls of the bourgeois domestic environment. What the new middle classes could not own for themselves, via early duplication technologies, they could, at least, become familiar with through the agency of public museums and galleries, and through travelling expositions and freak shows. It is at this point in history, with its emphasis on the Romantic sentiments of the individual, where tourism and the collection of souvenirs, as artefacts of travel and tourism, properly begins.

Initially, tourism set its sights on the spa and seaside towns of Britain, while the exotic destination of Italy appealed to the early eco–cultural tourist in the form of the Grand Tour (Shields 1991; Urry 1990). By the turn of the nineteenth century, with the colonial project in full swing, the Grand Tour soon expanded to include more distant lands as explorers, gentleman travellers, missionaries and amateur anthropologists engaged in the colonial project.[2]

Tourism and anthropology

Concurrent with the Victorian development of tourism was the gradual professionalisation of anthropology. As Strain explains:

> The marketing of touristic pleasures in the pre-cinematic era helped popularise a coherent set of strategies for viewing cultural Otherness, a set of strategies which can only be analysed in the context of a culturally-shared world view and late nineteenth-century developments, including the professionalisation and popularisation of anthropology.
>
> (Strain 1996: 72)

Long associated with the circus and travelling freak shows, that exploited the booty collected from abroad in human form, the mutual benefits of study and profit yielded the great expositions of the Victorian era in Paris, Brussels, Chicago and New York etc. (Torgovnick 1990; Impey 1977; Pearce 1995). These extravaganzas provided a scent of the exotic to would-be tourists who, without leaving home, could see elaborate exotic dioramas and living villages. Here the living human specimens of exotic cultures were encouraged to engage in their daily activities and perform their ceremonies under the passing gaze of domestic tourists. Strain (1996: 82) notes how in the 1880s the *Jardin d'Acclimatation*, on the periphery of Paris, provided a 'Parade of Ashanti's, Hottentots, Cossack, Lapps, Senegalese, Somalis, Dahomeans and Sudanese' that attracted 'Hundreds and thousands of spectators yearly', and that this enabled anthropologists in Paris ready access to 'ethnographic exhibits'. Behind the scenes the academic documentation of the 'specimens' took place and lent their results to the quackery of the philosophy of the natural order. The scrutiny of exotic people and things from within safe, Western confines typified the engagement of the anthropologist during the bulk of the nineteenth century, just as it typifies the perspective of many contemporary tourists.

While a small number gained their experience from colonial outposts, most mid-nineteenth century 'anthropologists could be likened to armchair travellers' (ibid.: 70). This remained the method of study for those sedentary scholars of the science of man 'serv[ing] primarily as curators and interpreters for the resultant accumulation of facts, photos and artefacts' (ibid.: 80). At this time, ethnographic field studies primarily consisted of reports from missionaries and traders. As Strain argues, for instance, 'true travellers or fieldworkers were not men who would become anthropologists at major universities but missionaries and merchants' (ibid.: 82).

It was this ability to organise the world from the Western perspective and the emplacement of European man at the head of the hierarchy that fostered the confidence to travel in those with the means. Once the exotic had been consumed, as a spectacle in model villages and their like, and their position located beneath that of late nineteenth century European man, adventurous tourists could then venture into the dark corners of empire, if not confident in their mastery of the exotic subject, then at least with some prior knowledge. The residue of this model can be seen today in the television travel shows, brochures, and internet sites that provide the would-be tourist with extensive information and tamed picturesque images of the prospective destination. Indeed, the function of the picturesque diorama persists as a primary structure of all tourist information. The diorama is clearly related to the 'view through the window' in its framing and distancing technique and, above all, in the way in which it maintains the comfort zone of the viewer. The picturesque diorama intensifies the notion of the viewer at the centre of things, just as the contemporary tourist is the centre of attention at resort towns and theme parks alike, both of which are tempered, or constructed, for the visitor's benefit.

Anthropology, with its yearning for knowledge of others, is a discipline that shares the sentiments of the Romantic Grand Tourist and a historical development concurrent with contemporary tourism. Structurally, both are environmental engagements that absorb exotic cultures and places (that people develop a culture in partnership with their environment is at the heart of both engagements) and that extended periods of time are spent among exotic cultures is also common. Furthermore, the desire or imperative to record the experience, in some material form, is also shared with the contemporary tourist and more specifically the eco–cultural tourist.

Explorer art and tourist art in Australia

As with other geographical regions within the British Empire, in colonial Australian history the trading of material culture is dominated by the colonial explorer, the missionary and, later, the anthropologist. In Australia we are indebted to many famous anthropologists, missionaries and other early collectors of Aboriginal artefacts for the richness that lines the storerooms of state and national museums and art galleries. Not withstanding the difficult ghosts of British colonialism, the artefacts collected during and just after that period have, through time, assisted in a better understanding and appreciation of Australia's indigenous cultures.[3]

The specific conditions relating to the trade in tourist art and souvenirs are peculiar to the condition of the tourist and, moreover, the European notion of leisure and travel that arose during the mid-to-late nineteenth century. The contemporary anthropologist might argue that his or her profession is unrelated to the travel purposes of the tourist. The initial examples of tourist art and contemporary souvenirs, however, are to be discovered in the collections of early colonial explorers and anthropologists, as too, is the germ of what is now referred to as eco–cultural tourism. By far the most common practice, shared by the anthropologist and tourist, is the documentation of the site and people through the collection of material culture and images. In the collections of the material culture of other societies reside many artefacts that are both ethnographic artefacts and works of art, and they address the complex activity of tourism and souvenirs that challenges our notions of what art is. Just as Lippard

(1999b: 4) questions the relationship between art and tourism, asking why so few artists have recognised the affinities between art and tourism, so Torgovnick (1990: 75) has aimed a similar question at the exhibition of exotic material culture and 'primitive' art. Furthermore, it is important to discover a way to appreciate tourist art and souvenirs that overcomes the prejudices once accorded 'primitive' art and material culture, one that circumvents their common perception as cheap, tacky and kitsch and recognises the authenticity of the souvenir's unique system of visual communication, within the arena of tourism.

The reception and appreciation of artefacts of travel and souvenirs today runs against the grain of both art appreciation and taste, as well as the purity of authenticity accorded the anthropological artefact. Souvenirs are historical objects that, like the artefacts of the early modern *Wunderkammer* collections, are sometimes inducted into the museogallery system, following a considerable lapse in time and altered social priorities. Here they become categorised in collections of 'Other' or exotic cultures, in community history or folk craft, depending upon the culture of production and their place and method of collection. For example the R. Shott & Son collection, 1925, at the Queen Victoria Museum and Art Gallery, Launceston, Tasmania is an exemplary collection of early Tasmanian minor species timber souvenirs and a valuable part of the community history collection of the museum (see Hamilton 1984). Just as the plunder of early explorers provided suitable subjects for the work of Durer, so they may or may not influence the work of contemporary artists for their exotic or kitsch qualities or, more recently, contestation of colonial history. The common thread is the representation of people and place.

This key underlying aspect of the tourist gaze is foreshadowed in the documentary images from Cook's voyages to the Pacific and other colonial explorers, as the majority of tourist art, and much explorer art is/was executed by artists without formal training. As a result, many of the documentary images from Cook's voyages of discovery challenged accepted ways of representing the figure and landscape. This is, in part, due to the untrained eye of the image-makers and equally due to the intended viewer. Smith, B. (1992: 52–53), tells us that prior to Cook's voyages of exploration 'European artists did not look and were not encouraged to look, beyond Europe'. This was soon to change through the advocacy of the Royal Society, who for almost 100 years had been calling for the visual documentation of unknown lands. Eventually this saw the appointment of professional draughtsmen to ships bound for far voyages but 'It was Joseph Banks who first attempted to realise the possibilities' (ibid.). Even the work of formally trained artists, such as William Hodges, was considered to be counter to the rules of good landscape at that time. But Hodges' images were produced not for the salons and galleries of Europe but for men of science, including early anthropologists (Heathcote 2001). This is also true of later work from Eugene von Guerrard, W. C. Piguenit and other colonial artists, in that they accompanied scientific expeditions for the purpose of documentation rather than art making (Johannes 1992).

The study of tourist art and souvenirs requires a similar shift in the focus of the gaze. Like the images from Cook's expeditions, the intended exhibition of tourist art is not that of high art and taste, defined by the museogallery system, but the satisfaction of the tourist's gaze and subsequent viewers' gaze. What the documentary images of early explorers and travel art share is a priority to represent place and make it real to those that have not seen or experienced it. It is the intended audience – the official patrons of the colonial expedition and the family and friends of the tourist – that sets the works apart.

This common aspect of the production of explorer and travel art – the substantial contribution of artists without formal training – delivers a challenge to the notions of good taste and aesthetics that are jealously guarded by art institutions. Unlike the desired factual content that underpinned the images from Hodges and others, the representation of place, through the production of souvenirs, engages the maker's imagination and is bound by a different set of rules that enable an abstraction of the representation of place. In this way, the production of souvenirs may, quite rightly, be viewed as an experimental art practice in the representation of place. Imagination and abstraction are given freer rein in the production of souvenirs, while the need for factual content is not totally abandoned. In his thorough examination of the visual documentation of Cook's voyages to the Pacific, Smith, B. (1992: 53) notes 'three principal means by which drawing may be said to represent … call[ing] them inventive drawing, illustrative drawing and documentary drawing'. He then goes on to explain how all artists 'require a stock of visual memories drawn from their worlds' and how

> [i]n one sense, all drawing is illustrative, a visualising of verbalisations; all drawing is documentary in its recording of memories; all drawing is inventive in its translation of neural activities into a graphic code. It is better, therefore, to think of inventing, illustrating and documenting as actual or potential components of all acts of graphic representation. Considered in this way, inventive draughtsmanship is of a kind that stresses invention but minimises the illustrative and documentary components of perception. A documentary draughtsman, on the other hand, will endeavour to suppress the inventive and illustrative components of his perception and do his best to draw what he sees.
>
> (Ibid.: 54)

As far as tourist art is concerned, it is the sense of place that is stressed. This may take a number of forms, the most common being that the artist will begin with a material that is endemic to the site represented or that the artist will craft a recognisable representation of the site from non-endemic materials. In both respects it is possible to detect a clear relationship with the project of the colonial explorer and the anthropologist, and the documentation and material culture collections made by them to record the culture of the place. While the necessity for fact may be obscured somewhat, it persists beneath the surface of the souvenir object with its priority for the spirit of the place, for example, in the endemic material from which it is constituted. In this sense the artefact may be viewed from a postcolonial perspective, in that it harbours multiple and complex representations of place

– inventive, illustrative and documentary. Such meanings may comprise of one or all of the following: heritage, that is methods and systems of production now redundant that live on as spectres; the artist's interpretation of the site; and the tourist experience of that site. These two components are at the core of souvenir production that will become evident as this project unfolds.

I have shown, through this brief overview of the development of souvenir collecting, how it is founded on the colonial collection of 'Other' cultures. Furthermore, the colonial project has, since, given rise to a European heritage in former colonial lands, such as Australia. Here the study of souvenirs takes on another dimension and engages with the politics of white indigenaity. This may be summarised as the way in which the descendants of colonial Europeans view their own colonial past, but is more properly defined as the study of another, if infant, culture which has been the result of European migration. This will be explored further in the second half of this book, but for now I want to look more closely at the anthropological project, borne out of the colonial project, and its relationship to tourism.

3 Souvenirs and the anthropological gaze

The study and reception of souvenirs over the last half century

Introduction

This chapter takes a decade-by-decade look at the relationship between tourism and anthropology and identifies common links between ethnographic artefacts and souvenirs collected in Australia during the latter half of the twentieth century. I will achieve this through a survey of anthropological texts that have engaged with tourist art and souvenirs, and plot their influence on the study of souvenirs.

I have, so far, shown how the study of travel art and souvenirs finds its antecedents in the academic fields of anthropology and art history. This was first recognised in 1976 when Graburn (1976: 2) wrote of tourist art and souvenirs as 'one of the most neglected fields in the disciplines of anthropology and art history'. There has been some progress over the last quarter of a century or so, but there remains much work to be done. It has until recently existed behind the veil of anthropology, art history and other related disciplines (such as archaeology, social theory, psychology, history, cultural studies and museum theory) and recently it has come to light in specific studies in material culture and tourism. What these disciplines share is an engagement with artefacts and objects that have been collected as a result of institutional and/or independent exploration and travel. The objects collected have then been assessed and organised using the criteria that are foremost in the individual disciplines. These criteria are often found to be contrary to each other but are, in many ways, also equally complementary. This is best exemplified in the curatorial contrast demonstrated by the presentation of the same or similar artefacts found in art galleries, anthropological museums and souvenir shops. For the anthropological museum, the display of the object is preceded by the knowledge of its use and fit within the culture of origin; it is the apparent information available in the object that attracts the scrutiny of the anthropologist or ethnographer. For the art gallery, the formal and aesthetic qualities of the object are paramount.

Tourist art and souvenirs, however, seem to rest somewhere in between; it is the aesthetic and decorative quality of the object that attracts the tourist's eye, while the object's ability to refer to the experienced site and culture is of equal importance. These innate qualities bring together the aesthetic and informative gaze around the commercial exchange that takes precedence in the souvenir shop. In so doing, the souvenir describes a unique range of objects and artefacts designed for the purpose of satisfying an equally unique way of seeing.

Few academics and writers have, until recently, recognised tourist art as worthy of serious study and in Australia the study of tourist art and souvenirs is particularly slight. That which does exist is to be found, in brief references, within studies of Aboriginal art and these, initially, took a dim view of the negative influence of tourism on the production of Aboriginal art. Any in-depth study of souvenir objects that refer to colonial society is non-existent, or in a formative stage. So it is that this chapter begins with a survey of literature, in the broadest sense, that considers the subject of tourist art as it pertains to Aboriginal and other indigenous cultures and European contact.

As the artefacts of Aboriginal Australia began to emerge to a receptive Western audience in the mid-60s, a clear distinction between Aboriginal art and tourist kitsch was established. 'Kitsch' is a term that has dogged tourist art and souvenirs. The common perception is that all souvenirs are kitsch, but the meaning of this term is almost as varied as tourist art. It may mean to cheapen in accordance with the original German – *Kitschen*, (Sternberg 1972). But it is Broch and Geisz (1979: 17) and 'the concept of *Kitschmench* or kitsch man', extended to refer to the 'man of bad taste', the way in which a person of bad taste looks at, enjoys and acts when confronted with a work of art (either good or bad), that does most to secure a notion of what kitsch means with regard to the tourist. Geisz (ibid.: 156) extends this notion with clear reference to tourism, first offering his list of options for the meaning of kitsch as bad taste, dilettantism, unoriginal, thoroughly conventional, or 'overloaded with rather primitive, affected and superficial attractions'. He then brackets the souvenir and the monument together as 'memory fetish', writing that both 'provoke a kitsch perversion' of the tourists' sense of time and that both the monument and the museum and 'the souvenir simplifies this sort of pleasant ambivalence by means of its tangible reality' (ibid.: 170). The intention was to discriminate between genuine artefacts that showed evidence of traditional use, and were worthy of public and institutional collection, and those crafted trinkets produced for profit within the Western economic system. Most of these early studies were undertaken by anthropologists with the assistance of missionaries. This saw the emphasis placed on information rather than aesthetics that, in turn, treated the collected objects as ethnographic specimens and displayed them accordingly.

The sixties

In 1964, Ron Berndt, renowned anthropologist from the University of Western Australia, lamented the influence of tourism and tourist kitsch on the development of Aboriginal art, stating that:

> [p]seudo or imitative Aboriginal art is *not* art: and unfortunately, it is in this debased form, in the shape of commercially produced items for the tourist

> trade, that it appears to have made the strongest impression. This aspect is outside our scope in the present discussion, but we should remember that some of this material does go under the name of 'Aboriginal art', and is accepted as such.
>
> (Berndt 1964: 73)

Berndt's quest for authenticity is typical of many anthropologists of that era. This 'debased form' of Aboriginal art is at the core of this project and represents the historical grounding of this inquiry, in which the positive aspects of such modified art production and its external influences are explored.

Similarly, Tuckson, in the introduction to Berndt's essentially anthropological text, draws attention to the contortions made by Aboriginal artists to satisfy the demands of such a market, writing that:

> [t]he demand from the tourist trade has also been met partially by Aboriginal artists themselves, especially through the agency of mission distribution centres. In a minor way this has modified traditional style. Missions sometimes price the artists' work on the basis of size.... And to meet the current demand, the artist has now taken to shaping his bark as rectangularly as possible, so that it may be packed and transported conveniently together with others. Over encouragement of such art has tended to produce quantity rather than quality.
>
> (Tuckson 1964: 68)

Tuckson identifies the role of mission settlements as central to the introduction of the profit motive, noting the values by which art was subsequently promoted. But, most importantly, he recognises the significance of size and uniformity, as fundamental structural developments, in the definition of tourist art.

In the same year, Roman Black, another anthropologist, introduced his text, *Old and New Aboriginal Art*, in the following way:

> In thousands of Australian shop windows one can see examples of pottery, wooden boxes and trays, table-mats, textiles, and various knick-knacks and souvenirs decorated with aboriginal designs. To a visitor from abroad this is like a breath of fresh air; here at last is something that is different, that is typical of the country, that is good.
>
> (Black 1964: xxi)

Just as Tuckson documents the shaping of indigenous art to suit the dictates of transportation, so Black is equally alert to the principle that a souvenir must be 'typical' of the visited site. In this, Black is less critical of tourist art, preferring to focus instead on the aesthetic freshness and difference of Aboriginal-derived decoration and design. The contrast between the gazes of Black and Berndt and Tuckson is apparent. Black's perspective is much closer to that of the tourist, in that he is visiting the country for the first time. It is true that Black and Berndt

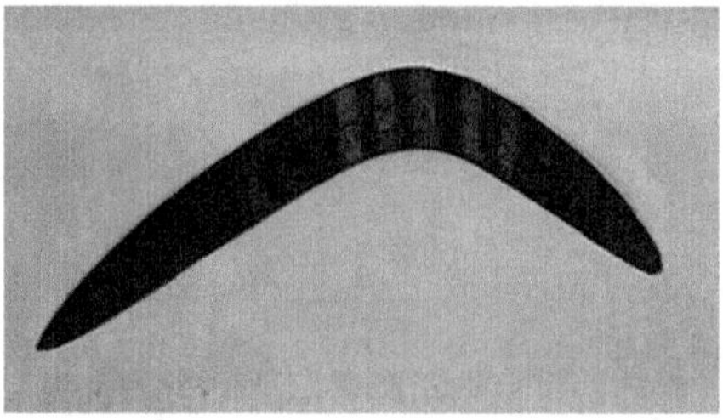

Plate 3.1 Multifunction Boomerang, wood and ochres. Collection: Berndt Museum, University of Western Australia, Cat. No. 2464.00.

Number 2464.00 Multifunction Object Boomerang

Country: Australia

State: Western Australia

Region

Place: Mowanjum

Description

The boomerangs are made from light coloured wood which is red-pink ochred. Painted designs occur on one side only. Designs mainly consist of 5Ó and ÒUÓ curves in yellow, outlined with fine white dots. Lengths: (from tip to tip)
60 cms; 52 cms.
Belief: The marks are just signs (waru) and tracks.
Function
Made for the tourist market (see slide reference below).
Boomerangs may be used for hunting, fighting and firemaking.

Collection: Luchich P

Originator: Worora tribe

Date 17.3.1963

Figure 3.1 Catalogue entry 2462.00, Berndt Museum, University of Western Australia.

both engage with the art of Aboriginal people from an anthropological perspective but there is, in Berndt's tone, an underlying desire for purity and authenticity in the art and culture of Aboriginal people. On the other hand, Black's view from afar welcomes the influence of trading routes and the exchange of ideas across clan and tribal boundaries and across the ocean. This is a particularly pertinent point, as Black dwells, for some time, on the pre-European contact and influence of Macassar and Malay culture on that of Arnhem Land Aborigines, and the introduction of figurative imagery into the latter's culture. Citing Berndt's 1947 collection of carved human figures from outside of Yirrkala, Black argues that '[t]he carving of human figures out of wood was introduced from Indonesia by Macassan and Malay traders who regularly visited this part of Australia' (ibid.: 17). This suggests that Aboriginal art (like the art of other cultures) has the capacity to adapt to outside influences and respond to changes, and also highlights the nonsense of Berndt's desire for cultural purity.

The distinction between art and souvenirs may also be found in the current records of the Berndt Museum at the University of Western Australia. Here, a small number of artefacts have been catalogued as souvenirs, made for exchange with the anthropologist that was engaged in the study and collection of artefacts. Examples include the following *Multifunction Boomerang.*

This artefact and catalogue entry, and two others from the Berndt Museum, situate the collector – in this case the anthropologist P. Lucich – in the role of the primary tourist, for this artefact has been produced, or at least adapted, as a personal gift for the anthropologist. This is an adaptation, by the maker, that points to the transition of the artefact from a tool, 'used for hunting, fighting and fire making' (ibid.), to one with the artistic representation of people and place as its priority. However, artefacts catalogued in this way, from this period, are rare.

The seventies

The first attempt to remedy this rather jaundiced perspective, and define the category of 'tourist art' as a genuine and unique artistic expression and style, occurred in North America with the publication of Graburn's ground-breaking *Ethnic and Tourist Arts: Cultural Expressions from the Fourth World* (1976). In this text, upon which it is fair to say the academic study of souvenirs was founded, Graburn establishes a structure of art production that locates souvenirs and tourist art as an identifiable genre of art, within the general field of art practice.

Graburn's initial problem was to identify how tourist art was distinct from what was then referred to as 'primitive' art. He managed this by invoking the concept of a 'Fourth World', which he describes as the 'collective name for all aboriginal and native peoples whose lands fall within the national boundaries and techno-bureaucratic administrations of the countries of the First, Second and Third Worlds' (Graburn 1976: 1). Then, in contrast to Berndt's insistence on authenticity, he argues that, '[n]ot only are they no longer isolated or autonomous peoples as they perhaps once were, but their arts are rarely produced for their own consumption or according to their own unmodified tastes' (ibid.). Here the author recognises the impact of colonialism and the modifications that have occurred that are demonstrated in the preceding example from the Berndt Museum. Graburn concludes:

> Thus, the study of the arts of the Fourth World is different from the study of 'primitive' art, characteristic of most earlier anthropological writings, for it must take into account more than one symbolic and aesthetic system, and the fact that the arts may be produced by one group for consumption by another. The Study of Fourth World arts is, par excellence, the study of *changing* arts – of emerging ethnicities, modifying identities, and commercial and colonial stimuli and repressive action.
>
> (Ibid.)

Within this precise statement, of what the study of souvenirs entails, Graburn clearly identifies points of divergence between 'primitive' art and tourist art, between anthropological artefacts and souvenirs. First, the myth of isolated cultural purity is anathema within the context of tourist art. Second, cultural identification and specification is tenuous within the Western framework of national boundaries. And, third, tourist art is produced for the consumption of visitors from other cultures, that is, the tourist. In terms of the focus of this book, it is this third component that is the most important detail from this extended quotation and does most to define the souvenir. For the principle, of art produced by one community for the consumption of another, is also applicable to the contemporary boom in the production of souvenirs by both non-indigenous and native peoples alike. This has become more evident, here in Australia, since the bicentenary in 1988 and the Sydney Olympics in 2000, in so far as certain non-indigenous groups may also fall into the same predicament outlined by the earlier categories of indigenous and/or minority representation within the national type. Graburn foreshadows this predicament by later tying the category of folk art to the same bundle as 'primitive' art. Elaborating on the notion of social interaction across cultural and class boundaries, he bases his premise on a theory of integration and differentiation, writing of integration and differentiation as two sides of the same coin. For Graburn it is:

> essential to the processes of solidarity within groups and between parts of groups that go together to make a part of larger entities. These groups or segments of society are called by many names: classes, castes, tribes, ethnic groups, identity groups etc., all of which are tending to merge in the contemporary world. The arts of these peoples have been called 'primitive' art and 'folk' art, depending on whether the creators are, respectively, members of a recently conquered group or of the long familiar 'lower classes' of complex societies.
>
> (Ibid.: 2–3)

In so doing, Graburn points clearly to the inclusion of the arts and crafts of former colonial societies, in which those with a historical base of economic migration and penal transportation, such as Australia and other former colonial states dominated by European descendants, may be included. Having established these broad, yet defining, parameters for the production of tourist art, Graburn presents a number of artistic typologies that define various styles and developmental stages of what we have come to know as souvenir production, as follows:[1]

1 Extinction

Graburn begins his typology by recognising extinct indigenous art; that is, art that did not survive the early contact years of colonialism due to the disruption of the indigenous social structure. This category has little relevance in the ongoing study of tourist art but it serves to demonstrate the benefits of tourism and how it may be crucial in the preservation of endangered artistic styles.

2 Traditional or functional fine art

Summarised as, 'traditional art form[s] … accompanied by some changes in technique and form, or even show[ing] incorporation of a few European derived symbols and images. As long as these do not disturb the transmission of symbolic meaning' (ibid.: 5).

This category is illustrated through Plate 3.2, in which the traditional boomerang form has been retained, as has the symbolic decorative crosshatch design. It is in the production technique that some variation occurs. Whereas, prior to colonialism, the recessed crosshatching was executed with stone or bone tools, it is highly probable that in this instance the decoration was achieved with the use of a metal or glass cutting device. As with many artefacts found in ethnographic collections, it is only possible to speculate about the tools used. Through a comparison with similar, pre-contact artefacts one can assess the edge of the mark for some evidence of the use of Western tools and then look for signs of wear and use – marks that will suggest some authenticity. However, signs of use should not preclude the artefact from this category. As Graburn informs us, antiquing, revivals and fakery are prevalent among many souvenir crafts. I will not determine objects and artefacts in this category as 'souvenirs' as Graburn sets out a distinct category for that title. Instead, I will refer to objects and artefacts that are, or have been 'souvenired', such as the boomerang shown here (Plate 3.2).

This category is more clearly defined by the term 'functional' in that the majority of souvenirs it embraces are utilitarian tools that have been appropriated into the souvenir market. They were made with a utilitarian purpose in mind, rather than the profit motive.

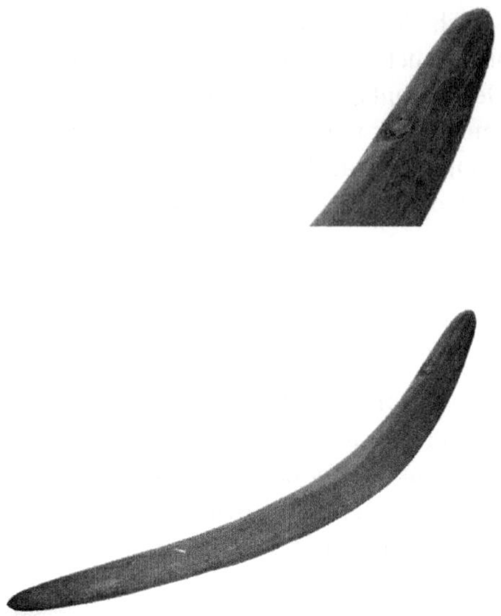

Plate 3.2 Multifunction Boomerang, wood with inscribed relief, 81 cm. Collection: Tasmanian Museum and Art Gallery, Cat. No. M3683.6.

3 Commercial fine art

An artefact described as 'made with eventual sale in mind but which adheres to culturally embedded aesthetic and formal standards' (ibid.: 5–6).

Eventual sale is also the motive behind many Aboriginal art works. I have shown in the above category how moribund tools are vulnerable to the souveniring habits of tourists. This is also true of this third category, but here intent is the key difference. For example, the coolamon (Plate 3.3) is a wooden vessel, initially used for collecting seeds and berries for food. Today these artefacts are produced specifically for the tourist market, augmented with various traditional designs, such as the dot-painting pattern on this example. They are also made in a number of sizes and with varying degrees of skill. What remains is the retention of the traditional form and design (see Brokensha 1987; Isaacs 1992, and Maruku Arts and Crafts n.d.). Other examples of art made for this purpose may be found in baskets from Aboriginal Australians, while the boomerang, as demonstrated above, is, today, also made with 'eventual sale in mind'.

4 Souvenirs

Objects of repetitive production manufactured 'when the profit motive or economic competition of poverty override aesthetic standards, satisfying the consumer becomes more important than pleasing the artist' (Graburn 1976: 6).

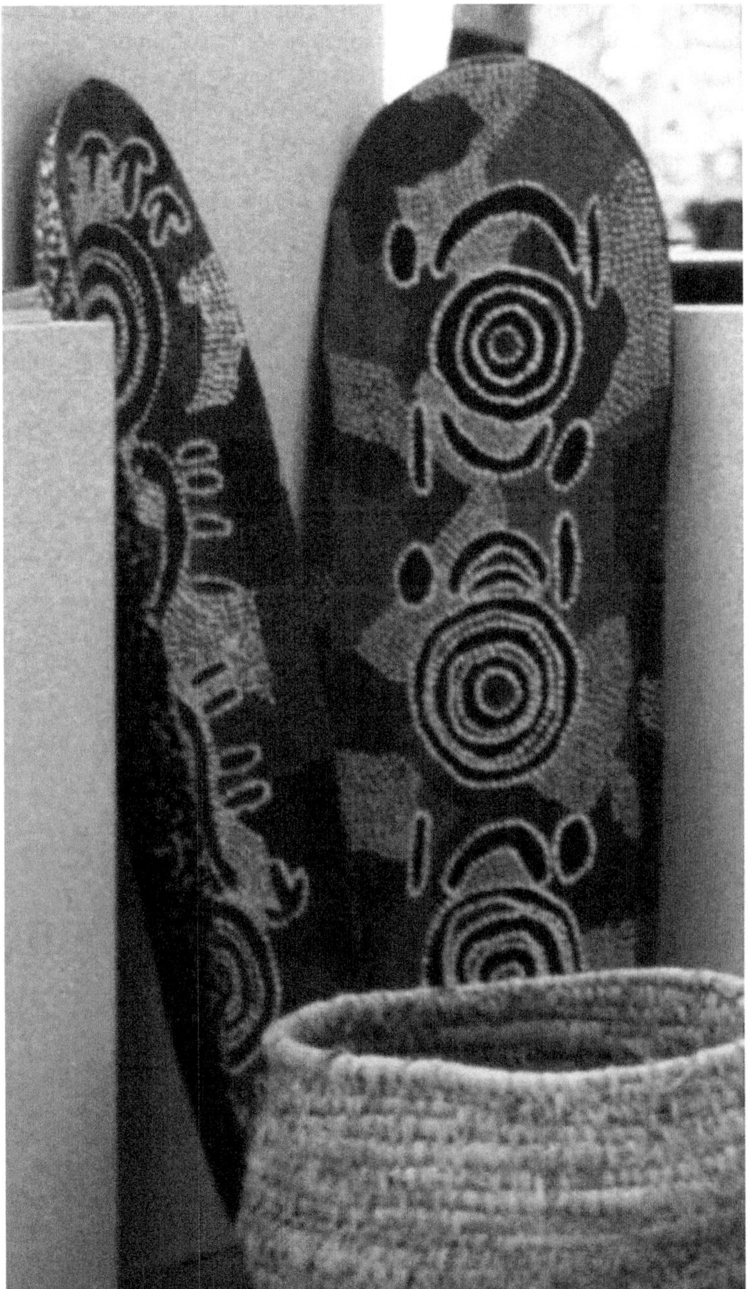

Plate 3.3 Mary Rose Nangala, *Coolamon*, 2000, acrylic paint on wood, with pokerwork detail on reverse, 63 × 18 cm. Private collection.

It is the repetitive production process that sets these artefacts apart from the former categories and, according to Graburn, it is this that most clearly defines the souvenir. The reliance on repetitive manufacture for this definition is problematic, as too is the notion of 'economic competition of poverty', which is assessed from the perspective and principles of Western economic development, imposed upon a different or alternative system of production. Unlike 'Traditional or Functional Fine Art', where the artefact is produced with no mind for its commercial exchange, or 'Commercial Fine Art', where the 'eventual sale' of the artefact crosses the mind of the maker, 'Souvenirs' are produced within a fully established capitalist exchange system, in which the sale of the artefact is the sole intention.

In the following examples, from the Keringke Arts Centre (Plate 3.4), mass produced pots and plywood model boomerangs are augmented with individual local designs where each design is unique and applied by hand with reasonable care and attention. However, there can be no argument that such artefacts are manufactured with the profit motive in mind, and that the intention of the work is, at least in part, to allay what Graburn calls the 'economic competition of poverty'. In the examples shown (Plates 3.3 and 3.4), the intention of the arts centre within a Catholic mission to integrate its members into a capitalist system should not be completely dismissed.

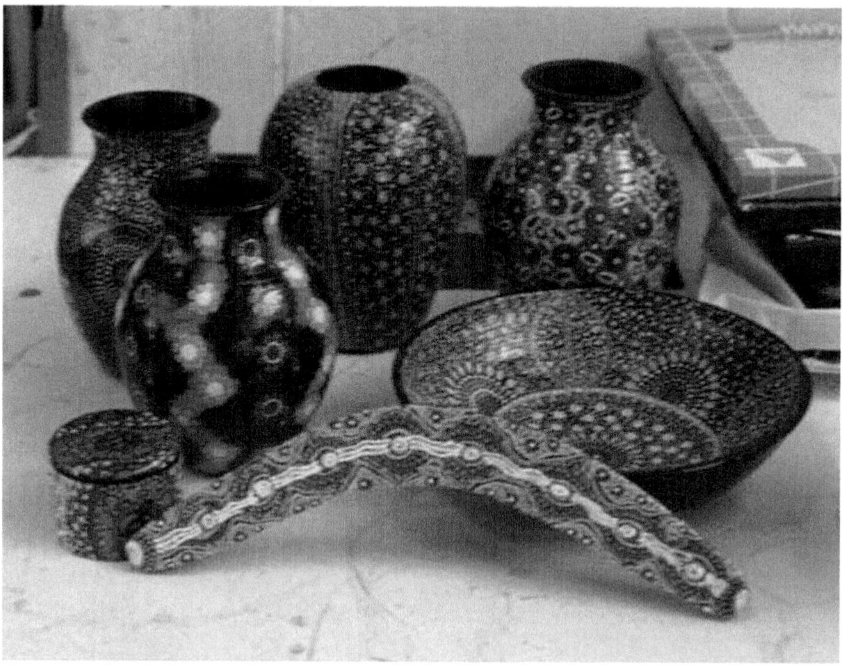

Plate 3.4 Keringke souvenirs-painted ceramic pots and wood boomerang, 2000, Keringke Arts Centre, Santa Teresa (Ltyentye Apurte) Northern Territory Australia.

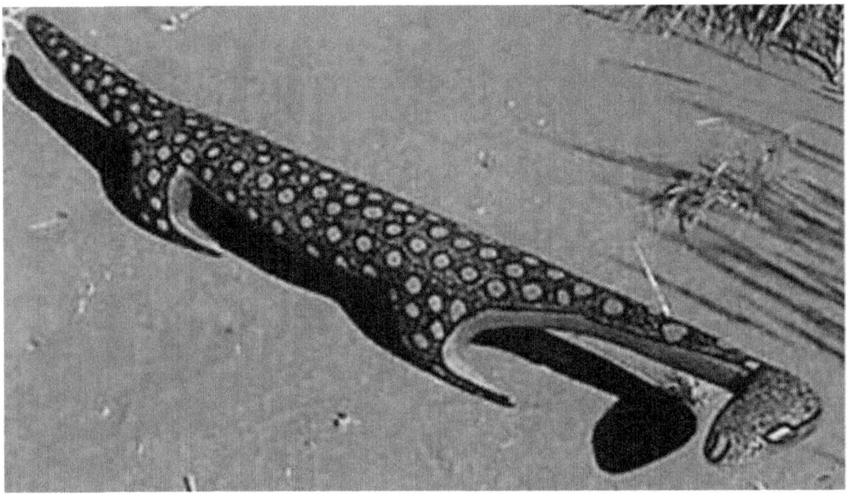

Plate 3.5 Topsy Tjulita, *Lizard*, undated, wood with pokerwork detail.

5 Reintegrated arts

Artefacts summarised as comprising of new art forms developed by indigenous people from introduced materials and methods.

It may be argued that most, if not all, indigenous souvenirs, such as the example pictured (Plate 3.5), conform to this description through the use of introduced materials and techniques, or methods that have enabled the work to meet commercial needs. The Pokerwork art, or Punu, of Central Australia, which I will examine more closely in later chapters, is a superb example, where traditional patterns are burnished onto the surface of the artefact by the use of heated lengths of fencing wire.

6 Assimilated fine arts

Artefacts summarised as made through the use of Western form and composition by indigenous peoples.

Graburn (ibid.: 7) cites Namatjira as a prime example here, illustrating his claim with Namatjira's Western style painting, *Ghost Gum of Temple Bar (1943)* and arguing that 'Namatjira painted landscapes in (*sic*) his aboriginal homeland, in the style of the white artist Rex Battarbee'.

Having listed the above categories of indigenous art that feed into the production of tourist art, the author provides some qualification by noting that objects contained within the above categories are not fixed but travel variously across the lines of definition that he has drawn up.

There is a fine line of division between each of Graburn's categories and in the case of both 'Commercial Fine Art' and 'Souvenirs' there exists a judgement to be made regarding the 'aesthetic standards' and their relationship to both traditional functions and the profit motive. For Graburn, the first category, 'Traditional or Functional Fine Arts' is characterised by the inclusion of post-contact materials, techniques and imagery, but they adhere to traditional functions, with no consideration of profit. They are artefacts that fall into the tourist art market after production and in this respect it is the tourist that makes souvenirs out of them. 'Commercial Fine Arts' are different, due to the secondary consideration of the artefact's commercial appeal, but they still conform to the function of transmitting traditional knowledge and retain significant symbolic meaning. Their purpose and conditions of production are identical to those of the previous category; however, it is the maker, rather than the tourist-as-consumer, that identifies their potential to operate as souvenirs within the Western economic exchange system.

In the third category, 'Souvenirs', the profit motive is the main purpose for the artefact's production and this is seen as having a marginalising effect on the object's symbolic meaning, function and traditional aesthetics. Artefacts of this type are framed as souvenirs by both the maker and consumer and therein rests the crucial definition of this category. Both, maker and tourist, recognise the remaining features of traditional function, aesthetics and symbolic meaning retained in the artefact, that allow it to operate as marker of people and place.

The eighties

The 1980s saw the flood of Central Desert Aboriginal dot-painting onto the international art scene. This, in turn, inspired a more expansive appreciation of other Aboriginal art forms, including that which had previously been labelled kitsch. In 1986, the exhibition, *The Dreamtime Today: A Survey of Contemporary Aboriginal Arts and Crafts* (Kintore Gallery) addressed Aboriginal craft in a less prejudicial way than Berndt and Tuckson, and not as wide-eyed and gawping as Black, in its documentation of similar, tourist-oriented work contained within the exhibition.

Alluding to the transition of the traditional art of predominantly hunter-gatherer communities, from transitory or ephemeral object into markers of people, place and time, the introductory essay of this catalogue remarks upon the 'seeming paradox of the desire of museums and art galleries to collect and conserve such pieces' (Megaw 1986: 9). This paradox may be further related to the artefacts of non-Western and Western heritage alike and carries a real significance to those artefacts framed as souvenirs. As the text continues:

> [C]ertain basic features may be detected in all Aboriginal visual arts. These include their basically religious nature, their perceived relationship to the past continuum of the Dreamtime and the all-important Dreamtime ancestors from whom stem essential aspects of Aboriginal life and thought; most important are the inextricable links between individuals and groups and the land.
>
> (Ibid.)

It is this expression of the relationships between people and place that supplies the starting point for the reception of indigenous artefacts as souvenirs and invokes a visual dialogue between host and visitor. Importantly, this dialogue situates the indigenous artist/craftsperson as the proprietor of the represented site. Similarly, for the settler descendant, it may be argued that the production of colonialist souvenirs enhances a sense of belonging to the represented site. In this way the colonial debate of ownership persists through the representation of place, which has further been complicated by the development of a recent inter-indigenous colonialism through the sale of artefacts, such as dot paintings, didgeridoos and boomerangs, to tourists in parts of Australia where such things are alien.

This catalogue makes further note on the relationship between tourism and Aboriginal artefacts with reference to a number of exhibits. One entry dates this relationship as beginning in 1945 with the initial figurative carving of a human figure atop a traditional Tiwi Island burial pole (Hart and Piling 1960, cited Maughan 1986: 89), stating that 'these artefacts soon realised a ready market within the tourist trade' (ibid.). In line with Tuckson's lament, and the qualifying feature of Graburn's 'Souvenir' category, the quality of the finished article is said to not only differ in its traditional representative style but:

> Poles made for tourists – or especially commissioned – can be even more flamboyant and even representational in style and decoration. This particular example is coloured with vivid yellow and the crude uneven carving and slapdash paintwork leave no doubt that it was intended for a European audience. Contrast this work with the following (Cat. No. 38A), a much more 'traditional' piece albeit also made for sale.
>
> (Maughan 1986: 87)

This development, out of traditional form and colour, is also recognised by Graburn (1976: 18) in the art of the Makonde of Tanzania, among others, and referred to as 'Grotesqueness'. He writes of it as the antitheses of the assimilated art typified by Namatjira and says that '[s]ometimes this leads merely to giganticism, the exaggeration of features or the creation of something "larger than life"'.

As well as symbolic and ceremonial artefacts, decorated utilitarian objects are also included in the sweep of this exhibition, Cat. No. 55 being a painted Coolamon, a traditional 'hollowed oval dish ... used for carrying seeds and berries', in this case 'made expressly for sale' (Maughan 1986: 43). Like the coolamon featured in Plate 3.6, this example and Cat. No. 63, a decorated boomerang, provide examples of artefacts that demonstrate how the enhancement of traditional tools, with traditional designs, increases their visibility and value within the cash economy of the tourist market. This is best typified by Cat. No. 71 – a woomera attributed to Albert Namatjira, similar to Plate 3.6, and recorded as 'made for the tourist market'. There are a number of further exhibits from this catalogue that fit within the framework of souvenirs, including greeting cards (Cat. No. 85–99) and another coolamon (Cat. No. 116) recognised as being produced especially for the tourist market due to its reduced size (ibid.).

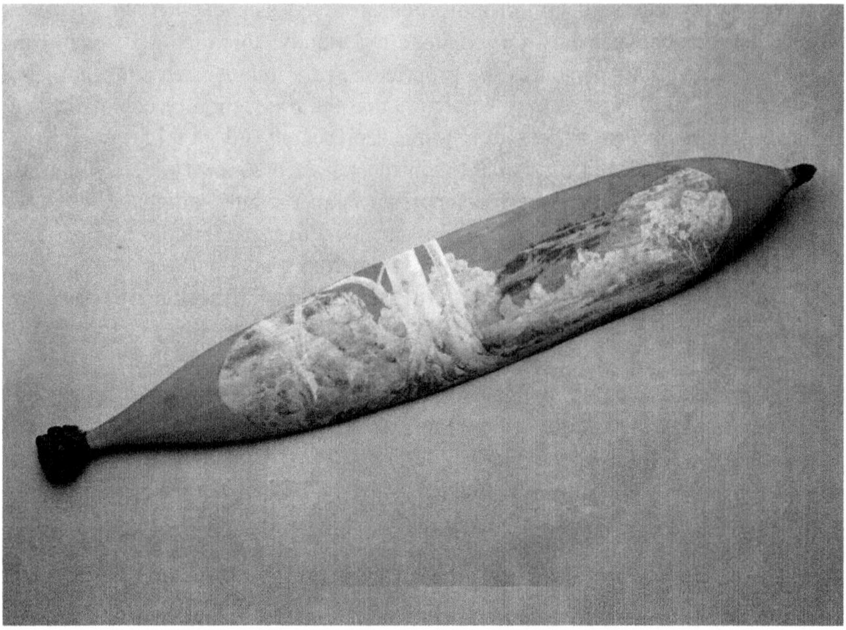

Plate 3.6 Albert Namatjira, *Woomera* (spear thrower), mulgawood/sinew/resin, painted by Albert Namatjira, Australia, 1945–1955. Collection: Powerhouse Museum, Sydney.

Changes in scale, and in particular miniaturisation, is a key focus of Stewart's text *On Longing* (1984), in which the author also dedicates some time to the analysis of souvenirs. This text deals ostensibly with why such things are collected; that is, the consumption of souvenirs. Stewart recognises how souvenirs 'serve as traces of authentic experience' (ibid.: 135) and how they are vital in documenting unrepeatable events, such as the once-in-a-lifetime visit to an exotic location. She also, quite rightly, asserts that souvenirs achieve this record through their ability to invoke narrative and argues convincingly that '[t]hrough narrative the souvenir substitutes a context of perpetual consumption' (ibid.). However, she warns that the meaning of the object will 'never be fully revealed' (ibid.). In this, Stewart is alert to the vagaries of narrative and its propensity for artifice over time. She goes on to highlight how, as a fragment of the site or event, the miniature operates in this system of memory and nostalgia, in that, as a fragment, it comes to represent the whole through the agency of narrative. In this elegant analysis of souvenir consumption, the author alludes to the relationship between the souvenir and the fetish, and frames her analysis of the souvenir in a terminology shared by the fetish. For Stewart the souvenir is a substitute, a fragment, and its narrative orbit is questionably repetitive. That is, its meaning is only fully understood by the collector, it 'cannot be generalized to encompass the experience of anyone; it pertains only to the possessor of the object' (ibid.: 136). As noted previously, another restrictive aspect of Stewart's analysis exists in her division of souvenirs into the basic categories of 'Sampled' and 'Representative' (ibid.). This simple division of souvenirs, together with their similarity to the fetish object and Stewart's conventional reading of the attendant narrative, needs prising open and I will attend to this in the next chapter.

The nineties

The formerly depreciated status of much Aboriginal art as tourist kitsch is confirmed by Morphy (1998), who, in his historical survey of Aboriginal art, makes a brief but positive mention of tourist art. Writing in reference to the period 1970–1980 (the period that saw the emergence of Contemporary Aboriginal art) Morphy (ibid.: 376) states that, '[p]reviously the only slot allocated for such work was the devalued category of "tourist art" '.

The author supports this claim through the work of Namatjira who, Morphy (ibid.: 269) tells us, was a major contributor to the field of tourist art during the 1930s and 40s, and 'was proud of his ability and sought to maximise his income.... He produced artworks in a number of different styles, including pencil drawing for visiting researchers and pokerwork engravings on artefacts made for sale'. Namatjira is possibly the earliest example of an artist who worked in both the souvenir and fine art market at the same time, and amongst the finest. This is something that only a few formally trained Western artists are today bold enough to do, but it is a practice that is widespread among Aboriginal artists. According to Morphy, the Aboriginal art of this war period, typified by the work of Namatjira, marks the establishment of a tourist art industry in the Central Australian Desert region, an industry that Morphy suggests was already firmly established during the interwar period in Southeast Australia and consisted of objects that:

> were often unfashionable in art world terms, straddling the division between popular art and tourist souvenir. Products included carved emu eggs, decorative feathers, flowers and applique bark pictures. Other crafts, such as basketry and boomerang manufacture have their origins in traditional practices, but were now directed towards the tourist and souvenir trade.
>
> (Ibid.:366)

Here Morphy, like Graburn, indicates how difficult it is to place tourist art within the broader field of fine art. He demonstrates how such art may, during one period, be discarded as tourist kitsch, only to subsequently come to rest in the collections of respected institutions, and to become entries listed in exhibition catalogues such as the *Dreamtime Today*.

A more recent analysis of tourist art and souvenirs appears in Phillips' and Steiner's edited collection of astute essays, *Unpacking Culture: Art and Commodity in Colonial and Postcolonial Worlds* (1999). Here, a global perspective on tourist art and souvenirs and their relationship to fine art is undertaken by a number of authors, including a reprise from Graburn of his foundational text. Like Graburn, the editors rest their argument on the opposition to the confining binary classification of indigenous art that saw most collections categorised as either 'artefact or ethnographic specimen and the work of art' (ibid.: 3). They go on to note how these classifications ignored the key activity of the artefacts as 'commodities circulating in the discursive space of an emergent capitalist economy' (ibid.). In this concern the authors address not just the production of the artefact and its drift from the 'authentic' ethnographic specimen, but also the consumption of those artefacts within the field of tourism and the Western museogallery system.

The display and presentation of tourist art and souvenirs within the museogallery system has provided a fruitful avenue for the academic study of such objects and artefacts. A notable contributor from the discipline of museum studies is Pearce (1995), who concurs with Phillips and Steiner in her criticism of the binary classifications, noting that the categories of 'Naturalia' and 'Artificialia' are inadequate for the analysis of tourist art and souvenirs. Like Phillips and Steiner, she identifies the need to expand these binaries that had emerged during the Romantic period, when the socially condoned collection of high art (Artificialia) and flora and fauna samples (Naturalia) was challenged by the collection of early tourist art by those engaged on the Grand Tour. Pearce (1995: 130–131) recognises that '[t]he accumulation of exotic and artistic pieces went hand in hand with a highly developed self image and the desire to create a world within a world'. Addressing the shift in the meaning of formerly utilitarian artefacts, she explains how '[o]bjects which were already seen to be "true relics" by reason of their "real relationship" with past people and events were transformed by the Romantic eye into a sensation of knowing the past'.

However, in her recognition of the need to establish a separate category devoted to the analyses of tourist art and souvenirs, which she labels Romantic, qualifying them as 'exotic objects of "primitive" and otherness' (ibid.), Pearce excludes the role of the fetish. For Pearce (ibid.: 32) the souvenir is the method by which 'the individual creates a Romantic life history', while she defines the fetish objects as objects that 'are allowed to create the self'. This viewpoint contests the argument put forward by Stewart (1984) and others, and will be discussed at length in Chapter 4, but for now I want stay focussed on the relationship between anthropology and tourism and examine more closely the changing meaning of the boomerang as an example of the influence of tourism on indigenous material culture.

The arc of the boomerang: a case study

Over the last 30 or so years, the most significant development in the study of tourist art has been Graburn's establishment of specific tourist art categories. In the following section, I will demonstrate these typologies through examples drawn from past and recent indigenous tourist art, in order to investigate, more thoroughly, how this structure may be applied to a contemporary study of tourist art and souvenirs.

Fleeting references to the boomerang have been made so far, but no project on tourist art and souvenirs, emanating from Australia, would be complete without a more detailed analysis of this, the best known, Australian souvenir. As Franklin (2010) points out, in his study of the Australian identity, both international and domestic tourists throughout Australia are presented with two dominant motifs: Aboriginal artefacts or Australian wildlife.

As we have discovered from the work of other writers, the souvenir has been shown to be an unstable artefact that confounds many attempts to categorise it by institutional terms and the boomerang is a case in point. The analysis of souvenirs is therefore best achieved by mapping the path they travel from production to resting. This proposition, I believe, is at the root of Graburn's categories, in that it is the shifts and alterations in the artefact groupings that distinguish one category from the other. This is informed and influenced by the qualities and characteristics invested in the work by the producer and consumer; that is the 'change incorporated … according to the tastes of the buyers and the efforts of the producers' (Graburn 1976: 14) that contributes to the movement of the artefact's perception from anthropological artefact to souvenir. Through the following case study, I will highlight the qualities of the souvenir object that bring about this restlessness and categorisation and, in turn, describe their path. I will attempt to locate the causes of these changes, whether they are occurring due to new technologies, cultural influences, or consumer demand.

In the case of the boomerang, shape is the key design feature. It is unique in this respect and that is a huge advantage in its operation as a souvenir. It may be made from anything, embellished in any manner, and only has to retain its unique form to be recognised for what it is.

I want to begin with four boomerangs selected from the collection of the Tasmanian Museum and Art Gallery.

Cat. No. M4238 (Plate 3.7) measures 80 centimetres from tip to tip and is hewn from a heavy durable timber, most likely Mulga or River Red Gum. It is decorated with a traditional, striated pattern that runs the entire length of the artefact. The patterning is like a continuous wave form of eight incised lines, with each wave striation separated by areas of sparse crosshatching. On close inspection it appears that the lines of the wave pattern are cut two at a time, perhaps with a tooth-edged cutting device. Known cutting devices include stone flints, animal teeth and introduced materials, such as glass and steel. Like the earlier boomerang from this collection (Plate 3.2), it is virtually impossible to discern what particular cutting device was used.

There appears to be no symmetry in the inscribed design but rather an increase in the density of crosshatching as the eye travels from left to right along the concave curve. It may be assumed, from the traditional design, execution, and patina of use, that this particular boomerang was produced for authentic purposes, being hunting and/or ceremonial use, and that its rightful understanding, in keeping with its mode of collection and storage within the museums 'Other' cultures collection, is as an anthropological artefact.

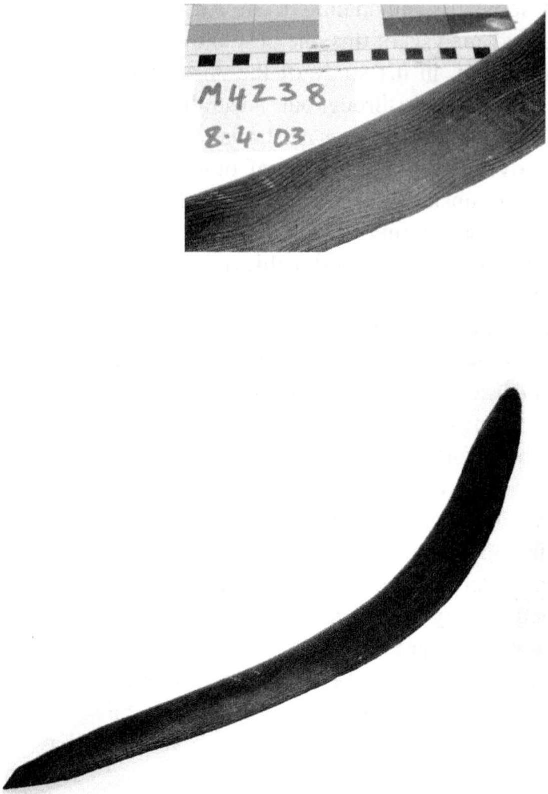

Plate 3.7 Multifunction Boomerang, wood with inscribed relief, 80 cm. Collection: Tasmanian Museum and Art Gallery, Cat. No. M4238.

In a second example boomerang, Cat. No. M2683.25, the decorative detail inscribed on the front convex surface seems less controlled and more crudely considered. It appears that the longitudinal centre, marked by two opposing crosshatched triangles, has been misjudged. Either side of this near central division are two similar shuttle designs that run in separate skeins to the tip of the artefact. These shuttle designs, that appear like connected elliptical leaves, are bounded on either edge by wave patterns similar to the first example (Plate 3.7).

As with the previous example, there appears to be some evidence of authentic use along the edges of this boomerang, which may lead one to consider them both as experienced artefacts. The difference between the two rests with the quality of workmanship.

The provenance of the next boomerang (Plate 3.8) suggests it was collected from the Northern Territory or Eastern Queensland. It is somewhat lighter in weight than the other examples and the decorative design is organised more openly along the 81 centimetre length of the artefact, while all the striations are

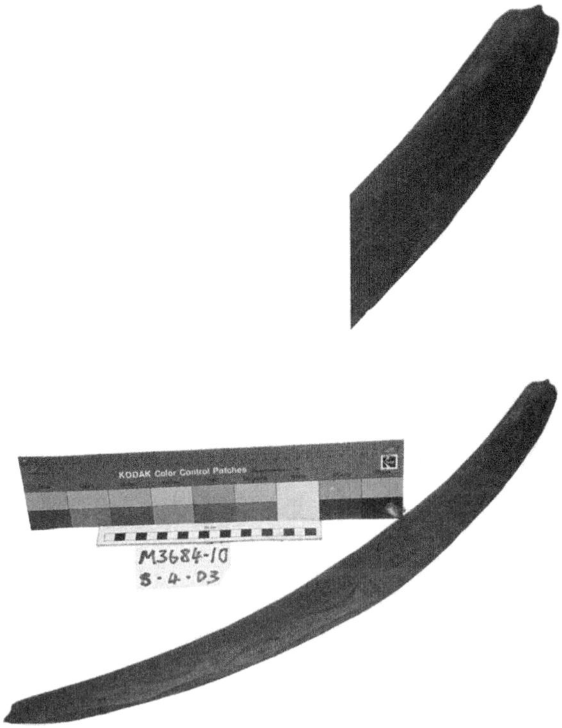

Plate 3.8 Multifunction Boomerang, wood with inscribed relief, 81 cm. Collection: Tasmanian Museum and Art Gallery, Cat. No. M3684.10.

shallower than in the previous examples. Like M3683.25 it is divided roughly in half by a row of four striated lines. This boomerang is also divided along its length by an extremely narrow, almost grass-like skein, resulting in a quartered division of the surface. Three of the quarters feature a shuttle or narrow leaf design, supplemented with simple crosscut lines, like those of a tally. The bottom right quarter, on the convex edge, does not follow this shuttle patterning, but instead features two continuous parallel lines in wave form.

Unlike the previous two boomerangs, the tips of this artefact are neatly clipped, which suggests the use of an introduced tool or cutting device. However, indentations along the edge may suggest some authentic use. In Graburn's terms the three above boomerangs demonstrate the 'Functional or Traditional Fine Art' category, due to the likely use of an introduced cutting technique.

The final boomerang, from the collection (Plate 3.9), also features clipped tips, but it is the decoration on the surface that says most about this artefact's production purpose. The inscribed design on the front surface of this artefact is

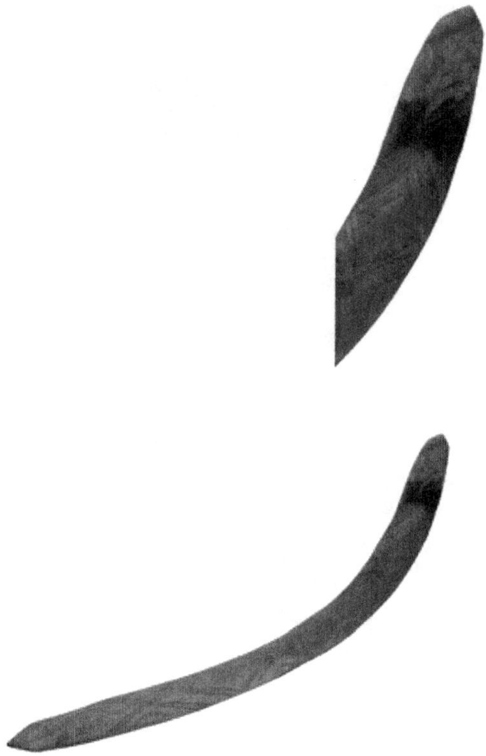

Plate 3.9 Multifunction Boomerang, wood with inscribed relief, 82 cm. Collection: Tasmanian Museum and Art Gallery, Cat. No. M4287.

fully developed in what amounts to a realistic figurative style, depicting single and double ovate leaves and on the right hand end, a stem or trunk with eight leaves branching from it. The figurative floral pattern is divided by diagonal crosshatching, while the incisions are deep, clean and by and large uniform. This boomerang, with its floral design and deep regular cuts, suggests more than any other example from this collection that it was produced with the aid of introduced tools and for the consumption of the colonial eye. Like the boomerang from the Berndt Museum (Plate 3.1), it can be assumed that this artefact was produced for exchange with colonial Australians or, perhaps, as a type of proto-souvenir, for there is evidence of what Graburn would term 'changes in technique and form … show[ing] incorporation of a few European derived symbols and images' (ibid.: 5). From the study of this selection it may be understood that the Tasmanian Museum's anthropological collection has, like many other state and national museums, ceased to collect boomerangs that show greater alteration from traditional form.

I now want to look at the more recent production of boomerangs in the photographic documentation contained within the *After 200 Years: Photographic Essays of Aboriginal and Islander Australia Today* publication (Taylor 1988). This documentation shows the varied meanings that the boomerang has to contemporary Aboriginal people and demonstrates the different motives behind the making of boomerangs in recent times.[2]

The following plates show images of a number of boomerangs; some are complete, others are in various stages of production. By studying the characteristics of these artefacts, it is possible to deduce the purpose of their production and intended resting place or market. In some cases the accompanying text provides most of the information required.

For instance, in the caption to the photograph *Tasman Snider Carving A Boomerang Outside His Home In Mantaka Watched By Leroy Diamond And Fleur Hobson*, the central subject, Snider, states that the main benefit, from the scene played out, is that of educating the young. He says, 'I could make a boomerang with my eyes shut' (Snider, in Taylor 1998: 115). The caption goes on to explain how he learnt to make boomerangs in the same way that the boy in the photograph is learning, by sitting around and watching. The role of this boomerang can be understood to have an educative priority that sustains the character of indigenous culture and social cohesion within. There is no mention, or allusion, to the souvenir market, or any other purpose for its production. This boomerang is not then identified as a souvenir by its maker but is more distinctly an ethnographic artefact. It does, however, rest in the 'Traditional' or 'Functional Fine Art' category, is made with non-traditional tools and has the potential to be recognised as a souvenir by a visiting tourist.

The second example drawn from this text (Plate 3.10) is the triptych, *Boomerang Making At Yaruman.* (Taylor 1988: 44). In these photographs the boomerangs are first roughed out with a tomahawk. The result of this process is shown in the second image. The third photograph shows a group of Aboriginal men working on the boomerangs at various stages of production. It is the supporting caption that provides the best insight into their purpose, telling us that '[w]e used to use them for hunting in the olden times but now we use them mostly for Law business' (Jampijin 1988: 45).

It can be understood, from this statement, that a shift has occurred in the intention of the tool: from hunting weapon to a tool for cultural organisation and cohesion. There is, however, a further potential shift in the purpose of these artefacts that moves them into the tourist art market. As Jampijin states, 'Sometimes we sell boomerangs in Halls Creek or Broome or Kununurra for might be 15 or 20 dollars for one' (ibid.).

There is no mention of decoration in this statement, so it must be assumed that the transition, from a tool for hunting and law business to souvenir, occurs with the boomerangs in the same condition. If this is the case, then these artefacts seem to retain their 'culturally embedded aesthetic and formal standards' and rest more closely to the category of ethnographic artefact rather than souvenir, as they have been produced, firstly, for use within the culture of their production, albeit for ceremonial purposes only.

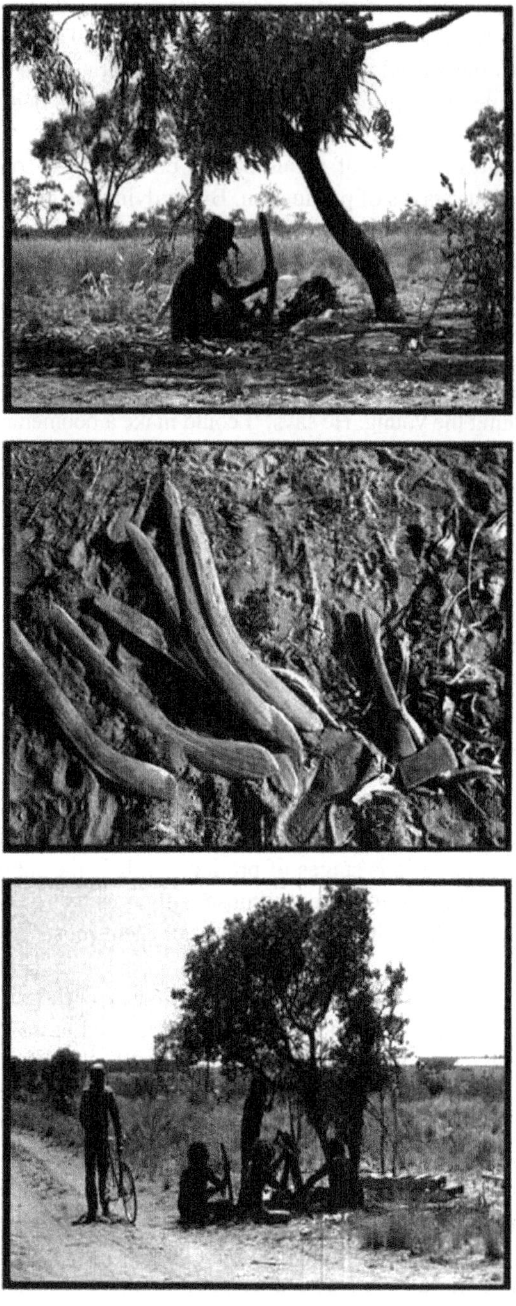

Plate 3.10 Jon Rhodes, *Boomerang Making At Yaruman*, 1988, black and white photograph.

However, as anthropological artefacts, such boomerangs are unlikely to demonstrate any evidence of their use within the culture of origin. Therefore, their inclusion in such a category is tenuous. Boomerangs made with this dual intention are likely to rest somewhere between Graburn's second category of 'Traditional or Functional Fine Art', and the third, 'Commercial Fine Art', as the level to which 'eventual sale', as the intended purpose of their production, cannot be gauged.

In the third example of a *Boomerang Factory at Robinvale* (Plate 3.11), the proprietor is unequivocal about the trajectory of the product. He informs us that the factory was set up with a loan from the state bank and a grant from 'the Arts Board in Sydney', and that '[w]e're aiming for the export market now' (Pearce, W. 1988: 223). This clearly situates these boomerangs and other Aboriginal objects from the factory within the souvenir market. Unlike the previous example, there is no pretence of use within the Aboriginal culture; rather, they are produced with sale to tourist outlets as their priority. What is interesting about this image is the assistance supplied by the Arts Board in the production of work clearly intended for the souvenir market. Not only does this link art and business together but it also identifies souvenir production as art, fitting it snugly into Graburn's notion of souvenirs, as the art of one culture produced expressly for the consumption of another, and category three, the 'Souvenir', defined as 'objects of repetitive production'.

There is also a second and more complex shift found in this photographic essay, which has to do with the raw material. The proprietor is denigrating of

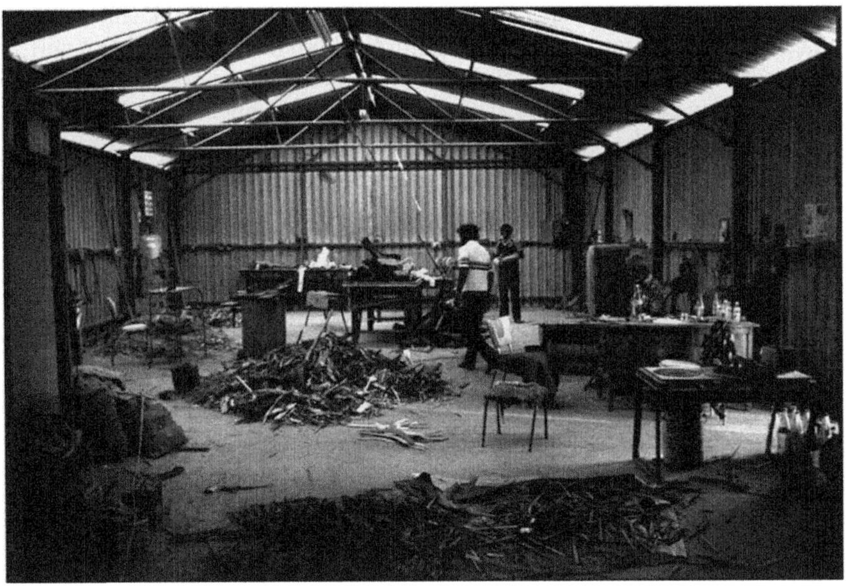

Plate 3.11 Michael Riley and Alana Harris, *Boomerang Factory at Robinvale*, 1988, black and white photograph. Collection: Michael Riley Foundation.

'those three ply ones', and also speaks of the change from using Mulga wood to Red Gum, saying, 'We used to go to outside Port Augusta on the other side of the Flinders Ranges to get the mulga. Now in the factory we use red gum, local wood' (ibid.).

This change in wood might say one or two things regarding boomerang production: it might suggest that Mulga provides the best wood for boomerang production, having characteristics such as strength, advantageous growth patterns, lightness and ease of carving; or it might suggest that Red Gum is a more marketable timber, being renowned for its durable quality and reified as the best timber to be found along the Murray River, in the same way that Huon pine has become a highly sought after and fetishised timber in Tasmania. Graburn (1976: 16) refers to this recognition of the importance of the raw material as an 'emphasis' placed on the 'valuable' material by the collector and demonstrates this through the relative values of Serpentine and Soapstone Inuit carvings in which the former attract a much greater price. What can be assumed, with some certainty, is that the boomerang form may be carved from many different species of timber from around Australia and, indeed, the world. At the same time 'aesthetic standards' are not necessarily compromised in the mass production of souvenirs. It is, in this respect, inappropriate to define souvenirs according to the reduction of culturally embedded aesthetic standards in favour of the need for profit.

I want to view one more example from the *After 200 Years* text before discussing the meaning of three boomerangs from the current souvenir market. In the photograph, *John Dixon Decorating a Boomerang For Sale at La Perouse*, the artist is burnishing a pattern onto a souvenir boomerang. Unlike the previous images, this photograph contains some finished product. Here, it is possible to see the decorative design of tourist influenced Western imagery, including a map of Australia and numerous animal motifs, blended with more traditional symbols. From the pokerwork technique, the commercial intention and the use of Western imagery, these artefacts show characteristics that span Graburn's second, third and fourth categories – 'Commercial fine art' 'Souvenirs' and 'Reintegrated arts' – and fix Dixon's artefacts, moreover, as genuine souvenirs.

In concluding this focus on the boomerang, I now present a suite of boomerangs collected during the course of this project. The first is an unassuming, three-ply boomerang, of the type denigrated by the proprietor of the Robinvale factory.

Made by '*Boomerangs* Down Under', this artefact (Plate 3.12) was purchased from a souvenir outlet in Alice Springs and is of symmetrical design, most likely formed on a bandsaw. It is light in weight and finished to a blond hue, with a tough commercial varnish finish. The label on the reverse states that it is 'Handmade to Return' and 'Designed by Paul Bryden – Australian Champion'.

This boomerang makes no allusion to authenticity and carries a rudimentary pokerwork design on the tip of each wing that has no symbolic meaning, but is purely decorative. The priority of this artefact is to demonstrate the utility of its design, which is that it flies in an arc pattern and returns to the thrower. By

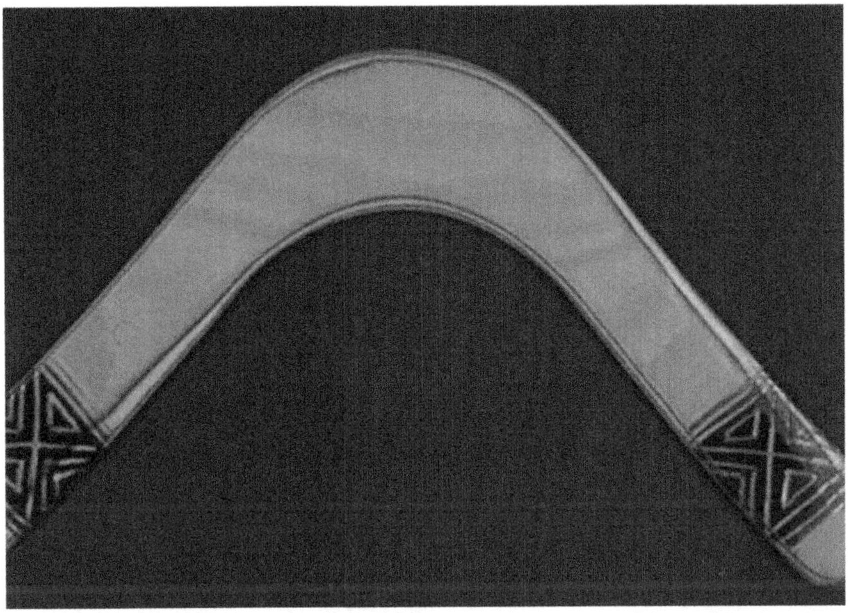

Plate 3.12 Paul Bryden, *Boomerang*, 2000, plywood with pokerwork detail, 35 cm. Private collection.

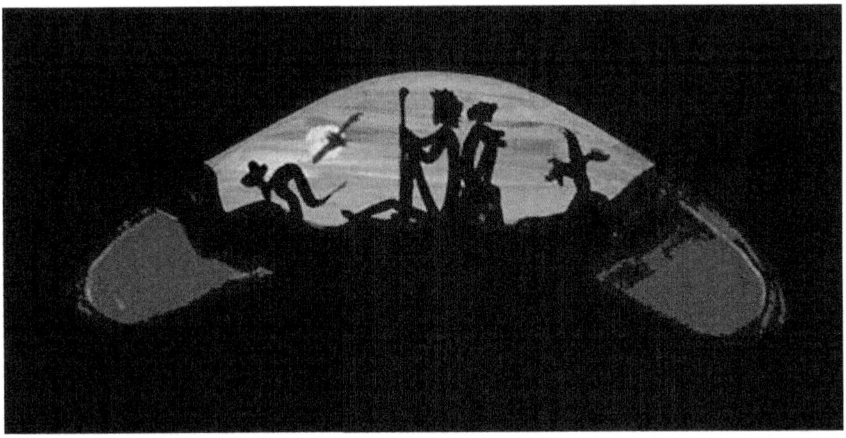

Plate 3.13 Fridge Magnet Boomerang, 2000, plywood, acrylic paint and magnetic strips, 12 cm. Private collection.

achieving this, it offers the tourist, as the intended consumer, a practical demonstration of ancient Aboriginal technology.

The second example (Plate 3.13) is not really a boomerang at all, but a model of a boomerang. It is also made from plywood and is only recognisable as a

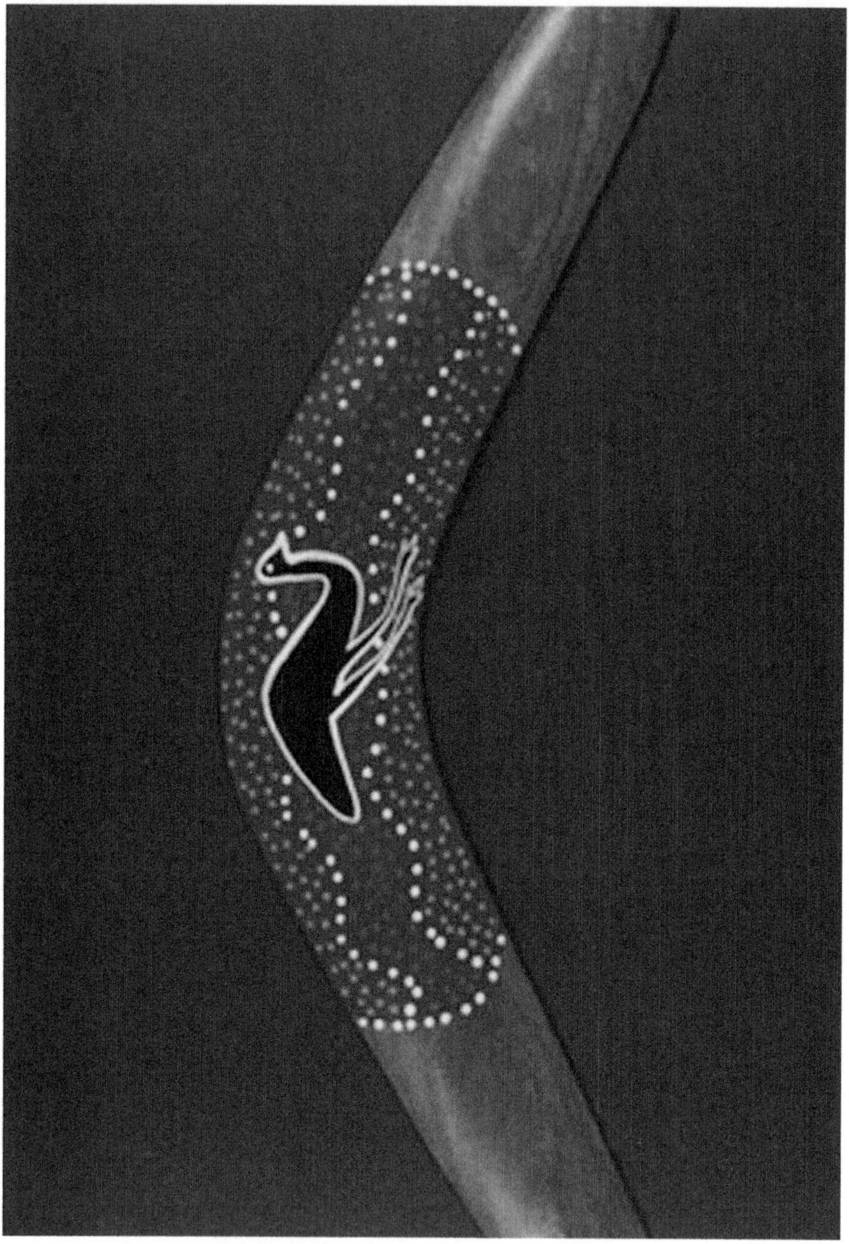

Plate 3.14 Simon Rose, *Boomerang*, 2000, wood and acrylic paint, 54 cm. Private collection.

boomerang through its unique shape. It does not describe an arc when thrown, nor does it return to the thrower. It cannot be conceived as a lesser-known, non-returning type, used for hunting in club fashion, as its size and weight would be of no use for this purpose. In reality, this artefact is a fridge magnet that utilises the familiar boomerang shape for the purpose of describing a stereotypical Aboriginal hunting scene on its painted surface. This truly decorative souvenir favours image over function and is implicitly aimed at 'satisfying the consumer' rather than 'pleasing the artist'. It is, however, hand-painted and so is not strictly a mass-produced artefact. Nevertheless, to the tourist it is successful in bringing to mind a picturesque sense of Aboriginal Australia.

This tendency, toward image over function, is also the priority of the third example (Plate 3.14). Made by Simon Rose, a descendant of the Birri Gubba and Goreng Goreng people of Queensland, this boomerang is of traditional design, obtuse angle and hewn from dense timber. The finish is imperfect and shows some small chips along its sharp edges.

The centre of the curved face is decorated with an Aboriginal-style design, featuring a black Emu with white outline, set against a sea-green background, augmented with orange, red and white dots. The dotted background lends itself to a notion of three-dimensionality in the scene, with two rows of white dots depicting the contours of hills, while the more generously spaced, central red band of dots provides the illusion of receding distance.

In his statement, provided on the reverse of this boomerang, Rose is unequivocal about the intent of his work, writing that his painting style is inspired by his culture's relationship to the land and expresses his happiness at 'fostering an appreciation of indigenous people' (Rose n.d.). Here the artist makes a deliberate engagement with the tourist market and recognises its importance in maintaining his culture across trans-cultural boundaries. This boomerang demonstrates the traditional sculptural and painting skills of the artist and is truly the art of one culture made for the benefit of another.

Summary

Despite the difficulties with Graburn's categories, identified above, they serve as a sound starting point for the study of tourist art, without which such artefacts would remain in a sort of limbo, between art history and anthropology, unwanted by both disciplines.

For his part, Graburn illustrates these categories with field studies from a number of researchers. They range across the globe, from his own foundational field study of the (*Eskimo*) Inuit art of Eastern Canada, to Williams' survey of Australian Aboriginal art from Yirrkala. What they share in common is a focus on the imagery of 'Fourth world peoples', whose way of life is under threat from acculturation and integration, and is vulnerable to the gaze of the tourist industry.

In her study of the development of the souvenir trade at Yirrkala, Arnhem Land, from 1935 to 1970, Williams, like Tuckson, points firstly to the establishment of the Methodist Mission settlement as responsible for the introduction of a cash economy and, subsequently, the marketing of Aboriginal arts (Williams 1976: 266). Detailing the goods transacted, Williams writes that:

> garden produce and other foods as well as clothing and desired small goods have become available in the mission. Aborigines obtained the money to buy these goods chiefly through wage labour and the sale of art objects (until recently predominantly the latter).
>
> (Ibid.: 268)

Williams continues providing a catalogue of art objects produced for sale during this period, consisting mostly of intricately carved wooden pipes, sculpted effigies of birds and animals, stone axes, wooden spears, painted spears and throwing sticks, boomerangs, didgeridoos and occasionally bark paintings (see Williams 1976: 273 for a complete list). With the growing sales of these items, she states that the mission station soon redefined its role to that of art dealer, going on to say:

> [t]he increasing demand for Aboriginal art that began in 1964 has continued to be principally the result of orders from business firms catering to tourists in Australian capital cities. These orders are preponderantly for inexpensive objects, mostly small carvings and suitcase size bark paintings.
>
> (Ibid.: 276)

In this way, Aboriginal art from the tip of the Northern Territory came to represent the broad expanse of Australia and to serve as markers of an engagement with a very different place. This demonstrates the ability of the souvenir to stretch the truth of the tourist engagement. Above all, it is the demand for suitcase-sized objects that clearly defines these objects as souvenirs.

Williams has documented the growth of commercial and tourist art at Yirrkala, with an emphasis on subsistence within the changing economic system. In the latter stages of her study she interviews a number of artists regarding their motivation to produce the art. Just as we have discovered a number of motives for boomerang production, Williams was informed by the interviewees that the work was firstly produced to maintain Aboriginal culture and identity, as a statement of land rights and to teach the young and, secondly, that the art was produced for financial profit, although the money earned was never enough to rely on by itself. It is clear from this that the affirmation of cultural identity and heritage was the primary intent of the Yirrkala souvenir makers. This is also true of Morphy's 1991 study, in which he points out that among the Yolgnu people of Yirrkala, sacred art and tourist art share the same social function and are equally important in maintaining the identity of the people. These motives are common to many other producers of tourist art.

In a comparative field study of Southwest American Indian art from the same period, Brody focuses on the revival of Hopi pottery and has recognised similar factors in the development or revival of indigenous art styles (Brody 1976: 75).

For Brody, the primary motive is the maintenance of cultural identity. In this respect, we may understand that the intimate consumption of the souvenired site by the producer is vital in the production of successful tourist art.

Whether it is Yirrkala bark paintings, Inuit stone carving, Hopi pottery or Aboriginal boomerangs, a vast range of tourist art product has been developed. Furthermore, some tourist art commands a high price, due to the quality of work, and is collected by art dealers, patrons, institutions and discerning tourists. It is repetitively produced for the consumption of the broad, tourist market but 'conform[s] to a preconception of what (art and craft) from that place is supposed to look like' (ibid.: 76). This almost parallel development of indigenous art at opposite ends of the earth has been found to be still in evidence some twenty-five years after the publication of Graburn's text. For instance, the establishment of the Keringke Arts Centre at Santa Teresa (Ltyentye Apurte), Alice Springs, has followed a similar pattern and today tourist art is produced in the same studio, in many cases by the same artists, as high-priced, painted canvasses. This process was evidenced at the Keringke Arts Centre, in which an enormous range of goods can be seen, from hand-painted model boomerangs to dot painted pottery, and other household items, fashion silks and highly detailed traditional paintings.

As with Aboriginal art from Yirrkala, the Catholic nuns of this former mission settlement also recognised the assimilatory potential of the arts and crafts and promoted them accordingly, modelling the work to the demands of the market (Keringke: 1999). This sensitivity is still uppermost in the mind of the present coordinator and reflected in the ongoing development of printed silk, designed for the tourist and fashion market. This enterprise occurred around 1981 and built on the development in the art of Batik that was happening at Ernabella (ibid.: 14).

A consistent factor in the production of tourist art, alluded to by Tuckson, is that of size and price. Both Brody (1976) and Williams (1976), together with Graburn (1976: 41–55), in their respective field studies of tourist art, cite the importance of uniform size, to facilitate shipping, and price sensitivity. Above all, the most vital definition of tourist art, demonstrated in the above surveys and others (Graburn; Maduro; Lathrap; Ben-Amos; Inglis; Batkin; Steiner; Littlefield Kasfir), is that tourist art is produced by one social or ethnic group for consumption by another.

The production of tourist art and the changing nature of indigenous art, brought about by the influence of new economic systems and later tourism, occupies the bulk of Graburn's text, and there is little consideration allotted to the study of the consumption of tourist art and souvenirs. What, other than size and price, attracts the tourist to certain souvenirs and not others, and where they end up, are central concerns of this project. Graburn's text is most insightful on the production of tourist art but falls short on the analysis of the activity of the tourist and how the subject experiences and consumes the site, ultimately selecting a souvenir by which to record the experience. This is the focus of the following chapters.

4 The souvenir and the fetish

Introduction

This chapter posits the idea that tourism and souvenir collection are structured along the same lines by which the fetish is theorised. This contention requires a slight alteration to the conventional understanding of the fetish, as I will argue that the conventional structure of the fetishistic narrative, as circular and restricted in its orbit of meaning, is expanded when the material anchor is a souvenir.

I have broken this chapter into individual parts that take their titles from facets of the fetish; namely: Narrative, Substitution, Irrational Belief, Surplus Value and Seriality. Additionally I have elaborated on certain facets, with resource to examples and classic case studies.

In the following pages it is my intention to demonstrate how the history of fetishism shares many common facets with the theorisation of the tourist as 'Other' and how this state is recorded through the collection of souvenir artefacts that may also be understood in terms of the fetish. I will also elaborate further upon the point of convergence between 'primitive art' and tourist art. This will include an examination of theories expounded in the writings of Marx and Freud, and later developed by other writers who utilise a contemporary theory of fetishism and investigate its relationship to tourism.

First used in 1757, by French philosopher Charles De Brosses, the term 'fetish' was quickly seized upon by German and French writers and applied to the analysis of primitive religion associated with the African continent. Both Marx and Freud picked up on this and applied the term to their own work on the primitive and irrational (Pietz 1993: 134). Given that both writers were, principally, engaged in the theorisation of modern society, it is reasonable to consider their theorisations of the fetish as methods by which to establish the 'Other' through the dominant discourse of the day. More recently, MacCannell (1992: 1) has argued convincingly that 'tourism is not just an aggregate of merely commercial activities; it is also an ideological framing of history, nature and tradition', while Barnard (2002) argues for the recognition of '[h]unting-and-gathering society: an eighteenth-century Scottish invention' as a way of recognising a mode of production 'other' than modern.

A key proposition in the study of tourism is 'that myth and fantasy play an unusually large role in the social construction of all travel and tourist sites' (Rojek 1997: 53–54) and, furthermore, that:

> [t]he emerging sociology of tourism and travel has not really got to grips with the role of the unconscious in colouring sights … there is much in how our ordinary consciousness of tourist sights (*sic*) functions to suggest that we draw on a collective fund of unconscious symbols, images and allegories.
>
> (Ibid.)

This claim is grounded in Urry's argument that tourist destinations are culturally constructed, in that they are formed from a dichotomy that reads the domestic domain as 'ordinary/everyday' and the tourist site as 'extraordinary' (Urry 1990: 11) (see also Graburn (1977) who theorises the same shift as a Sacred–Profane disjunction). In his claim, Urry establishes a clear relationship to the nineteenth century anthropological construction of 'Otherness' that is materially anchored and typified by the fetish object. This is supported through Rojek's ensuing analysis of tourist behaviour, in which he points to the character of current social conditions as 'fragmentation, differentiation and now de-differentiation', and continues to cite the way people associate with each other around brand names but without actual contact (Rojek 1997: 61). This equates to the fetishes of consumer society or, as Rojek puts it, 'the material register of our inner fantasies and dreams'. On this, Rojek (ibid.: 58) provides a critique of cultural theorist, Walter Benjamin, and writes 'Benjamin sees capitalist culture as suffused with the direct expression of the unconscious. Wish fulfilment and repression are integral to capitalist processes of exchange and distribution … it is also the material register of our inner fantasies and dreams.' Rojek then makes the point that these 'social conditions of anonymity' are typical of the 'virtual collectiveness' that gathers around tourist sites, referring to such temporary social groupings and the sites around which they meet as 'pulpy', in that they retain a plasticity of ever-changing meaning (ibid.: 61). Here there is a dexterity of meaning that, in the last chapter, was discovered to exist in the souvenir, itself a fragment of the site.

Before the tourist even experiences the site, however, he or she has developed a perception of the site from fragments of information gathered through various tourist and anecdotal sources, such as brochures, billboards and, increasingly, television and other electronic media. What can be seen here is that the fragment not only characterises the souvenir, but that it also underwrites the structure of contemporary tourism at its onset, including the construction of the site. Even in the case of a small island, like Tasmania, those attractions and views listed and promoted by the tourist industry represent only a tiny fragment of the island, yet they are framed in such a way as to represent the entire island state. Marketing terms, such as 'See Tasmania in Ten Days', in fact support the idea of creating the whole from the fragment. I will scrutinise these issues more closely in the following section. For now, I will focus on the souvenir as a fragment of the visited site and culture. Stewart (1984: 135) provides an account that utilises a Freudian schema, positing that the artefact of tourism operates within a logic of substitution, writing that:

> Here we find the structure of Freud's description of the genesis of the fetish: a part of the body is substituted for the whole, or an object is substituted for a part, until finally, and inversely, the whole body can become object, substituting for the whole.
>
> (Stewart 1984: 135)

As Stewart points out, the fragment and the souvenir are always incomplete and reliant upon the imagination to complete the narrative they suggest. The souvenir, like the fetish object, exists as the material anchor from which the narrative emanates. For Rojek (1997: 53) this narrative construction is fundamental to the tourist's appreciation of the site and represents the manner through which, in the author's terms, the tourist 'indexes their experience'. Such indexes or markers take the form of 'visual, textual and symbolic representations', that is fragments of the original, not uniform fragments, but rather media 'and conventions associated with signifying a sight'.[1]

As an indexical item, the souvenir's effect on the psyche of the collector relates to the activity of the fetish, in that it is a fragment that refers to the whole, from which a narrative, albeit conventionally a limited narrative, is generated. This activity, of attaching narrative to a material fragment, is the most apparent point at which the two objects, the fetish and the souvenir, come together. It is also a contentious issue within the study of tourist art and souvenirs.

This point is debated from one angle by Pearce, S. (1995: 32), who partitions the souvenir from the fetish object on the grounds that the fetish object remains dominant and constructs the personality of the collector. She contends that 'the objects are dominant and the collector responds to his obsessive need by gathering as many items as possible'. She argues that the souvenir enhances the personal experience of otherness for the collector, who 'creates a romantic life history by selecting and arranging personal memorial material to create … an object autobiography, where the objects are at the service of the autobiographer' (ibid.). On the other hand, Stewart (1984: 135–136) suggests that the souvenir is not only clearly related to the fetish object, but that the relationship confers a historical feature upon the fetish that was previously denied.

In the following section I will demonstrate the fundamental relationship that exists between the fetish object and the souvenir. I will achieve this through a focus on how such objects sustain and integrate the holiday experience into our daily routine once the holiday is over. I will then explore how such objects develop from the initial fetishistic impulse that is at the root of their collection. Furthermore, I will show that there is a very close relationship between the two types of objects, and that theories of fetishism can inform our understanding of souvenired objects. I will argue that souvenirs construct the experience of the collector and are endowed with the same supernatural powers of the fetish. I will then show that such objects remain dominant in the narrative construction of the collector's past experience of the visited site. But first it is necessary to gain some insight of the compositional features of the fetish and how they relate to souvenirs.

Substitution

Substitution is the first component I want examine. For Freud the idea of the fetish finds its root in the Oedipus complex and, more precisely, in the fear of castration at the sight of the naked female body (Freud 1962: 154).[2] As Stewart (1984: 135) notes, the base structure of the Freudian fetish is dependent upon the notion of substitution for that which is not available. In Freud's notable example, that which is lost is the mother's phallus. The concept of substitution occurs in the unconscious and sets up an enduring material 'memorial' for that which is unavailable or denied materially. In touristic terms this structure relates to the activity of souvenirs, as a fragment of an actual, rather than an imagined experience of place and otherness (Phillips and Steiner 1999; Stewart 1984).

Freud's theory of the fetish takes as its starting point an experience that never was. Instead, this experience is imagined during the early stages of ego development, during which the child subject comes to recognise (him)self as the centre of his world and the measure of it. It is this centrality of the self that also resembles the condition of the contemporary tourist in his or her real travels and experiences. In later sections I will elaborate on how objects and artefacts displayed according to the seventeenth century structure of the *Wunderkammer* conform to this idea by situating the collector at its epicentre. It is in the action of substitution, however, that a method of organisation is to be found that parallels that of the souvenir.

Substitution is, then, the first point at which the souvenir and the fetish converge. This process of substitution begins prior to the collection of souvenirs, and is a primary condition of the tourist or holiday-maker's activity. As the tourist disengages from his or her daily routine, a replacement behaviour emerges. The mundane routine, summarily divided into equal daily sections of work, rest and play, may be characterised in terms of the subject's emplacement within the contemporary mode of production. It is an emplacement that is predicated on the notion of a capitalist exchange economy. In this system the subject, the intentional tourist, exchanges his or her labour in order to profit through increased purchasing power. In other words, the subject gives in order to take, or produces a product in order to consume another of his or her choice. This system is suspended in the holiday mode, and replaced or substituted for one that is based entirely on consumption, which renders the tourist as 'Other' with respect to those still engaged in the mundane system. For Rojek (1997: 55–56), this suspended state is characterised as 'escape activity' which, he argues, deserves more scrutiny than is often afforded it, on the grounds that the appeal of tourism is 'partly related to the switching of rules practiced in our domain cultures with contrasting rules'. This argument is further strengthened through Rojek's reading of Kracaeur and Virilio in which he makes the point that the tourist's ability to travel vast distances today, for the purpose of visiting tourist attractions, 'caters to our desire for stimulation without demanding that we make serious important personal commitment' (ibid.). In the context of my argument, the lack of 'serious important personal commitment' may be understood as characteristic of an outright consumer mode of being. More interestingly, Rojek pursues this convincing line of thought via an anecdote about Freud visiting the Parthenon. Citing a brief tourist memoir, in which Freud recalls his visit during his forties, Rojek explains how, from listening to tales about Ancient Greece from his father, Freud had long harboured a desire to see the Parthenon. These stories had made a deep impression on his unconscious, but the young Freud, believing that he would never see such sites, had placated this desire by repressing them, 'except as objects of imagination' (ibid.).

This switching of rules demonstrates the holiday-maker's need to fill the structural void of the holiday with a substitute set of rules; a set of rules that is focused on the consumption of the destination or event. In other words, for the period of the holiday, the holiday-maker is relieved of the need to produce or give anything back that is concrete. It should be noted, however, that the holiday is not unproductive. What the tourist produces is narrative; those ubiquitous travel stories that are augmented by, and made more believable when given material form through, the souvenir. This substitutive action is investigated further in Freud's study of belief systems, in which the role of the concrete artefact takes centre stage.

Belief

An insight into the believable nature of tourist narrative, augmented by the souvenir, is to be found in Freud's analysis of organised religion. Here the founder of psychoanalysis speaks of placation through unsubstantiated belief and lists a number of mechanisms – such as powerful deflections, substitutive satisfactions and intoxicating substances – that placate our misery and, in part, fulfil our wishes (1962: 74–75).[3] Indeed, it is the 'powerful deflections' of the holiday that cause the holiday-maker to forget the routine of work, and other chores, that characterise the domestic environment.

In the holiday environment the tourist is relieved of the drudgery of housework. This is replaced by the intoxication of exotic places that permeates the subject's being while on holiday. It is this initial alleviating measure that I now want to investigate in order to show how the tourist's relationship with the visited site provokes the collection of souvenirs.

Early anthropologists were informed largely by a pre-modern theory of hierarchical evolution that situated European people at the apex of civilisation (Phillips and Steiner 1999: 7).[4] This hierarchical model of human evolution, anchored within Western society, provided the basis for Freud's theory of psychic development. Many interpretations of the Freudian formulation of the fetish have been made as derivations of this evolutionary theory. Freud's use of the artefacts of other cultures to illustrate his theories makes him an important figure in the present argument. Torgovnick explains the associative value when commenting on the figurines that littered Freud's study:

> For Freud these statues were more than mere decor or possession. They were containers of myth and clues to human nature, collaborators in the stories Freud told about men and women, morality and sexuality, civilisation and the forms of life that went before it.
>
> (Torgovnick 1990: 196)

In this illuminating chapter, Torgovnick elaborates on how Freud's study was set out in order to exhibit his collection of artefacts for the specific purpose of suggesting to the analysand a narrative progression from uncivilised infant to civilised adult (ibid.: 197).[5] So it is, with the collected artefacts of travel, that the display of souvenirs demonstrates the structural organisation of the collector's experiences of foreign places and cultures that amount to the tourist's foray into otherness.

That hierarchy of 'primitiveness to civilisation' has a particular bearing on the success or prevalence of fauna-derived souvenirs as markers of a pleasure-seeking period. This is alluded to, for instance, in Ranashoff's captions for the photographs of Freud's study in which she states that: 'Here above the chair where Freud sat listening to his patients are … mythological figures: a centaur (half man – half horse) and Pan (half man – half goat). They represent aspects that are primitive, phallic, and pleasure-seeking in human nature' (Ranashoff, cited Torgovnick 1990: 196).

Reflected in these mythological figures is not only the link between pleasure and animal nature, but also the illustration of incompleteness. This suggests the image of such mythological creatures and, for that matter, fauna-derived souvenirs, as unique types of souvenir, that record a period, or periods, of lapsed civilisation on behalf of the collector. There are a significant number of souvenirs, from many parts of the world, that engage the tourist with the idea of becoming part animal such as Kwakwaka'wakw (Kwakuitil) masks from the West Coast of Canada and many other First Nation tourist arts (Jackson Rushing III 1999). Other souvenirs suggest an engagement with the fauna of the tourist destination through motif and figurine, such as Spanish bulls, kangaroos and koalas, Micky Mouse, etc. As I have suggested above, the holiday is in many aspects a suspension of civilisation, as typified by the mundane domestic routine. But, above all, what is illustrated through Freud's Romantic construction of history is the power of objects and artefacts to make real and believable a desired narrative.

It is quite apparent from Freud's writings, and the above insight into his study, that he rarely took a holiday. And why should he? Torgovnick's survey shows he had no need to absent himself from work for he had, throughout his study, the artefacts that contemporary holiday makers collect in order to organise and integrate their moments of deviant discontentment. This is emphasised further in the opening line of *Civilisation and its Discontents*, in which Freud (1962: 3) writes, through the voice of a friend, of the 'unbounded' feeling, that he describes as the sentiment of religion, 'a feeling which he would like to call a sensation of "eternity", a feeling as of something limitless, unbounded – as it were, "oceanic"'. The use of four descriptors – 'eternity', 'limitless', 'unbounded' and 'oceanic' – suggest the difficulty of describing the feeling, a feeling that most clearly resides in the unconscious alongside the fetish impulse. For the tourist this sensation is that which is sought from the visited site and the sensation of travel. It is 'freedom' from the order of the mundane that is evoked by the holiday.

This limitless sense of freedom is demonstrated today in the specific example of the eco-tourist who, seeking to satisfy a desire for freedom, will immerse him or herself in the so-called wilderness. Many of these destinations are not, in actuality, wilderness sites but are little more than theme parks, framed through legislation rather than perimeter fences, and dedicated to delivering a wilderness experience. They are the playgrounds of the biophilic fetishists, for him or her to explore, to develop and enhance their experience of nature. They are experiences that are lost at the completion of the holiday but are recovered, or made clear, through the sensual process of fetishism. Such experiences are frequently sustained in the material form of fauna and flora fragments or, more commonly, landscape photographs and images into which the tourist may project his or her presence. In order to comprehend this notion at a deeper level, I want to substitute, as Torgovnick (1990: 205) does, the idea of the missing maternal phallus for our estranged relationship with nature and the wilderness.[6]

Nature and landscape form have historically provided illustrative examples of the birthing process. Much has been written regarding the landscape imagery, perspectives and representations that draw their inspiration, mostly, from the female form.[7] These images frequently depict lush valleys, caves, grottos and other such pictorial compositions that are read as metaphoric vaginas. These gendered perspectives have informed and influenced the shape of many souvenirs. Prints, postcards and other reproductions of such images have found their way into the souvenir market. One of the most renowned painters to interpret the landscape in this way was Gustave Courbet, 1819–1877, whose gorge and grotto images clearly parallel the vagina and offer a primordial engagement with the landscape, or as Fried (1990: 209) argues:

> [S]cholars have often noted an analogy between Courbet's depictions of caves and grottos and certain overtly erotic paintings of female nudes centered on the vagina, most notoriously the *Nude with White Stockings* and the recently rediscovered canvas … *The Origin of the World.*
>
> (Fried 1990: 209)

In her discussion of Courbet's *L'Origin du Monde*, Nochlin (1986: 77) argues that 'nothing could be more Freudian than … the quest for a lost original'. Here, Nochlin is referring to both the search for the original painting and the subject of the image, the naked female torso, which she, like Fried, equates to Courbet's earlier grotto paintings.

Other landscape theorists, including Bermingham (1986), also recognise the dominance of the male gaze in the formulation of the conventional landscape composition and particularly the features of 'promise, refuge and threat', so prevalent from the early Romantic picturesque (Bermingham 1986: 63–85; see also Appleton 1978). This compositional style has persisted through the development of contemporary tourism and has one single aim – to provide the tourist with a sense of unbounded liberation from the mundane. A survey of most promotional tourist literature will show how two of these features – 'refuge' and 'promise' – are inscribed into the images of tourist brochures and other promotional media. These features vary in presence, depending on the destination in question; the resort tourist tends to prioritise toward refuge, with some degree of promise and a minimum of threat, while the eco- and adventure-tourist engages with a higher degree of threat, supported by promise and imagined refuge.

In each case, the promotional images must cause the would-be tourist to believe that the desired attractions exist at the destination. The postcards featured here – *Bruny Island* (Tasmania) (Plate 4.1) and *Cephissus Creek In Upper Pine Valley, Du Canne Range, Tasmania* (Plate 4.2) – are typical touristic images that demonstrate these compositional features to differing degrees. The *Bruny Island* postcard (Plate 4.1) offers the promise of a deserted, sunbaked beach, accessed along a cleared path. There are two points in this image at which threat may be conceived. In the distance the landscape appears impenetrable and dangerous; here the sense of threat is dramatic. However, from the point in the

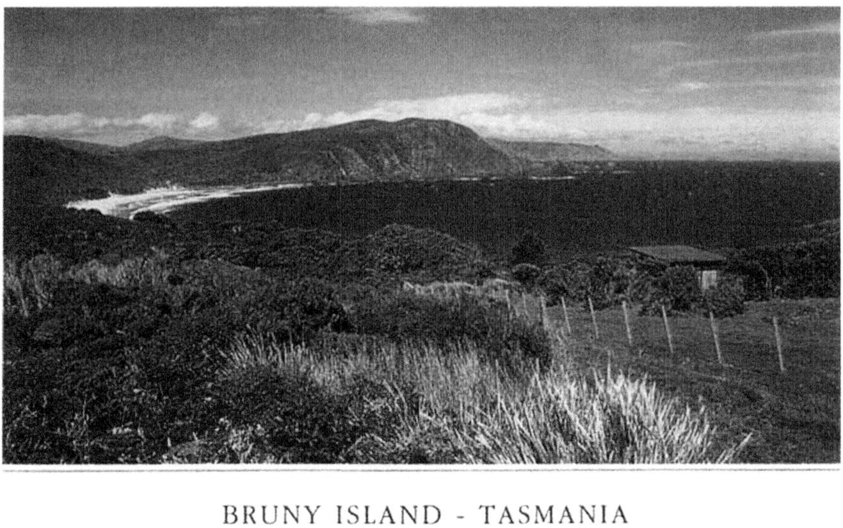

Plate 4.1 Geoff Murray, *Bruny Island*, 2002, postcard, 14.2 × 10 cm. Private collection.

foreground where the path disappears into the coastal heath, the viewer must trust that the path is constant in its definition and gentle slope. The sense of threat in this instance is one of becoming lost and ensnared in heath. Refuge is provided by the small hut, which also serves as a navigational aid by which the tourist may find his or her way back.

The viewer may become lost in this postcard image, subsumed by nature; however, there is a greater likelihood of that in the following postcard image of *Cephissus Creek In Upper Pine Valley, Du Canne Range, Tasmania* (Plate 4.2). The composition of this image offers no gentle access along a cleared pathway. Nature closes in on both sides and there is no promise of a distant, sunbaked beach. The central feature of this image is the narrowing Cephissus creek. It is like Courbet's *Source of the Lou* grotto paintings,[8] in that it features an expanse of onrushing water in the foreground and recedes pictorially into unknown primordial darkness. In their compositional qualities, this postcard, in common with many other popular wilderness images and Courbet's *L'Origin du Monde* and grotto paintings, shares a symbolic reading that offers the viewer a 'panerotic mode of experience that perceives in nature a female creature' (Hofmann, cited Fried 1990: 210).

In these two postcards, the natural environment is framed as remote and alienated from the tourist's mundane routine. They represent an estranged engagement with the natural environment or wilderness that Freud refers to as

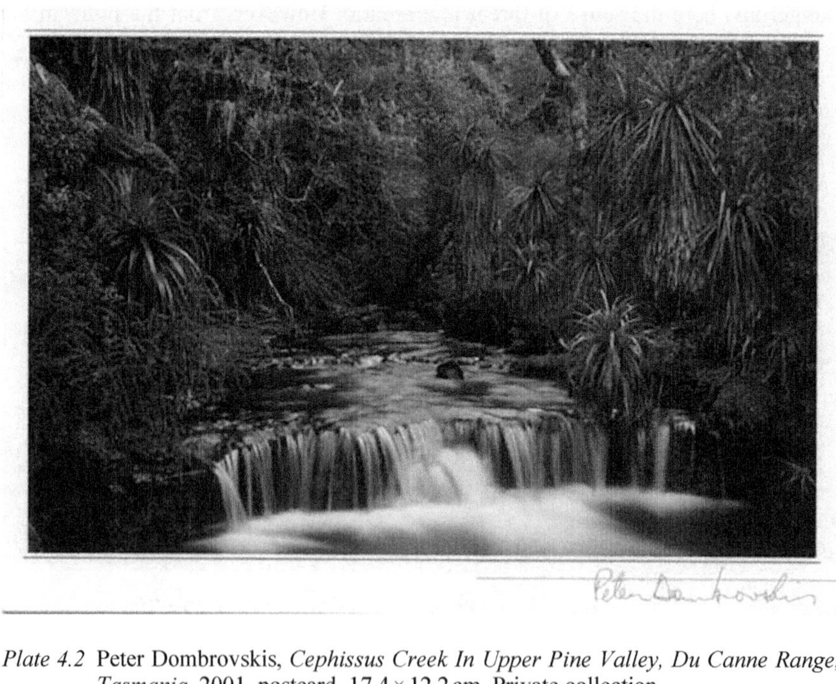

Plate 4.2 Peter Dombrovskis, *Cephissus Creek In Upper Pine Valley, Du Canne Range, Tasmania*, 2001, postcard, 17.4 × 12.2 cm. Private collection.

sensations of unfettered freedom and oceanic connectedness with the natural environment. This absent relationship with the birth phenomena, that is nature, is commonly engaged with through the activity of tourism, in particular all degrees of eco-tourism, of which sightseeing is a fundamental recreation (Urry 1990; Crawshaw and Urry 1997).

The notion of substituting a fragment of what is denied for the entirety of the experience is sustained in the field of tourism and, moreover, in the consumption of souvenir objects, as fragments of the holiday experience. Just as the artefacts in Freud's study are understood to describe the journey from primitive to civilised being, so souvenir artefacts are invested with the task of representing the visited site and/or culture. The souvenired object may then be understood as a fetish object that replaces the finite experience of the destination. The disavowal of loss is now complete and the experience has been given material form. This lost experience becomes comprehensible through the inscription of narrative onto the surface of the souvenir, as a memorial to the trauma of loss. Then, by installing souvenirs of visited sites in the domestic environment, the collector is able to rekindle the state in which the mundane is suspended. But, unlike the narrative props in Freud's study, the initial direction invoked by the souvenir takes the collector back to a deviant period characterised by the 'primitive'. These periods of deviant behaviour are, according to Soper (1995: 117), founded on 'Holy days [that] are after all feast days, when the normally forbidden excess is permitted and even prescribed', and are typical of the condition of the tourist and plot the development of tourism from Christian holy days as the initial relief from the drudgery of the mundane. For MacCannell (1992: 180), these periods represent a 'search for the authentic self, characterised as the *savage* or *primitive* figure viewed as close to nature' (see also Urry 1990; Rojek 1997; Shields 1991).

This state of 'primitive' or primordial engagement, this sensuous experience of place and people, is consistent with colonial formulations of the African fetish object, as structured by the colonial and early anthropological interpretation of exotic people and places. The tourist's engagement takes place outside the socially authorised constraints of time and place. As discussed previously, it is also commensurate with the rise of the tourist sublime during the Romantic period, that best defines the condition of the tourist. For the sublime too is a sensuous engagement in which the subject is overawed by a sense of oneness, in which the structured order of being is suspended in favour of a state of innocence or freedom.

It is my contention that the understanding of the fetish as a childlike, unstructured, unknowable and irrational belief system is bound up in the modernist prejudice toward the art of non-Western cultures. An aspect of this kind of prejudice is the misunderstanding that what were formerly referred to as primitive cultures were absent of historical development. Furthermore, I contend that the circular movement that defines the conventional account of the fetish is flawed. It is my belief that the fetish contains within it a space that only appears to be vacant, but is really loaded with knowledge and expression; that is not unavailable or impenetrable to the outside viewer; it is simply difficult to comprehend from the viewer's current standpoint. The root of this prejudice resides in Freud's inability to conceive of multiple histories, coexisting side by side, and his assumption that 'primitive' societies lie outside of historical processes. This notion of coexisting histories is seen as incompatible with that of the West and, as a result, remnant 'primitive' societies are locked into a continuous cycle of repetition, or, as MacCannell (1976: 91) terms it, 'Staged Authenticity'.[9]

The nineteenth century anthropological underpinnings of Freudian psychoanalysis are somewhat discredited today and non-Western discourses are accepted today as history. In the tourist's suspended state, he or she is liberated from the history that characterises the non-tourist or domestic emplacement within the world. The tourist creates an, albeit brief, other self under the conditions of the substituted regulations, one that is 'unbounded' and liberated from the mundane routine, and approaches the 'authentic' self that exists elsewhere in other 'historical periods and other cultures, in purer, simpler lifestyles' (ibid.: 3). It is an alternative emplacement within the world that shares many of the attributes allotted to those societies formerly viewed as primitive. For instance, the tourist often uses a foraging mode of consumption, believes in the magical powers of the fragment to create the whole, what might be referred to as a 'primitive' and irrational belief system, and finally, there is the propensity for the substitution of the governing social structures or norms. All of these aspects of tourist behaviour contribute to, and can be identified in, the psychoanalytic formulation of the fetish. There remains, however, one sticking point in the psychoanalytic formulation, and that is its insistence on the circular and impenetrable nature of narrative.

Narrative

The narrative activity of the fetish presents a significant problem for the associative analysis of souvenirs. According to Freud's formulation, the fetish implies a narrative that is forever circular and never expands its meaning beyond the personal. For Freud the fetish never breaks out of its circular orbit and is therefore unappreciable to anyone, other than the collector of the fetish object in question. Freud is unequivocal on this private aspect of fetishism, writing that:

> The meaning of the fetish is not known to other people, so the fetish is not withheld from him: it is easily accessible and he can readily obtain the sexual satisfaction attached to it. What other men have to woo and make exertions for can be had by the fetishist with no trouble at all.
>
> (Freud 1962: 154)

Not only do we see the root of Pearce's reading of the fetish, as an object that remains dominant, but also an economy that exists solely in a closed loop between the subject and the object. The problem in comparing souvenir objects as fetish objects is clear, in that the secondary purpose of the souvenir is to situate and express the collector's experience of the destination within the private and public realm. This can only be achieved if the souvenir can be seen as operating in a more expansive way than the conventional fetish. As we have discovered, narrative, within the field of fetishism, has been restricted by the belief that the narrative is always circular and non-expansive. This is embodied in the writings of Freud, for whom it is incomprehensible that concurrent histories, times and places can exist like some sort of overlapping mosaic of transparencies, which is challenged by later interpretations of the fetish.

Apter (1993: 3), for example, argues that fetishism is typified by the 'Eurocentric voyeurism of "other" collecting' and is 'always a meaningful fixation of a singular event; it is above all a "historical" object, the enduring material form and force of an unrepeatable event'. In discussing the European coloniser's search for 'aura soaked signs' of African otherness, Apter directs our attention to the rise of the tourist sublime and the character of the fetish, and how they have 'emerge[d] as a trope of 'wish fulfilment' an expression of oneric nostalgia for archaic substrata of the self' (ibid.). This is what MacCannell (1992) terms the 'authentic' self, discovered in the activity of tourism, through an engagement with 'primitiveness'.

Apter first deals with the political activity of looking, likening the tourist gaze to that of the coloniser. As with Stewart (1984) and Pearce (1995), she recognises the souvenir as backward looking in the first instance, but then notes the close relationship of colonial invasion and tourism, pointing to the present and future action of the souvenir. She sees the souvenir as a device for remembering, and making present in every day life, a period of time and an engagement with another place and culture, that permitted and fostered a behavioural pattern informed by the sensuous unconscious (Apter 1993: 5). In this interpretation Apter alludes to the condition of the tourist and the developmental character of the fetish. But the decisive point at which Apter draws the fetish and souvenir together is in the ability of the fetish object to act as 'the enduring material form and force of an unrepeatable event', for, as Stewart (1984: 135) argues, souvenirs also mark unrepeatable events.

In Figure 4.1 I have sought to illustrate this developmental quality of the fetish. The conventional circular narrative structure is represented by the small inner circle. Within this circle I have plotted the conventional fetish object and the limited scope of its narrative, which placates the trauma of loss in the unconscious and is restricted to the personal domain. Under the unique conditions of tourism, represented by the souvenir, this narrative will travel to the outside of the inner circle and become manifest in the form of the souvenir. At the boundary of the conventional fetishistic space, the fetish gathers up a narrative structure, a simple uttered narrative, and projects the object into the private communal space and then broader society. That is, from the personal space into the domestic space, exemplified by display in the private home.

Once the object has broken the confines of the conventional fetish and the narrative is understood by others close to the collector in the private or domestic domain, the anecdotal momentum is unstoppable. This momentum, propelled by narrative, sees the fetish object expand its meaning into the thoroughly public

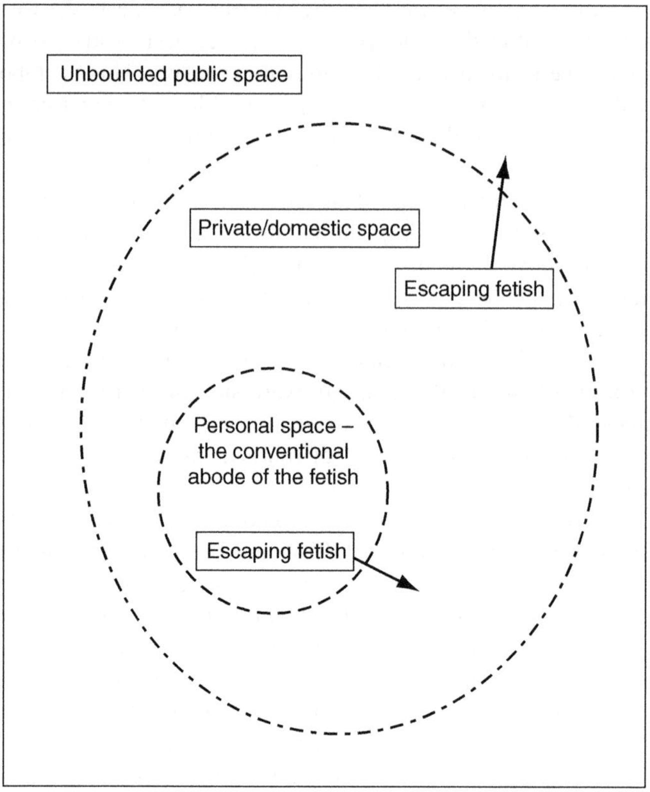

Figure 4.1 Showing the travel of the fetish from closet to sideboard to museum as personal, domestic and public sites of exhibition.

domain and take on a meaning and value that is consistent with the public or communal authorisation of the icon. One can see in this process the development of museums from private collections.

In Figure 4.1 I have defined the conventional boundary of the fetish using a simple dash-dash circle, while the nominal boundary between the private and public space is defined with a dot dash line. The purpose of this is to illustrate that the object contained within the private domain tends to travel more easily into the unbounded public domain than the conventional fetish can into the private domain from the personal.

The initial attraction of the souvenir, for the collector, is fetishistic, in that it is a substitute part for the entirety of the tourist experience of the destination. Firstly, it satisfies the tourist's need to organise his or her emplacement within that space and then it further serves to sustain that experience through irrational belief. Like the fetish object, the primary role of the souvenir is to memorialise and placate a difficult memory. For Freud, the fetish object placates the trauma of the castrated female form, whereas the superficial activity of the souvenir soothes the reality that the holiday and the experience of the destination must end. That is the supernatural power, or value, that narrative brings to the material presence of the souvenir. It is evident from this that souvenirs and artefacts of travel always refer to a destination or place, while the fetish object is less insistent on place. If experience is attached to a site of occurrence, then further similarities between the two objects will be discovered. Freud notes that '[i]n very subtle instances both the disavowal and affirmation of the castration have found their way into the construction of the fetish itself' (Freud 1962: 156). The idea of affirmation is consistent with the notions of memorial and placation, foreshadowed above, but it is also suggestive of a future narrative expansion.

In the postcards, *Bruny Island* and *Cephissus Creek In Upper Pine Valley, Du Canne Range, Tasmania* (Plates 4.1 and 4.2), I have demonstrated the prevalence of the male gaze, showing how they share the same compositional features with Courbet's grotto paintings. I have also pointed to the relationship between the figurative reading of Courbet's grotto paintings, his *L'Origin du Monde* and the two landscape postcards, suggesting that they all offer the viewer a figurative engagement with the unknown that brackets together the female form and nature. This relationship is extended further through the narrative of origin, and the provenance of *L'Origin du Monde*.

In his repeated grotto paintings, Courbet positions a dark void in the middle of his canvasses, just as Dombrovskis draws the viewer into the narrowing reaches of Cephissus creek, shrouded by the increasingly dark, lush vegetation. In the truncated female figure of *L'Origin du Monde*, the vagina is the central focus, while Dombrovskis makes the syrupy Cephissus creek, with its foreground of mist, the central feature of his landscape. Both *L'Origin du Monde* and *Cephissus Creek In Upper Pine Valley, Du Canne Range, Tasmania*, provide the viewer with a rich point of departure, from which to develop an expansive narrative, that Nochlin (1986: 77) frames as Freudian and refers to as 'the quest for a lost original'.

It is this state of connectedness – Freud's 'oceanic' condition – that the tourist, and especially the eco-tourist, seeks to engage with and record through the selection of a souvenir. The foot fetishist is able to make whole the female form by attributing meaning to the fragment, a meaning that assists the integration of the female form with his own. Likewise, the tourist's activity of souvenir collecting enables him or her to sense a connection between the exotic or extraordinary visited site – in this case the Tasmanian wilderness – and the more familiar or ordinary, and subsequently to sustain the experience of the entire site, through the attributed narrative. The provenance of *L'Origin du Monde* and the reception of Dombrovskis' wilderness photography demonstrate this travel of the fetishistic narrative.

While attempting to trace the whereabouts of Courbet's infamous painting, Nochlin discovered that 'the work was bought in about 1910 by Baron Francis Hatvany of Budapest', who 'had seen the painting at Benheim Jeune Gallery in a double locked frame, hidden by a panel representing a "castle in snow"' (ibid.: 80).

The fact that the painting was 'hidden' is a clear indication of the way the furtive and fetishistic nature of the work was retained while it was on display in the public sphere. She then recounts Maxine du Camp's sighting of the painting in 1881 'at the home of its then owner, the notorious art collector Khalil Bey', who notes that '[i]t was viewed in his "dressing room" and kept hidden under a green veil' (ibid.: 81). Both the highly personal setting of the 'dressing room' in 1881 and the concealed manner of display in 1910, at the Benheim Jeune Gallery, point to a limited reception of this work, that is commensurate with the travel of the fetish, demonstrated in Figure 4.2. In the first case the image was displayed in a personal space; 31 years later it was still veiled but in a more open and commercial environment and today it hangs in a public museum, the Musee d'Orsay, where it is flanked by two of the greatest public works of art that Courbet created – *A Burial at Ornans*, 1849–1850 and *The Artist's Studio: A Real Allegory Determining a Phase of Seven Years of my Artistic and Moral Life,* 1855.

The evolving reception of Dombrovskis' landscape photography is somewhat different, yet is equally convincing in showing the developmental nature of the fetish. His most famous image, *Rock Island Bend, Franklin River, Southwest Tasmania*, is composed in a similar manner to the earlier example, *Cephissus Creek In Upper Pine Valley, Du Canne Range* (Plate 4.2). It features a swirling mass of foggy water in the foreground, bounded, this time, by sheer cliffs that focus the eye into the centre of the image, where the river narrows, beyond which a light mist shrouds the background. The site of this image – the Franklin River, Tasmania – was, during the 1970s, the destination of small groups of rafting enthusiasts, early eco-tourists and wilderness photographers.

In the late 1970s the Tasmanian State government proposed a plan to flood the area for a hydroelectric dam. This brought about a conflict that pitched the Tasmanian Wilderness Society into opposition with the government of Tasmania, and a protracted political battle ensued. Both parties sought to garner the support of the people through an evolving publicity campaign. A major turning point in the ongoing campaign was the worldwide publication of Dombrovskis' *Rock Island Bend, Franklin River, Southwest Tasmania* image, which is credited with mobilising opinion regarding the beauty of the river to a much wider audience; which in turn contributed significantly to the river's protection and subsequent world heritage listing as a key tourist attraction.

The images created in the Southwest of Tasmania, during the early 1970s, circulated among the few that ventured into this remote part of Tasmania and their friends. The reception of the images, at this stage, can be seen as existing in what I have illustrated as the domestic sphere. Following the publication of *Rock Island Bend, Franklin River, Southwest Tasmania* in the national and worldwide media, the narrative attached to the image has, like that of *L'Origin du Monde*, ascended into the public sphere, as shown in Figure 4.2. Both images were once restricted to the viewing pleasure of a few but are now overwhelmingly ensconced in the public psyche. In both cases the images have achieved great notoriety. They have accomplished this by appealing to the viewer's desire for a sense of connectedness with nature.

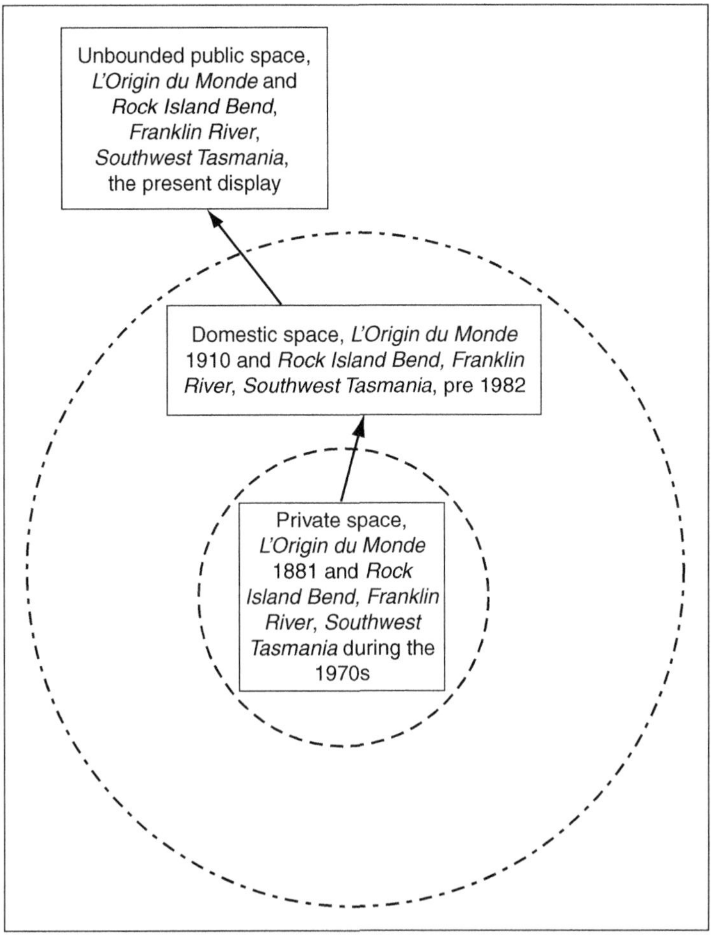

Figure 4.2 Showing the developmental nature of the fetish embodied in Courbet's *L'Origin du Monde* and Dombrovskis' *Rock Island Bend, Franklin River, Southwest Tasmania*.

The shadow of the holiday's early structure survives today in the habits and desires of contemporary tourists in general and, in particular, the eco-tourist, that specific band of tourists that engages with the natural environment. The holiday today is a period of time during which the participant disengages from the life-long activity of socialisation through work and other regular activities that establish and enhance his or her status within the everyday community. It is this mundane routine that alienates the subject from any sense of unboundedness. The need to sustain the ego through the accumulation of goods forces the subject's id into submission for long periods of routinised time. That is to say, the ego, the conscious calculating forefront of the mind, is dominant for around forty-eight weeks a year, leaving little time for an unbounded or oceanic spiritual engagement, invoked and organised, or rather dis-organised, by the unconscious id. During the brief periods when the order of work is suspended, the subject often becomes a tourist, engaged with the rules of extended leisure, and demonstrates many behavioural patterns that are the antithesis of those dictated by the work ethic and its attendant routines. The tourist will: overvalue his or her temporary place of abode; eat, sleep and drink on impulse; experience heightened erotic sensations; and collect objects with little or no utilitarian value. Rojek (1997: 60) addresses this sensuous engagement of the tourist as a state in which 'mass culture reduces the ordinary consumer to the position of an addicted consumer of reproduced objects, packaged events and other manipulated stimulants'. The tourist will, in general, behave in ways that do not suit or fit the usual mundane routine of work or expected social behaviour. Indeed, just like the fetish object, the souvenir is, at heart, an object that engages with the collector at a sensuous level. This runs counter to the imperial argument that states that primitive society is characterised by its lack of art and pure creativity, for the arrangement of discrete periods of tourist activity may be seen as an escape from a 'primitive' state of being within a contemporary, Western-style society. This is because the tourist finds him or herself in a condition that is characterised by leisure, sightseeing, consumption, the collection of souvenirs and, above all, a sense of otherness. This is a condition in which a sensuous engagement is promoted and one in which most tourists retain a 'faith' that their needs and desires will be met, that are the opposite to a lifestyle dominated by work and security. This notion of faith of belief in magic is the next feature I want examine.

The magic of material objects, art and souvenirs

At this point I want to consider the tourist's sense of otherness and his or her faith in the souvenir's ability to record this sensuous state. First I will look at the so-called magical power of the material fetish through anthropological case studies and then I will show how artworks and artefacts of contemporary tourist art function as fetish objects.

Stewart (1984) provides an insightful account of how, in particular, Freud's theories of fetishism inform our understanding of the attraction of tourist art and souvenirs (see also Pearce 1991; Phillips and Steiner 1999; Clifford 1994). After showing how the fetish operates by substituting 'a part of the body for the whole', she demonstrates the correlation between the fetish object and the souvenir, writing, '[t]he souvenir is by definition always incomplete' (Stewart 1984. See also Pearce 1991; Phillips and Steiner 1999; Clifford 1994.) Stewart argues, for instance, that a model of the Eiffel Tower, while not a sample of the tower but a representation of it, still operates as a sample of the experience (ibid.: 136). As a representation it retains the power to invoke an expansive narrative of the experience, an experience that is irretrievable without the supernatural powers discovered in the structure of the fetish.

It is Pearce (1995), however, who, having earlier distinguished between the fetish object and souvenir, provides the clearest link between the activity of both forms of object, and their capacity to transcend the personal space of the fetish, to the sacred state of communal museums and art galleries. For her, it is all a matter of magic and illusion. The fetish object, in terms of 'primitive', animistic belief, is endowed with supernatural powers that define the adherent's situation or emplacement within the world. It is the sacred object around which all else is organised. In contemporary Western society, these reified objects are gathered within the walls of museums and art galleries. Pearce (ibid.: 406) refers to these artefacts as 'the sacred collection … stored within its shrine through its successive historical manifestations'. Here Pearce situates the museogallery system as the final resting place for those artefacts that the community hold in the highest esteem. But she also suggests that, in their 'successive historical manifestation', such valued artefacts existed at a less valued level, gathered by individuals without communal covenant (ibid.). In this state the collection may be housed either in the closet, sideboard, or perhaps dressing room, the personal or private space as depicted in Figure 4.2.

I have shown, in Chapter 2, how, during the sixteenth century, this personal space for the storage and display of valued possessions took the form of the *Studiola* or *Museo* in southern Europe, the *Wunderkammer* in Germany and later the 'Cabinet of Curiosities' in England. These variously described repositories of the weird and wonderful bear a significant similarity to the closet in that the *Studiola* and *Wunderkammer*, in particular, are described as dark windowless rooms, often situated in an out-of-the-way part of the house.[10] In the first instance such collections were confined to the powerful but, with the advent of the industrial revolution, the Romantic period and the democratisation of travel (notably the Grand Tour), the capacity to gather and store such collections soon spread to the growing middle classes. Many of these collections now form substantial parts of state and national museum collections.

Once ensconced within the the museogallery system, the collection performs for the public and, as Pearce (1995: 406) argues: 'Here it acts as the community's endorsements of its own value judgements about aesthetics, knowledge and history. The museum collection acts as the touchstone for the authenticity of physical evidence upon which, in the last resort, understanding rests.' In other words, the collection is endowed with the magical ability to make things real – judgements about art, knowledge and the past. It conjures a reality for a history that can only be imagined. This is true also for the private collection. As Pearce again argues:

> For the individual his own personal collection does much the same, validating his judgement of his own life and linking this to the broader judgements of the community as he may or may not wish to do. In both dimensions the collected objects both reflect our ideas about ourselves, and act with their own magical power to reinforce and enhance these ideas.
>
> (Ibid.: 406–407)

Here she recognises the magical power of the object, which in its sacred state operates as a fragment of the past, which presents the illusion of an unbounded state across time, place and cultures.

It is in Pearce's astute use of the word 'reflect' that we find not only the genesis of the unbounded or oceanic state, but also a conflict with her earlier notion of the activity of the fetish. It is, as the title of this section suggests, all done with mirrors. For it is only in the reflected image of the self that we may actually view ourselves set within the context of our environment. Once achieving this, either through a direct reflection in a reflective surface or a captured image such as a photograph, we are able to gaze upon our physical selves as subject, as part of the environment and, as Pearce says, to validate our judgement of our own life. It is this process, of self-reflection, that the souvenired object fosters through its materiality of the experience. Like magic, the souvenir has the ability to imaginatively transport the collector back to the time and place of the experience. It conjures an experiential past in which the collector is able to imagine him/herself situated as an indelible part. In this sense one can see that the fetish object, in the form of the souvenir, is also capable of contributing toward the personality of the collector. This capacity becomes more dominant over time, as the recollection of the experience begins to rely, more and more, on the conjuring ability of the souvenired object.

As the fetish object escapes the confinement of circular narrative and becomes familiar to a larger audience, it does so without loss to its fetishistic worth – defined through its status as a fragment with unsubstantiated value. There is, however, a shift in the make-up of its definition as a fetish object. Once out of the closet, as we have seen in the case of Courbet's *L'Origin du Monde* and Dombrovskis' *Cephisus Creek*, the narrative of the object becomes familiar to a broader audience and continues to expand until it is appropriated into the museogallery system. The object is now more complete and distanced from its fragmentary fetishistic status as this narrative expands. This is, however, balanced by the object's assumed and increased, but unsubstantiated, worth, validated by the museogallery system. The 'magical power', so frequently allotted to the fetish object, is not, therefore, diminished or dying, as both Pearce and Mulvey would suggest, arguing respectively that it is vulnerable in domestic or public display (Pearce 1995: 32), or said to die when exposed to 'new economic conditions' (Mulvey 1996: 3), but instead altered or transformed. The fetish object and the souvenir alike, have, as MacCannell (1992: 176) writes of tourism, 'the capacity to make dizzying leaps over existing political, cultural and social class boundaries', and, in the process 'enmeshing a great diversity of local groups, community, artefacts and natural attractions in its expansions'.

In pursuing this point, MacCannell then draws our attention to the typical tourist town as an example and presents an excellent demonstration of how the fetish may survive outside the personal space. He says, of the tourist village, that it 'resembles an empty meeting ground: where people live and tourists visit, a place that has been decorated to look like an ideal town of some sort, but no one is related to anyone else' (ibid.). In other words, while the village appears to be a normal village, developed through a communal history, that history is absent, or at best incomplete, just as it is for the fetish object. In Rojek's terms, it is 'pulpy' and, if one follows Mulvey's and Pearce's notion of the dying fetish, then the tourist village has lost its integrity and exists now only as a commodity of tourism. Gone is what, for the tourist, is the attraction of the tight community and simple social values that typify village life. But, is the fetish dead under the public gaze of the tourist? According to MacCannell, it is only the 'primary function of the village' as 'the base for human relationships' that is altered; it has now transformed into 'a detail in the recreational experiences of a tourist from out of town' (ibid.). So, in MacCannell's terms, the fetish persists in the private and public space, as shown in Figure 4.2, as a historical detail.

For historical support for this claim I want to turn to the annals of structural anthropology. In his study of magic and religion, 'The Sorcerer and His Magic', Levi-Strauss (1958: Chapter IX) examines the activity of narrative among the tribes of Brazil and later the role of the shaman in Kwakwaka'wakw (Kwakiutl) society on the West Coast of Canada during the 1930s. He begins by explaining that the intention of sorcery is to cast out the evil that is manifest in the patient. This includes exiling the subject from friends and relatives, and from the community that provides the routine referencing system of self-awareness. Levi-Strauss (ibid.: 138) terms it as the 'withdrawal of multiple referencing systems' that, in effect, confirm life. This action is similar to the isolation of material and substances that occurs in the discipline of Western science, where subjects of study are subjected to the microscopic gaze, removed from their interrelated context. This isolating gaze is evidenced quite clearly in the sketches of exotic flora and fauna executed by the illustrators that accompanied the voyages of many early explorers.

The withdrawal of these social support systems render the subject dead, 'cast into the world of shadows', which even 'physical integrity' cannot overcome. The subject's own knowledge of self cannot overcome this status of 'the dissolution of the social personality'. While death does not actually occur, a state of suspension does; as Levi-Strauss argues, physiological shifts in the subject do occur. They take the form of a drop in blood pressure, rejection of food, dehydration, and general trauma and anxiety. The author typifies these symptoms as psychosomatic, in that they are not completely imagined but are enhanced by the imagination, and that such symptoms are prevalent in unstable societies (ibid.). In the nature of an unstable society, there are clear similarities with that of the community of tourists, because the ephemeral community of tourists is, perhaps, the most unstable of temporary societies within the broader, contemporary Western society and symptoms of instability do affect its participants. For his part, Rojek (1997: 61) refers to this condition as one of 'Virtual collectiveness' or 'Social anonymity' describing it as a collectiveness that is temporary and based on the immediate emplacement of the subjects, rather than historical and social understanding. Relph (1976: 149) provides a useful commentary on how travellers come to know a strange place and put down shallow roots in a couple of days.

In the curing of these psychosomatic symptoms, shamanism finds great success. While Levi-Strauss refers to a society reliant upon the vagaries of hunting and gathering and the uncertainty of where the next meal is coming from, the tourist finds him or herself in a similar situation, in an unfamiliar environment. Indeed, upon arrival at the unknown destination the tourist engages in a frenzy of activity devoted to mapping the site and allaying such anxieties; the degree of desired instability varies considerably, depending on the type of touristic engagement. Tourist brochures and other related information not only tell the tourist of the wondrous sights that he or she may experience, they also present the homely (that is familiar) comforts that are to be found – such things as toilets, bathrooms, restaurants, shops that might allay the onset of homesickness. In short, and like that of Levi-Strauss's tale, the tourist is cast willingly into an environment that is less stable than home.

These theories are illustrated in two further accounts drawn from Levi-Stauss's research. The first occurs in the jungles of South America (1958: 169). This story involves two disparate small bands of tribes that come together due to difficult or unexplained circumstances. In this, too, we find a similarity with the ephemeral community of tourists. Levi-Strauss tells how a member of the newly formed group fails to return to camp after a day's foraging. A number of reasons for his absence are discussed and, after a protracted period of time, he is discovered shivering in the forest. He is then brought back to camp and eventually recounts an unlikely story. Each section of the newly formed group considers his fantastical tale and it is soon integrated into the composite group and has the effect of assimilating the two groups into one. This, Levi-Strauss refers to as the 'the means of objectifying subjective states, of formulating inexpressible feeling and of integrating inarticulated experiences into the system' (ibid.: 172).

This story runs parallel to the condition of the tourist, and particularly the eco-tourist, albeit, in most instances, in a somewhat less traumatic fashion. For the tourist is subject to the magic and sorcery of the destination and is bewitched by it. By embarking on a holiday in an unknown destination, the tourist engages with the temporary relief of his or her 'social personality' as it is confirmed by the familiar referencing system of family, friends and colleagues. The tourist exists in two worlds: the familiar and the exotic. In order to integrate both, the experience of the exotic is recounted in a similar way to the holiday tale. The holiday anecdote serves as a type of immaterial souvenir that permits the integration of both worlds. In the above story, and in the case of many tourists, this is the integration of the private experience into the public, through the agency of narrative, an integration that is solely reliant upon the listener's wish to reach agreement about its meaning and understanding. In the Levi-Strauss story it is a matter of blind faith, a faith that can be confirmed by the presentation of some sort of physical artefact as evidence of the experience – that is, a souvenir. This progression is the subject of the next tale.

In *Structural Anthropology*, Levi-Strauss (1958) expands on the power of magic in 'primitive' societies and, in so doing, presents a further example that speaks to, and is analogous to, the principles and power of material culture as it operates within tourism. This narrative, and its orbit around an unlikely artefact, makes clear what the author refers to as the 'Shamanistic complex' and how it clusters around extremes of experience: on the one hand, the intimate experience of the shaman and, on the other, the consensus of the group.

This story occurred among the indigenous communities of the Canadian West Coast and focuses on an apprentice shaman by the name of Quesalid. Learning his craft from the shaman community of his own tribe, Quesalid is sworn to secrecy about the methods and deceits used in the shaman healing ceremonies. Central to these ceremonies is a piece of fluff or 'down' that is hidden in the mouth of the shaman. He induces in himself a trance-like state, through dance and chanting, during which he bites the interior of his mouth, by which the 'down' becomes covered in blood. The bloodied down is then spat from the shaman's mouth as the material form of the illness that was afflicting the patient. Having learned this, Quesalid later comes into contact with another tribe and community of shaman. They show him their ways, which involve simply spitting saliva into the hand as the representation of the illness. Quesalid is coerced into demonstrating his craft and, upon doing so, is hailed as a great shaman and his technique is adopted.

While this is an advancement in the practice of shamanism, it also demonstrates the power of materiality, in that belief in sorcery is more likely with the presence of a material object. This is what Levi-Strauss (ibid.: 172) explains as the magic of materiality that supersedes 'blind faith'. It is in actuality a development in the science of traditional healing based upon material evidence. This is also true of the souvenir, in that it provides material evidence of the event. Levi-Strauss then shows how the power embedded in the narrative structure is enhanced by the material form. This is a threefold process described as a 'fabulation consisting of procedure and representations' (ibid.: 175), and detailed as:

1 The shaman undergoing psychosomatic states
2 The sick person, who may or may not get better
3 The public perception of enthusiasm and intellectual and emotional satisfaction that begin a new cycle.

(Ibid.: 172–178)

By stripping away the specifics of Levi-Strauss's research and focussing on the narrative structure, it is possible to detect certain similarities that address the condition of the tourist experience and, moreover, the purpose behind collecting souvenirs. Beginning our analogy, at the end point of the above, one can see how Levi-Strauss's process equates to:

3 The site is perceived and understood by the public through the images, artefacts and literature of tourist brochures as offering 'intellectual and emotional satisfaction'.
2 The tourist may or may not achieve the above.

1 But the site will, through the agency of the host, be presented as a state relative to the psychosomatic state of the shaman; that is, not totally imagined but certainly framed, edited and enhanced to capture and hold the attention of the tourist.

Quesalid's success is directly related to the attitude of the group; that is, the communal consensus that the bloodied piece of down is the sickness. This is also typical of the souvenir, in that its success corresponds to the belief that it is a fragment of the visited site. In other words, the 'intellectual and emotional satisfaction' of the site must be represented in the souvenir artefact, and the allusion of these characteristics must be believed – firstly by the collector, then the ephemeral community of tourists and subsequently the broader society – once the tourist has returned home.

It is due to this need for communal recognition that souvenirs are standardised in some way. This normally occurs through raw material, image or reference to heritage, or through all three. In Tasmania and many other parts of Australia these qualities are profoundly embodied in material drawn from the flora and fauna, such as minor species timber souvenirs. But what is most apparent, in the above example, is how belief, formed through narrative, may give rise to an inflated value for material objects such as souvenirs and fetishes, and this is the subject of the following section.

Surplus value: the economy of the fetish and souvenir

Marx defined fetishism in his early writings as '[t]he religion of sensuous desire' (1951). This phrase is neatly analysed by Pietz, who writes that:

> The term 'sensuous desire' … was thus theoretically fraught. Not only is 'desire' the term for the purpose-forming subjectivity that characterises the ethical world of humanity, but 'sensuous' indicates that immediate experience of lived reality which is the primordial mode of experience (the object of aesthetic feeling).… 'Sensuous desire' is thus the direct 'aesthetic' expression-apprehension of purposes and intentions within the subjectively objective world of immediate experience.
>
> (Pietz 1993: 140)

From this interpretation of Marx's formulation of the fetish it is possible to discern the condition of the contemporary tourist. Fundamental to the tourist is a desire to experience the 'Other' in terms of culture and environment. The tourist seeks or desires to be taken out of his or her own routine environment and to experience that which is unfamiliar. In such a case, the tourist is then required to initially engage with the visited place in a primordial, sensuous mode until the unfamiliar site is mapped, gridded and made familiar, through a rational system of mind's eye cartography.[11]

At the end of the eighteenth century, 'Otherness' and a primordial mode of experience were the domain of the 'primitive', while the so-called Enlightenment logic understood fetishism as an animistic belief system, associated with 'primitive' cultures in Africa and other differently developed parts of the world. Pietz (1993: 131) tells how the 'theoretical narrative of the world history of religion was established in European intellectual culture by the end of the eighteenth century' and how '[h]istorians of religion around the turn of the century … discussed fetishism extensively as the earliest stage of religion'. He also informs us that:

> the very distinction that constituted Enlightenment rationality was responsible for a contradiction in the way it conceived its unenlightened Other: fetishism was defined as the worship of 'inanimate' things even though its paradigmatic historical exemplifications were cults of animate beings, such as snakes.
>
> (Ibid.: 139)

During the colonial period, artefacts collected from non-Western cultures were used to support this imperialist view of the evolution of humanity, situating races, cultures and environments in a hierarchical order, otherwise referred to then as the 'chain of being'. From this dominant Eurocentric position there appeared to be no earthly or spiritual rationale for investing supernatural, god-like power in animals, and particularly inanimate objects. It was with this perspective in mind that Marx formulated his notions of 'surplus value' with respect to the Western capitalist system of commodity production. For, '[a]lthough Marx's materialism and his social theory went far beyond those of Enlightenment thought, his synopsis of the historical progress of people … bears an eighteenth-century pedigree' (ibid.: 130–31). This understanding of both 'primitive' fetish objects and Western commodities as containing supernatural powers suggests an economy that contains an unsubstantiated surplus, a value that, according to the laws of capitalist economics, is irrational. The economics of souvenirs supports this theory, as those artefacts are always priced over and above their rational value and even beyond that circumscribed by Marx's notions of 'surplus value' bound in the capitalist system of exchange.

In recognising the sensuous engagement and unbounded relationship the 'primitive' exhibited with the environment, Marx discovered a similar relationship between 'moderns' and money. For Marx, money was the single most fetishistic feature of modernity that facilitated the 'mystical character of commodities' (Marx 1954: 76). He explains how the property of the commodity exists as an unintentional by-product of the producer's labour, only knowable through the process of exchange, and that it 'has its origins … in the peculiar social character of the labour that produces it' (ibid.). For exchange to take place, and for exchange value to occur, the artefact must be of some use to the maker and others (ibid.: 78). For Marx, the unsubstantiated exchange value occurs only under the condition of capitalism, because 'the whole mystery of commodities, all the magic and necromancy that surrounds the products' exists only while they 'take the form of commodities' and dissipates in 'other forms of production' (ibid.: 80–81). In terms of the souvenir, this exchange value is dominated by the expression of people and place, which is not directly addressed in Marx's critique but to some degree exists in the mystical and magical properties of the artefact.[12]

Marx's next step involves the way goods were produced and received in the West prior to the capitalist exchange system. He asserts that in the Middle Ages, goods and labour had no value as exchangeable commodities. Work was carried out, goods produced and a benevolent payment was made by the sovereign, as God's agent (ibid.: 81). He then argues that the religious world is a 'reflex of the real world' (ibid.: 83) and suggests that commodity exchange under capitalism is a natural development along this spiritual path (ibid.: 83–84). If this is so, then tourism – with its developmental base in the religious pilgrimage, holy days and the desire to discover oneself and its associated artefacts – must be seen as a type of secular, post-modern, religious practice, a practice that includes the investment of magical powers in inanimate objects and animals. In other words, tourism is an occasional, quasi-religious engagement with 'Otherness', whose experience and surplus or irrational values are embodied in the souvenir, just as Christianity is embodied through the crucifix and other fetishised commodities, including shrines and other buildings and historical sites.

In spite of the discrediting of the hierarchical theory of evolution, and even as testimony to the far-reaching structural nature of the fetishistic desire, souvenir objects and artefacts still function to standardise the representation of the culture of origin. Those representations often provide a false, simplified and generalised picture of the experienced culture. This occurs on a macro and micro level as the representation of nationalities, religions, cultural groups, and, as MacCannell (1992: 176) has argued, as villages. It is, in essence, the attraction of the visited site and culture that the tourist seeks in the souvenir. Today the natural and cultural heritage of Western and non-Western cultures is found to be represented by many fetishised crafted artefacts; such as totem poles, Tibetan rugs, boomerangs, Scottish kilts, masks, Spanish bulls, Mickey Mouse and other inanimate objects. This organisation is not a conscious decision, but in effect demonstrates the function and value of the fetish that Pietz (1993: 120), reading Levi-Strauss, says, 'informs a particular mode of social organisation without themselves being objects of consciousness'. In this way souvenirs also may be viewed as artefacts that are 'fundamental organisational structure[s] of a given society' (ibid.: 120). That is, they serve as the organisational structures of the social narrative that, in Graburn's terms, both differentiates and integrates the identified culture according to fundamental structural features.

As we have seen, for the anthropologist today, as in the colonial period, objects of 'Other' cultures and proto souvenirs function as an index of the social organisation of societies. But today, the society organised by these artefacts and objects is, moreover, that of the ephemeral community of tourists and, more broadly, the developed Western, post-modern, mobile society.

This understanding of fetishism's role in consumer culture is further elaborated upon in Mulvey's study of commodity fetishism, in which she asserts that:

> Both Freud and Marx use the concept of fetishism in an attempt to explain a refusal, or blockage, of the mind, or a phobic inability of the psyche, to understand a symbolic system of value, one within the social and the other within the psychoanalytic sphere.... One, the Marxist, is derived from a problem of inscription. How, that is, does the sign of value come to be marked onto a commodity?... the Freudian fetish, on the other hand, flourishes as phantasmatic inscription. It ascribes excessive value to objects considered valueless by the social consensus.
>
> (Mulvey 1996: 2)

Here the subject of inscription and the problem of the commodity's value are set out as common to both Marx's and Freud's interpretation of the fetish. Mulvey continues, a few lines later, to outline the difficulties of analysing the points at which society and its consciousness part, and the relationship between people and things begin. She writes (ibid.: 3) that:

> [t]he cultural analyst, while trying to draw attention to these 'points' and make them visible, may only be able to begin to reach them when new economic and social conditions come into existence, rendering the dying fetishisms easier to grasp.

Here, as we have discovered, Mulvey concurs with Pearce in seeing a fetish as a finite thing of restricted meaning, suggesting that it cannot exist beyond its deeply personal confines. However, the most interesting point is that Mulvey suggests that clarity occurs in death. Surely the author's meaning is not literal here but alludes to a moment of transition, that in the early Romantic poet William Blake's sense is understood as passing from innocence to experience through a sublime moment.[13]

Mulvey's study takes film as its subject and while her understanding of the fetish is conventional, the suggestion of 'new economic and social conditions' might well refer to the developed state and democratisation of tourism and travel, and the effect it has on visited cultures. This renders her reading of Marxist and Freudian concepts of fetishism pertinent to a study of the commodities of tourism. For it is notions of disavowal and estrangement – as she writes (ibid.: 3) '[t]he process of disavowal (Freud) and estrangement (Marx) [that] produces an over-valuation of things, and the over-valuation flows onto and affects an aesthetic and semiotic of things' – that provide the process for the recovery of loss, of those precious moments of deviance, through the selection of souvenirs via their semiotic inscription. In this way, the tourist seeks to reconfigure, or stay, the onset of time through the material presence and magical powers of the souvenir.

Time

Time is a further point at which tourism intersects with this early formulation of fetishism, in that both are ahistorical. As we have seen, the post-Enlightenment theory of fetishism is grounded in studies of African animism, the worship of creatures and things said to be lower in the chain of being than humanity (Pietz 1993: 133–135). These are the objects and artefacts, like souvenirs, that are endowed with supernatural powers in order to organise alternative belief systems. To the early explorers of the day there seemed to be no discernible evidence of religious development (according to the European model of progression from animism to polytheism to monotheism) and so such societies were deemed to have no history and to exist outside of time. While this notion is quite rightly discredited today and, as I have already stated, alternative histories are increasingly recognised, the notion of existing outside of time is fundamental to the activity of tourism. The tourist does, indeed, attempt to achieve just that, and seeks to stave off the onset of time, uttering such lines as 'do we have to go home tomorrow?'

As I have discussed, in psychoanalytic terms, this sense of being outside time is interpreted as 'unboundedness' and takes its narrative lead from the Oedipal crisis. In this narrative, new-found manhood is the metaphor used to signify a limitless state outside of time (Torgovnick 1990: 205). This state is applied more precisely to the condition of the tourist by Baudrillard (1998: 151), who writes that the concept of time 'occupies something of a privileged place. The demand for that special kind of good equals the demand for almost all others taken together.' In both ways – by experiencing an environmental site or inanimate object as the key structure, fixed in time, from which the site radiates, and the desire to exist outside of routinising time – the tourist fulfils the role of the primitive in the discourse of post-Enlightenment and early modernist philosophy. It is the role of the souvenir, as a fragment of the experience, to preserve the memory of such 'unrepeatable events', and to provide for the incorporation of them into the normal daily routine after the fact. In this way the souvenir suggests the notions of unboundedness and connectedness, and above all assists in sustaining the holiday sensation after its termination.

Here, once again, it is possible to see Graburn's notion of the souvenir as differentiating and integrative. It is the tourist's desire to exist in a static moment that, in many ways, fosters a system of museumification throughout the tourist industry. For instance, both indigenous and non-indigenous cultural groups, as the subjects of the tourist gaze, are encouraged to promote former lifestyles through fabricated artefacts and performances. These have become less integral to their social structure, and therefore of less real value, but are vital in the tourist's perception of their society and so accorded a surplus value that is realised only in the process of exchange.

In Marxist terms this is achieved by the tourist, through the action of the commodity's overt indexing of its process of production; that is to the place, time and activity that surround the souvenir's making. In this way the souvenir serves as a representation, and reminder or mnemonic device, for the recovery of a lost, past or unrepeatable experience. It is consistent with the fetish, encoded with mystical powers, the powers of projection that subsequently enhance the collector's spiritual and sensual life and knowledge. The souvenir also functions in accordance with the Freudian interpretation of the fetish to disavow the notion that the experience is lost, or performance ceased, and cannot be regained in the foreseeable future, if at all.

Fulfilling the role of a memory jogger or aide-memoire, the souvenir is invested with the wealth and value of the associated experience. The souvenir provides a surface that is subsequently inscribed with the narrative of the experience, thus sustaining a relationship with the place and time of the experience or event. However, unlike the Marxist fetish, the souvenir is not reliant upon the total erasure of the mark of production. Indeed it is crucial that the souvenir retain some identification of its production process, reference to its culture of origin and, in the best example, the thumb print of the maker.

In recognising the tourist's capacity for excessive consumption, and preference for the hand-made, the craftsperson is often inclined to place a mark-up on the souvenir that is in excess, that is a surplus to that which the product would cost in a standard or routine exchange system. This may, in part, be justified because of the seasonal nature of tourism, in that the craftsperson may only find a market for his or her goods during three or four months of the year, when tourists are plentiful. However, if, as is most often the case, the craftsperson works for him or herself, then the surplus value accorded to the alienation of labour does not exist, for there is no contractual exchange of labour involved in the manufacture of the goods.[14] In other words, many crafted souvenirs are produced in a way that is more similar to the mode of production that existed prior to industrialisation and the capitalist system of mass production. The crafted souvenir is, moreover, 'hand-made'. Today there exists a value attached to the phenomenon of the 'hand-made' and this is important in any discussion of the fetish or souvenirs.

Looking backward to an exchange system just before the industrial revolution and the advent of what is recognised as the industrial capitalist exchange system, we find ourselves in a period when almost everything was produced by hand and displayed the variables of being hand-made. During this period the location of the fetish existed in what has formerly been labelled 'orientalia'. Hand-made artefacts from other cultures – artefacts produced through production processes and/or from raw materials unknown to the collector. It is the appeal of the unknown, or unacquainted techniques, and the resultant end product that attracts the collector, just as it was the appeal of mass-produced goods and commodity fetishism that propelled the modern age of production.

One is able to detect, here, the distancing of hand-made production in the industrial age and its relegation to a mode of manufacture clearly associated with pre-modern modes of production and 'Other' cultures, those considered to be at a 'primitive' stage of development. Today's souvenir labelled 'hand-made' will, in most instances, attract the eye and touch of the tourist as it references a period prior to the advent of industrial and mass production, and thus associates the visited culture with the former, pre-modern period and in turn museumifies it. This attraction of things produced in the ways of the past, and the fetish for 'hand-made' things, explains not just the allure of non-Western artefacts, but also objects from the history of Western culture, such as colonial and convict artefacts and models. This sensuous attraction, accorded to the hand-made souvenir, does not, however, translate to the unique or one-off, as even hand-made souvenirs must conform to what is expected of the visited culture.

Within this system, the souvenir provides an exemplary object for, as I have noted, the tourist, the consumer of souvenirs, who is more than willing to purchase a souvenir without regard to its real value, that is the value it would attract within the world of mundane ordinary things. The tourist finds him or herself in an unreal world of expenditure – that is consumption, with little or no concern for income – and an enhanced need to record his or her experience. As a result, the tourist produces little other than narrative, that is made more believable and persistent when given material form.

The product that the tourist purchases is inscribed with a value that is in excess of Marx's surplus value. This is due to the tourist's suspension of the mundane and to the environment in which the souvenir is exhibited to the tourist. This constituent surplus I will refer to for now as 'leisure value', for the tourist is always reluctant to re-enter the domain of routine existence, that is dominated by work and other mundane chores, until the prescribed end of the holiday. In this respect the tourist is an excessive consumer, in that he or she will consume all that is offered by the holiday destination and return little or nothing. Given this attitude of avaricious consumption, in which the tourist will spend, spend and spend until the allotted money is consumed, he or she is more than prepared to pay more for the souvenir than the product is worth within the normal capitalist exchange system. This is in order to, first, sustain the unreality of the leisure period that is the holiday and, second, to make sensible that period upon return to the mundane. Furthermore, it is also necessary for the tourist to demonstrate a sense of belonging and social cohesiveness among the ephemeral community in which the tourist finds him/herself. To achieve this, the tourist engages in certain behavioural patterns characteristic of excessive consumption, including the purchase of same or similar goods.

Seriality

Seriality is yet another point around which the fetish object and the souvenir congregate. Like the collection of fetish objects, the method of souvenir collecting is characterised by repetitiveness or seriality in which, according to Freud, the collector will gather the same object and allot to it the same powers of representation. A representation that induces a sense of completeness developed from the fragment, for instance the sexual desire allotted to an article of clothing, takes repeated form in the fetishist's ongoing collection. In terms of the souvenir, the collection of spoons, charms and badges operate in a similar manner.

Steiner (1999: 90–96) has highlighted this purchasing habit of tourists, noting, in his case study of Ivory Coast tourists, that the tourist will seek the same or similar objects and ignore the one-off product. He suggests that this is due to the overriding need for the souvenir to represent the character of the visited site and culture among the disparate community of tourists. Here the souvenir not only needs to carry the narrative to the collector, but it must also be recognised for what it is by other tourists that have experienced the same site. It must, in other words, be characteristic of the experience and place it represents. To that end, the singular or one-off artwork fails as a souvenir, unless it includes a reference to the site by style, image or specific medium, as is the case in Steiner's own example of Ivory Coast masks, in which style alone is the binding factor. He makes no mention of the quality or specific character of the wood from which the masks are made, which may or may not be a feature of their 'Ivory Coast-ness'. For just as we have discovered how the Romans sought rare timbers from far away places in Chapter 2, I will demonstrate shortly how the character of specific timbers represents what is typical of the visited site. In this propensity to collect that which is seen to be worthy under the conditions of tourism, an unusual creature is born, in that a type of collective fetish is authorised by the loose community of tourists that is related to commodity fetishism for brand names. This shows a clear movement of the fetish as souvenir toward the public realm, one that is propelled, initially, by the authorisation of other tourists. The tourist does not seek a one-off piece; he or she seeks an object that above all speaks of its place of manufacture, that bears the mark of the maker, be it individual or collective. Steiner is succinct about this stating that:

> Because an object's economic worth in the African art market depends not on its originality or uniqueness but on its conformity to 'traditional' style, displays of nearly identical objects side by side underscore to prospective tourist buyers that these artworks indeed 'fit the mold'. There is no room left for ambiguity in this visual exhibition of iconographic reiteration and its attendant display of formal juxtapositions. In this scheme, the unique object represents the anomalous and undesirable, while a multiple range of (stereo) types signifies the canonical and hence what is most desirable to collect.
>
> (Steiner 1999: 96)

For a souvenir to represent a site, it is reliant on some element of continuity and replication. The object must be recognisable as coming from the visited site. Huon pine artefacts are a case in point as the species of tree is only found in Tasmania and therefore anything produced of its distinctive timber will automatically be associated with Tasmania, just as the boomerang form always references Australia.

The action here is allied to the activity of both the souvenir and fetish object, in that the souvenir, like the fetish, is a fragment from the place or experience it pertains to represent. From this action, it is possible to see that while it is true that some souvenirs conform to Freud's personal and inferior interpretation of the fetish, others develop a thicker narrative that sees their representation transcend the personal and come to rest in the private and public realms of display (see Figures 4.1 and 4.2). This has been noted in the case of anthropological collections, for while the anthropologist may exercise his or her particular fetish during the gathering of the collection, as in the example the Pitt Rivers collection of vessels, once the collection is recorded as a collection in the name of the collector, the collector's name then comes to represent the entire collection. The effect that this has is that the collector's fetish becomes the subject of a public fetish and is invoked by the utterance of the collector's name.

This attraction of the multiple, this ethnographic priority among tourists, brings into play notions of authenticity and debates regarding the aura of the original. Like other writers dealing with material culture, Steiner refers to the initial work on this subject in the writings of Benjamin (1969), who claims that 'the unique value of the 'authentic' work of art has its basis in ritual, the location of its original use value'. What then should be made of so many duplicates lining the shelves of souvenir shops? For, like the masks in Steiner's example, the boomerangs and didgeridoos of Aboriginal Australia, or the cedar masks of the Canadian West Coast, have their roots in ritual as the basis of their original design and use. It is this association with ritual basis that attracts the souvenir hunter and satisfies his or her desire to mark the experience of the 'Other' and exotic culture. This debate is made more complex by the nature of certain timber souvenirs in that, like the limited nature of the work of art, the 'hand-made' wood souvenir (such as the Huon pine fruit bowl, boomerang and cedar mask) is essentially also a one-off, due to the unique grain pattern of each piece of timber.

I want to conclude this chapter with a brief examination of how the producer of souvenirs sensuously consumes his or her own space and expresses his or her own fetishistic consumption of that space in the souvenir. I will then present concrete examples of this process in the following chapter, in which I focus more precisely on the transmission of cultural exchange embodied in the souvenir objects of museum collections.

The transmission of the fetish from producer to consumer

As noted previously, for Marx the ultimate fetish of modern society is simply money, as the icon of a capitalist exchange system. This conforms to Marx's early interpretation of the fetish as 'the religion of sensuous desire', a religion that finds actuality in an exchange system 'in which people's ability to produce the object of someone else's desire becomes the means of satisfying their own desire. The general form realising or reifying this social network of desires and their objects as a market system is money' (Pietz 1993: 141). This passage points to the process by which the craftsperson first satisfies his or her own desires in the production of the goods, prior to the satisfaction of the tourist (as consumer), by the creation of a proto narrative.

The crafted artefact represents the craftsperson's concept, sensual consumption and representation of their environment, that is the producer's 'oceanic' or 'unbounded' sensation of his or her environment. Such a concept is most often realised in idealistic form and refers to a heritage or part thereof that the craftsperson finds engaging and chooses to identify with, in the same way that an artist selects a medium. That which is communicated is always a selected portion, a fragment. It is the part of the site's heritage that the producer wants the tourist to see. This editorial control causes the souvenir to be overvalued in the very instance of its conception. Like the isolated flora sample, subjected to the Western scientific gaze, it is designed to command the total attention of the viewer, or in the case of the multiple, the viewer is overwhelmed by the specific features of the design or medium. In either case an excessive value is attributed to the object/artefact through its eventual isolation, fragmentary state or seriality.

The souvenir, with its reliance on the communication of heritage and, more precisely, place, situates it in some form outside the capitalist exchange system, in that its over-valuation fails to conform to the broad social consensus of the value of things. Likening the nature of social consensus and repetition regarding the African tourist art market to Krauss's (1986) commentary on Western contemporary art's constant rediscovery of the grid, Steiner (1999: 102) writes:

> In the tourist art trade in Africa, repetition is equally inescapable because the demands of the market are such that tourists, on the one hand, require the validation of multiple exemplars to authenticate their acquisition of souvenirs, and, on the other, the canons of 'authenticity' in African art as set by outsiders are such that the styles and forms of the past take precedence over developments that may rise in the present or future.
>
> (Steiner 1999: 102)

Rather than the fetish of cash accumulation through labour, which Marx fixes as the primary fetish of modern society, the souvenir is reliant, in the first instance, on the successful representation and communication of place. It is in this representation that the desire of both the producer and consumer, the craftsperson and the tourist, must manifest in a sensuous form, so that the needs of both fetishists are met in a dialogue that is inscribed onto the surface of the souvenir. In other words, this initial production process requires the sensuous consumption of the souvenired site by the craftsperson. That is, a sense of oneness is achieved with the site and the chosen material. Most often this is not a conscious decision but one that is in part collectively authorised by the maker's culture and is dependent on the maker's particular skills as an artist/craftsperson. The consumer then senses a part of the maker in the object, that, in Benjamin's terms, would be referred to as the 'aura' but is better called *inua*, a Greenlandic term meaning the spirit of the maker within the object (Hinnerson-Berglund 2002). The tourist recognises this *inua* and completes the souvenir through the inscription of his or her own touristic narrative.

This aspect of the souvenir conforms, moreover, to the notion of a primordial engagement or sensuous experience of place, promulgated in MacCannell's (1992) study of touristic desire and the aforementioned early anthropological representations of 'Otherness'. In this instance, and particular to crafted souvenirs, the sensuous experience represented in the artefact is firstly that of the host – the first layer of fetishism. This can be seen in the same way that, say, certain non-Western cultures have developed an iconography around fauna and flora that are prominent food sources and lend themselves to the forms of daily routine and lifestyle. Similarly, settlers to Tasmania have developed an iconography drawn from apples. More broadly, settler Australia may be considered to have once been represented through the image of sheep. In this way the once real social and economic value of the exampled object is sustained by this form of publicly authorised fetishism.

Where the stated examples diverge is in the exchange system within which they operate. Carved apples from rare timbers are deliberately, that is consciously, produced for the souvenir market in Tasmania, there is no traditional ceremonial history, while the products of non-Western cultures are often initially framed as souvenirs by a highly developed tourist industry. To discover more about this process, one needs to investigate early artefact exchanges between explorers, missionaries and anthropologists. It is there, between the pages of anthropological notebooks and museum catalogues, that the seminal exchanges that have developed into a sophisticated souvenir market are to be discovered.

Much of the ground work here has begun to surface recently through the work of contemporary scholars such as Potter (1999), who surveys the post-contact development and reception of Inuit representations of place and culture, citing the shift from stone-carving to print-making in order to better market their images. Batkin's (1999) study of Pueblo Pottery traces the opportunistic trade in curiosities and their instalment in domestic spaces of the Victorian era. Similarly, Lee (1999) investigates the Victorian penchant for the display of indigenous artefacts in the home environment. Many of these case studies take the form of appraisals of the historical contextualisation of indigenous art in the home, museum and gallery, but also recognise the value of the artefact in keeping traditional ways alive.[15]

The desire to represent the visited site and culture does not always require an intermediary in the form of the host or craftsperson. Souvenired objects may take the form of pebbles and sea shells gathered by the tourist directly from the beach. Such objects fulfil the same 'sensuous desire' to mark an experience of a site, but are more directly related to the interpretation of fetish objects in the discourse of early anthropologists on African cultures. Here the relationship of the souvenired artefact to the collector is principally animistic, in that extraordinary supernatural powers are allotted to such artefacts. That power brings to mind the entire experience of the site, making it relatable to others through the physical presence of the object. In this form, the souvenir is more consistent with the psychoanalytic interpretation of the fetish and the scientific motivation of early explorers, in that the object, say a pebble or sea shell, comes to represent the geology and fauna of the experienced site – what might be called the pre-culture of the place. The history of this form of souvenir is to be discovered in the samples gathered by botanists and other scientists attached to the parties of early explorers (such as Joseph Banks) and, moreover, how such examples have come to be read as synonymous with their site of collection.

This relationship circumvents Marx's theory of people–commodity relationships but extends the notion of 'sensuous desire', in that the souvenir may take the form of a direct relationship between tourist and object without the intermediary of human labour. It occurs, instead, as an object of nature, or of unmediated production, such as the aforementioned sea shells and pebbles. In this instance, the relationship extends from collector to object to place, in that it is the intention of the collector, as tourist, to consume the site by conjuring the experience through a narrative inscription placed directly upon the blank surface of the souvenir. In other words, the artefact acts as the conduit for the interpretation and memory of place and demonstrates how place is understood, without the negotiation of the host. On the other hand, the crafted artefact demonstrates the interpretation of place through the agency of the producer – the artisan, artist, or craftsperson – who must consume the site as resident or host in order to re-present it in the artefact, and later to the consumer. Then the consumer, on purchasing the artefact, invests it with his/her narrative, thus imaginatively re-inscribing, or over-inscribing, the object with the marks of interpretation and fulfilling the intention of the artefact as a souvenir. The fundamental components of this narrative include: where the souvenir was purchased; what it is made of; and the associated activity or event. As the consumer, in the form of the tourist, inscribes more and more of his/her own narrative with each telling, the narrative of production may be paradoxically obscured as it is woven into the retold narrative of the end consumer – the tourist. A fetishistic relationship then develops between the collector and the artefact, which is more often referred to as 'sentimental value'. Within this trade and negotiation of narratives, the fetish assumes a transactable value (Marx's exchange value) between producer and consumer that circumvents the notion that the fetish is stuck within its own circular narrative.

For Freud, fetish objects are bound within this notion of a non-expansive narrative that remains personal and inferior, in that it is comprehensible only to the collector, and that the replacement of the whole with a part occurs without any loss of power and meaning. The recovery of loss here provides a common meeting point for the Freudian and Marxist theories of the fetish. For as Freud theorised that the fetish evolved to mask the absence of the imaginary maternal phallus, so the souvenir may be understood as functioning to disavow the absence or loss of the touristic experience once the tourist has returned to a routine life style.

The common action of all souvenirs and fetish objects is to represent the experience, memory, beliefs, understanding and stories of the owner, and, in so doing, to make sensible periods of deviant and irrational activity – sensual desire. In this respect, the souvenir, like the fetish object, is indeed an artefact of the irrational unconscious, encumbered with certain magical powers of illusion that serve as a bridge between the unconscious and the conscious, the irrational and the rational, across which the traffic of narrative flows. To view a collection of souvenirs is to peep into the maker's and the owner's unconscious; this will be explained in the following chapter, when I scrutinise a number of artefacts that, at one point in history, fulfilled the role of the souvenir but have since found their way into respected museums and galleries.

5 Contexts of display

Tourist art in recent museogallery exhibitions

Introduction

In this chapter my aim is to challenge the assumption that ethnographic artefacts, souvenirs and works of art constitute three unrelated groups of objects and to highlight the connection between them. This will be illustrated by bringing together a number of case studies, looking at a range of artefacts presented within the museogallery system. I will begin with two examples of Aboriginal art from Alice Springs that demonstrate the tourists' demand for authenticity, and how it may be established and enhanced according to the location of the artefact.

The second case study examines indigenous artefacts from the Canadian West Coast that were initially collected towards the end of the early Modern period. Both studies involve the transition of moribund tools into representations of culture and place and the replication of ceremonial art objects for the satisfaction of the Western and/or tourist gaze.

Following this I present a number of artefacts from Aboriginal Australia and examine their status as ethnographic artefacts, souvenirs and works of fine art. I will illustrate the relationship between these objects, demonstrating how they move from one group to the other, how what were once classified as ethnographic artefacts become souvenirs and then ultimately works of art displayed in museums and galleries.

This chapter will then conclude with a study of the enhanced aura afforded these artefacts by the museogallery environment in which they are housed, outlining the way they operate as miniatures to fulfil the needs of the tourist gaze.

So far I have shown that souvenirs, as artefacts of travel and representations of place, fall somewhere between those things described as art, reliant upon their aesthetic qualities, and those objects displaced by a more recent means of production, that refer to past or changing modes of production. In Chapter 3, I have demonstrated how souvenirs maintain the identity of minority and under-represented groups and respond to their changing circumstances under the pressure of colonialism. I have also demonstrated how innovation in the field of tourist art draws the work closer to the arena of fine art and confuses the artefact's operation as a souvenir. In this chapter I examine this relationship more closely.

The primary attraction of souvenirs, like works of art, is their aesthetic quality. Also, their purpose and meaning is predicated by the collector's experience and/or perception of the visited site and culture, of which the souvenir is, in one way or another, a fragment. This attraction is based less on the quality of work but more on what is typical of the site and by the quality of what is brought to mind by the typicality of the work. It is the power and knowledge imparted by the object, through the information contained and invoked by it, that gives the souvenir its significance. It is this ability to render power and knowledge that is shared with the anthropological artefact, in that the latter also provides evidence of the experience through a material manifestation of the visited site and culture. This is the activity and meaning of the souvenir as it is consumed by the collector. Phillips and Steiner (1999: 3) argue that it provides 'an imagined access to a world of difference, often constituted as an enhancement to the new owner's knowledge, power and wealth'. Objects from exotic worlds are collected for different reasons and come to rest in various sites and are understood in different ways through time.

In the previous chapter I have argued that yesterday's fetish object may, with the aid of time, transcend the furtive collection of the fetishist and come to rest in public galleries and museums. The historical variation here, between fetish, souvenir and museum relic, relates to the ownership and the proprietorship of the enhanced 'knowledge, power and wealth' exuded by the object.

Ceremonial artefacts and displaced tools, rendered redundant by changing economic and political circumstances, provide a good example as they are vulnerable to re-interpretation as souvenirs and are, today, reproduced specifically for the souvenir trade. Such artefacts, made specifically for the tourist trade, may later be discovered as valued artefacts within museum or gallery collections. The flow of artefacts between these institutional sites of display and their subsequent investment of 'knowledge, power and wealth' must be considered in any study of souvenirs and is a key focus in the work of Phillips and Steiner (ibid.) who write:

> For the past century or so, the objects of cultural Others have been appropriated primarily into two of these categories: the artefact or ethnographic specimen and the work of art.... As a construction, however, this binary pair has almost always been unstable, for both classifications masked what had, by the late eighteenth century, become one of the most important features of objects: their operation as commodities circulating in the discursive space of an emergent capitalist economy.
>
> (Ibid.)

This discursive space is clearly demonstrated today in the shop windows and displays of art and craft galleries and souvenir outlets that have proliferated in clusters around tourist precincts the world over.

Johnny Possum Tjapaltjarri: artist and souvenir maker

In commercial outlets, artefacts can be discovered that transcend the binary division of art and ethnographic specimen. An example of this is the display of a hand-crafted boomerang in the window of a souvenir outlet in Alice Springs (Plate 5.1). This artefact, made by Aboriginal artist Johnny Possum Tjapaltjarri, is a throwing boomerang of authentic size, decorated with stylised traditional markings. The decoration is executed with commercial acrylic paint and, in the light of such artefacts examined previously, demonstrates the transition of the artefact from ethnographic specimen to a work of art, while the decorative design affirms the maker's sense of place, his belonging and, indeed, his ownership of that place. Tjapaltjarri is no mere carver of cheap tourist trinkets for, like many indigenous and some settler producers of tourist art and craft, such as Namatjira before him, he is also engaged in the production of high quality, high price fine art work. In the painting, *Possum Dreaming* (Plate 5.2), Tjapaltjarri, a brother of the better known Clifford Possum Tjapaltjarri, illustrates a more complex story of place. Significantly this canvas, measuring approximately 80 × 50 cm, provides the artist with about fifteen times the surface of the boomerang. That the story of possum hunting in this image is more elaborate than the simple Eastern Arrente Aboriginal motif on the boomerang is due to the surface area that the artist has to express his story of ownership. The painting is also clearly perceived by the predominantly Western consumer group as a work of art, fetching somewhere between $3,000–$7,000, while the boomerang demonstrates the instability of the souvenir object, as an ethnographic specimen and work of art, and sells for under $100. This price and the artefact's discovery in a blatantly commercial souvenir outlet should not and does not undermine the artefact's position as a work of art, while the attached label makes clear its operation as an ethnographic artefact, stating that it is 'Hand made by a genuine Aborigine'. Similarly the content and style of the painting provides the viewer with some ethnographic knowledge, while its presentation and medium locate it in the field of fine art. Nevertheless, this should not detract from the work's potential to operate as a souvenir.

My point is that the presentation of these two works – the painting in a gallery setting, hung in a contemporary gallery style, against a neutral space with discrete lighting, and the boomerang lodged in the corner of a shop window amid a jumble of other souvenirs – frames the way in which the objects are consumed. It is, therefore, worth dwelling on the play that oscillates between these two artefacts for a moment longer and to consider their contrasting reception. The boomerang's reception is predicated upon its form, in that it is firstly recognised as the partially redundant iconic form of the well-known Aboriginal tool; that, to many tourists from overseas, signifies a generic Aboriginality across the continent and, by extension, the entirety of indigenous and settler Australia.[1] For what is brought to mind by the boomerang form is first and foremost Aboriginal Australia, and then Australia.[2] This simplified and all encompassing myth of the boomerang demonstrates how the tourist narrative seizes upon an instantly

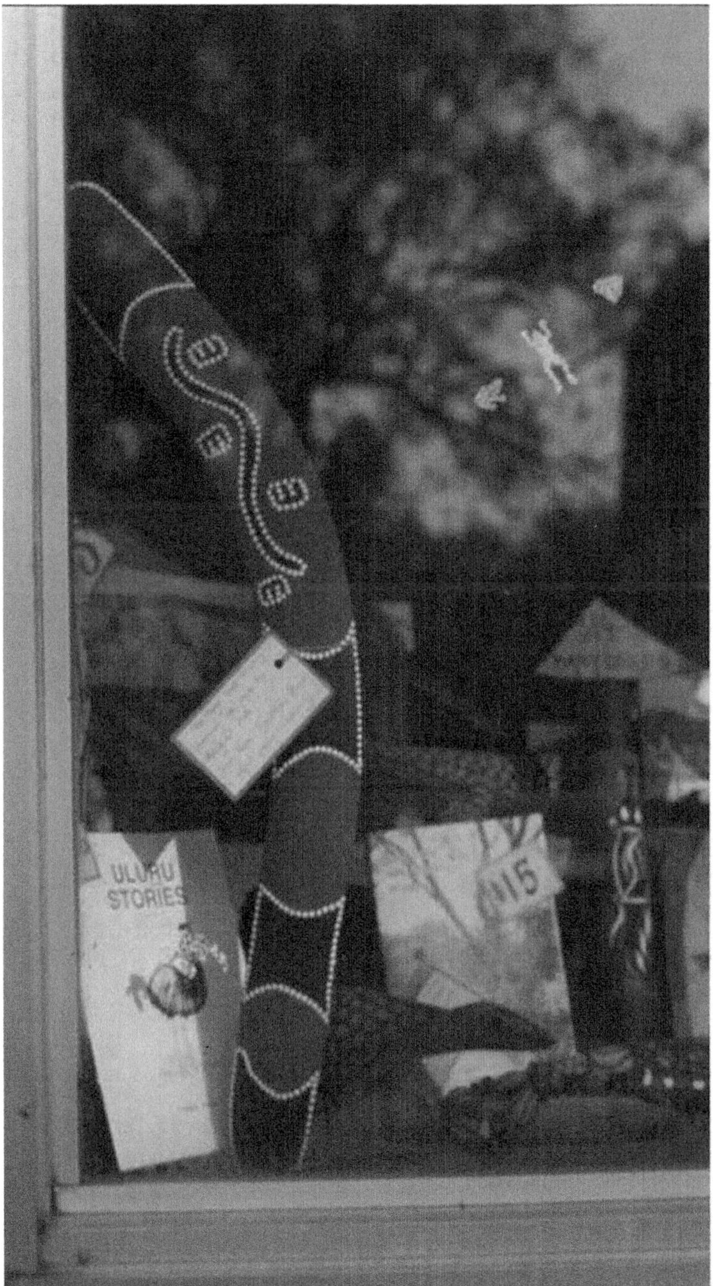

Plate 5.1 Johnny Possum Tjapaltjarri, *Hand Crafted Boomerang*, 2000, wood and acrylic paint, 60 cm.

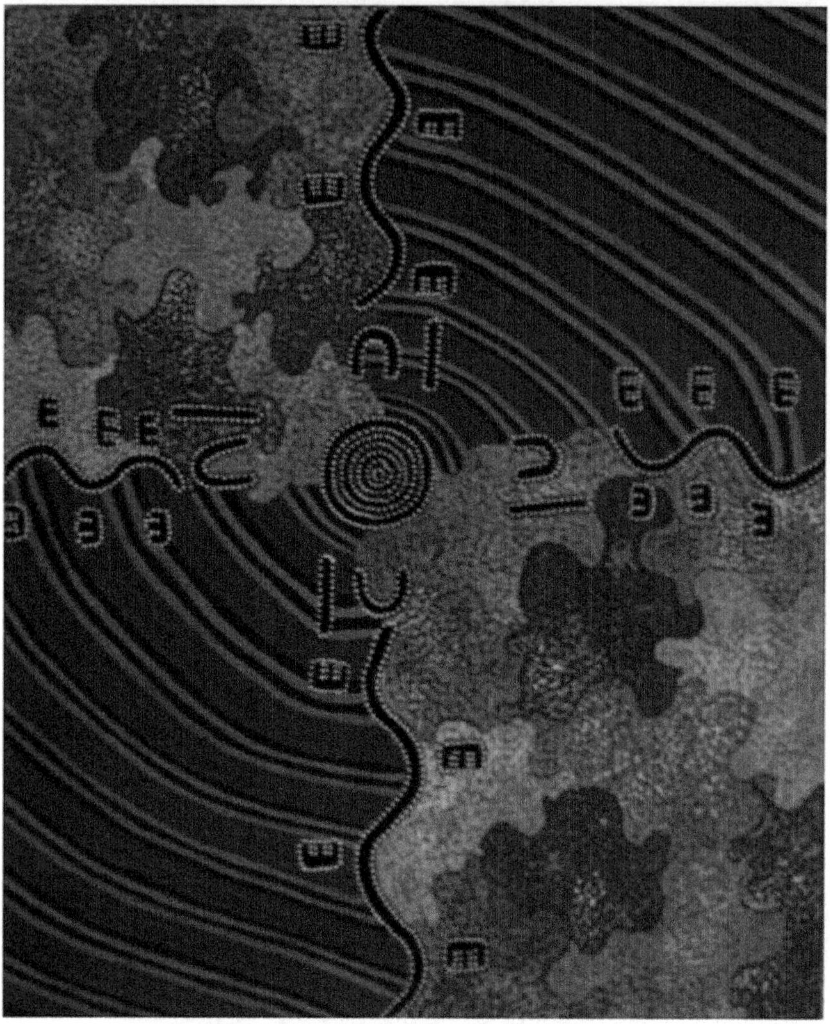

Plate 5.2 Johnny Possum Tjapaltjarri, *Possum Dreaming*, 2000, acrylic paint on canvas, 80 × 50 cm.

recognisable image – the symbolic content – and expands that image to represent all Aboriginal groups. The decoration, however, remains peripheral, even impenetrable, to most tourists and is of little consequence in the ensuing narrative. This decoration is specific to the maker's tribal group or clan, but this is of little interest to the average tourist, other than the fact that the painting adds to the artefact's visual appeal. This therefore leaves the boomerang more closely related to the consumption patterns of the ethnographic artefact in that it is simply a boomerang, an authentic example of ancient Aboriginal technology. It is 'authentic' because it is what is expected. The flow of information from the maker is likely to stop there and be picked up by the consumer's own experiential narrative. It acts as a marker of the tourist's visit to Alice Springs, from which other stories of the experience of the visited site and culture will flow.

Tjapaltjarri's painting, however, is dominated by its function as fine art. The form of its rendition is shown to be less reliant on the traditional means of production as it has already made the transition from the traditional surface of the desert floor to canvas, from pigments derived from the natural environment to acrylic paint, without any loss to its status as fine art, 'authenticity' or aura. Indeed, through this transitory process the painting has achieved a portability and durability that would be impossible or tenuous were it rendered in the traditional materials of ochre on sand.[3] In making this transition, the artist has come to recognise two key characteristics in the production of tourist art and souvenirs: portability and durability. The emergence of Aboriginal art on to the global market necessarily engaged with these two key criteria of tourist art; through its traditional style and by framing the work within the field of Aboriginal fine art, authenticity has been established without the need for the crass label that accompanies the boomerang.

Without further research and an understanding of Eastern Arrente society, this painting remains largely impenetrable and decorative and, like the boomerang, provides only a shallow amount of information, in that it is rendered in Central Desert Aboriginal style, by an authenticated Aborigine. At best, both the boomerang and the painting offer evidence of the collector's, that is the tourist's, passing engagement with an exotic 'Otherness' and the world of difference that is dominated by the consumer's superficial experience of the site and culture. Both works are, however, what has come to be expected in terms of the art and craft of the site. In other words, they are typical, and that is really their purpose.

The symbolic content – that of Aboriginality – and the appeal to tourists of both objects points to a history of the souvenir as an object of 'cultural Otherness'. Their real value is in the demonstration of the collector's 'knowledge, power and wealth', authorised by the collective fetish of tourism for that which is traditional or typical. While neither artefact is a copy, they are accepted as authentic, in the same way that eighteenth century travel books were validated by what Steiner (1999: 90–93) terms 'descriptive convention'. In other words, if the site is described in a certain way in a previous text, then the current text must recognise similar features for it to be perceived as genuine. So, too, the style of Aboriginal art and souvenir artefacts to be found in Alice Springs, such as dot paintings and boomerangs, must conform to what is perpetuated in the tourist literature and guide books as typical, if they are to function as souvenirs.

This calls for a high degree of seriality and, as previously discussed, is a key point around which the fetish object and the souvenir congregate. As with the collection of fetish objects, souvenir collecting is bound in repetitiveness or seriality. The collector, therefore, seeks a representation that induces a sense of completeness from the fragment. Duplication is also a key principle, integral to the production and consumption of tourist art. Steiner summarises this as tourist art's 'canons of authenticity – a self-referential discourse of cultural reality, that generates an internal measure of truth value' (ibid.: 95). He goes on to argue that the souvenir must, like the ethnographic artefact, be characteristic of the experience and site and culture it represents. To that end the singular or one-off artwork is limited as a souvenir unless, like Tjapaltjarri's painting, it includes a reference to the site by style, image or specific medium that is perceived as typical.

This fetishistic attraction of the multiple among tourist art and souvenirs then brings into play notions of authenticity and debates regarding the aura of the original. Famously Benjamin (1969) argues in his classic text *The Work of Art in the Age of Mechanical Reproduction*, that there is an emptying of meaning in the duplication of art. This emptying is centred on the erosion of the aura which, in turn, is taken to be the fundamental index of authenticity (ibid.). Prior to the mechanical reproduction of art, authenticity was, according to Benjamin, based on ritual and tradition. The subsequent reproduction of original work was believed to dislocate the copy from this base and in turn dilute the aura of the original (ibid.). Taken at face value, this argument situates tourist art and souvenirs as denigrated copies. However, tourist art does not operate according to the measures of authenticity set out in the discipline of art history. The authenticity of tourist art is, as Steiner (1999) observes, reliant upon its perception as typical of the visited site and culture. Its authenticity, in other words, can be likened to that of the ethnographic artefact and must take the form of what is expected by the tourist. Authenticity will be confirmed by the presence of likeness or, as Steiner (ibid.: 102) puts it, 'the demands of the market are such that tourists ... require the validation of multiple exemplars to authenticate their acquisition of souvenirs'. In effect, tourist art exists in a paradox of unauthenticity, caught between 'two conflicting principles' that argue, on the one hand, that innovative work in the tourist art market is not authentic because it fails to match what is expected and, on the other hand, that copies of work that are deemed typical or traditional are viewed as unauthentic because they are simply copies dislocated from their ritual basis of artistic production.[4]

In the following examples I examine a number of objects caught between these two conflicting principles of authenticity. Objects that Graburn (1976), Clifford (1994), Morphy (1998) and Phillips and Steiner (1999), respectively, point out refuse to rest permanently in either form: as either fine art or ethnographic artefact. This is particularly so of non-Western objects that, as Clifford (1994: 198) writes, have, '[s]ince 1900 ... generally been classified as either primitive art or ethnographic specimens'. Objects which, as Clifford goes on to say, were, '[b]efore the modernist revolution ... differently sorted – as antiquities, exotic curiosities, orientalia, the remains of early man, and so on' (ibid.). Despite the seeming elitism, that causes the souvenir to oscillate between fine art and etnogragraphic artefact, it is reasonable to argue, as Ben-Amos (1997: 128) does, '[t]hat tourist art is not the visual equivalent of "simplified foreigner talk" but is a communicative system in its own right'.

This seeming elision is typical of the souvenir and suggests that the two sides of the same coin, that Graburn (1976) calls 'differentiation and integration', are equally interchangeable. This takes us to a point prior to Graburn's separation of 'primitive' art and tourist art, to a period when the two intersected. Here one might ask what the collector's intentions were. Is the collector collecting 'antiquities, exotic curiosities, orientalia' or 'the remains of early man'? And, as Ben-Amos (1997: 128) asks, 'how and why these forms arise, what are the patterns of development, how is communication accomplished and what are the rules governing the creation and acceptance of new forms within the system'. It is in the collections of state and national museums that the answers may be unearthed.

Behind the mask: the creativity of the First Nations of the Northern Pacific Rim, at the Tasmanian Museum and Art Gallery 2001

In her 1995 text, *On Collecting*, Pearce argues that there were two socially condoned spheres of collecting before the eighteenth century: 'the ethnographic specimen and the work of art', and defines these by the terms, 'artificialia' and 'naturalia'. The first consists of high art objects, such as paintings and sculpture, and the second comprises of flora and fauna as samples of natural history (Pearce 1995: 124). It was this narrow authorisation of collecting that saw many artistic objects like Tjapaltjarri's boomerang and painting described as 'antiquities, exotic curiosities, orientalia' or the 'remains of early man' and their artistic qualities ignored. As Pearce goes on to explain, there was no place during this period for 'historical and exotic' material within the venues of public museums and galleries. She makes the point that '[t]hrough very roughly the eighteenth century and into the early nineteenth, two strands became visible. One, morally respectable and intellectually acclaimed, occupied the collecting high ground; it concentrated upon art and natural history' (ibid.: 124).

As the eighteenth century progressed and the industrial revolution developed into what is commonly referred to as the modern industrial society, Romantic sentiments also came to the fore. It is here that Pearce identifies a third mode of collecting, 'which concentrated on historical and exotic material,... its exhibition was commercially organised and, especially in the bigger cities of England, it became a regular element in popular culture' (ibid.). Here, with the heightened sense of individualism that was fundamental to Romantic sentiments, came the desire to collect things that would, as Pearce (ibid.: 129) writes, 'enhance the experience of the individual'.

The exhibition *Behind the Mask: The Creativity of the First Nations of the Northern Pacific Rim*, at the Tasmanian Museum and Art Gallery in 2001, featured artefacts from the early 1900s, Frank A. Wilkes, collection of contemporary traditional art and recent replicas of ceremonial artefacts that are now housed in the Australian Museum in Sydney.[5] With the inclusion of artefacts from the early 1900s, it can be seen how artefacts collected for personal or fetishistic consumption have now become valued artefacts within the public realm. This exhibition raised a number of issues regarding the changing meaning of the works as they are brought into the public sphere from the private collection of an individual. In the light of the preceding argument, the 'authenticity' of many works in this exhibition is questionable, while the aura accorded them by the museogallery environment may also be debated. Should the contemporary artefacts be accounted for in a different way to those that were made by earlier craftsmen, which played a more central role in the ceremonial life of the maker; are the works from the earlier period more 'authentic', or should one consider these different bodies of work as equally 'authentic' but produced from a different system of visual communication?

The Wilkes collection was gathered by Colonel John A Stacey from 1912–1913.[6] The provenance of this collection demonstrates the establishment of an interest in the collection of crafted artefacts of exotic 'Otherness' that is consistent with the recording of individual experience lauded by earlier collectors. This collection is also consistent with *Wunderkammer* collections gathered during this and earlier periods. Within the context of Western museums, these objects from the beginning of the last century are clearly artefacts of exotic 'Otherness'. The date of production of many artefacts from the Wilkes collection is unknown; so, too, are the names of the artists that produced them. As with most souvenir artefacts, it is from their time of collection that they are dated, while their construction may have occurred much earlier.

Among the ethnographic artefacts on display from the Wilkes collection are an unattributed Wolf Headdress and a Shaman Rattle. These are contained within one display cabinet, which also contains a Seal Bowl created by Calvin Hunt and a recent Shaman Rattle made by Glenn Rabena, both contemporary Canadian First Nation artists. This combination of the old with the contemporary raises many questions regarding the understanding of such objects as art or artefact.

The Seal Bowl and recent Shaman Rattle have a different purpose to the Wolf Headdress and Shaman Rattle from the Wilkes collection. The works from Hunt and Rabena are intended as objects of art and they demonstrate and express the history, philosophy and continuing presence of the First Nations of the Canadian West Coast. They were made to be consumed by non-indigenous collectors and, in that regard, they share a common purpose with many souvenired objects of a similar kind. As Graburn (1976) has argued, they were made by one culture for consumption by another. In this respect it may be argued that they are dislocated from their ritual basis.

In comparing these recent replicas from Hunt and Rabena to the Wolf Headdresses and Shaman Rattles from the Wilkes collection, it is evident that their primary difference exists in the quality of finish. Hunt's and Rabena's work has a smoother surface and the colours are more vibrant, while the Wolf Headdress from the Wilkes collection shows some unworked, or raw, edges and faded paint. The anthropologist might suggest that the Wolf Headdress exhibits signs of age and use and that, given this evidence of fit and use within the culture of origin, it should be attributed with great worth because of its demonstrated 'authenticity', because it comes from a period when the ceremonies for which it was created dominated and, possibly, stood alone in the social structure and culture of the indigenous people of the Canadian West Coast. This headdress may therefore be understood in Clifford's terms as a 'relic of early man' or, more succinctly, a pre-modern work of art based in ritual.

Now where, in the light of that ethnographic consumption, does that leave Hunt's Seal Bowl? Is it purely an artistic representation of times gone by, a modern reproduction? To answer that question in the affirmative is to deny the continuing presence of the Canadian First Nation people and culture. It also suggests that the recent Shaman Rattle and Seal Bowl are souvenirs, in the broadest sense of the term, that have found their way into the Western museogallery environment because of the political demand for the contemporary representation of indigenous people.

Light is shed on this problem of production, reception and consumption by Townsend-Gault (1999) who poses a similar far-reaching question, asking:

> Is the art of the Northwest Coast great art in the present, or is it the relic of a great past, a hidebound tradition with a contaminated present?… Can such matters, which are about a kind of power, be separated from Native identity politics or the politics of land rights, and sovereignty, without coming adrift in the postmodern flux?
>
> (Townsend-Gault 1999: 113)

The pressures of contemporary indigenous politics and native identity are further addressed in the *Behind the Mask* exhibition and again involve the work of Hunt. Consistent with the project of the souvenir, this exhibition is both historical and contemporary, and blends unattributed artefacts with the work of contemporary

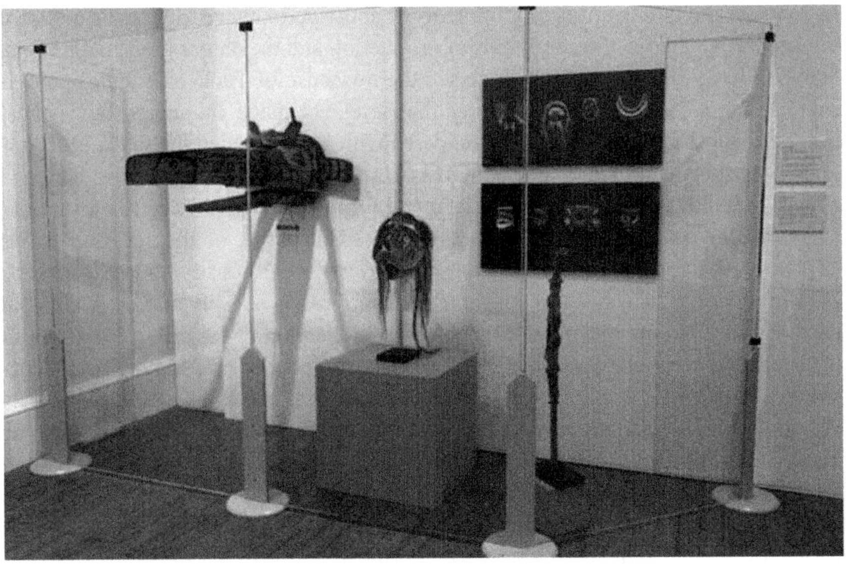

Plate 5.3 Calvin Hunt, *Raven Mask*, and *Echo Mask*, from the exhibition *Behind the Mask: The Creativity of the First Nations of the Northern Pacific Rim*, Tasmanian Museum and Art Gallery 2001.

artists. Many of the objects on display comfortably straddle that artificial divide, while there are others that provoke more intriguing questions about the real and the artificial; the ethnographic artefact and the souvenir; art and souvenirs, and authenticity. Hunt's immaculately crafted Raven Mask and Echo Mask (Plate 5.3), are particularly good examples of this.

Sitting squarely between the ethnographic artefacts and the contemporary art of this exhibition are these two replica masks from Hunt: Raven Mask and Echo Mask. I use the term 'replica' cautiously for they are, actually, copies of originals, and yet the process of their production is, to a degree, 'authentic', while being also thoroughly contemporary.

Hunt is a Canadian First Nation artist from a notable artistic family and was commissioned to produce these works to facilitate the repatriation of the originals – gathered as part of the Wilkes collection – back to their rightful owners.[7] Their exhibition highlights the 'authenticity' conundrum inasmuch as it poses questions about the nature of display and how that might affect the meaning and value of the artefacts. For there is, in this exhibition, a remnant of the old elitism that saw European fine art displayed in art galleries, while the fine art of non-Western cultures was consigned to the cabinets of anthropological museums. At the same time, while the attribution of Hunt's name causes the work to be consumed as fine art in today's terms, the artifice of his work may not warrant a second glance from the ethnographer.

As with Hunt's Seal Bowl, if we compare these recent replications from Hunt to the Wolf Headdress from the Wilkes collection, it can be seen once more that their primary difference also exists in the quality of finish. Hunt's work, for instance, is again of a smoother finish and the colours are more vibrant. However, to compare the two is unfair, for the tools of construction have altered, as too have the decorative media, the conditions of production and the nature of Canadian First Nation society. Here it is possible to see the nonsense of Tuckson's anthropological bias (see Chapter 3) in claiming that artefacts made by indigenous people expressly for the souvenir trade are rendered with less care than the 'authentic' ethnographic specimen. Hunt's elaborate masks are clearly crafted with great care and adhere to 'culturally embedded aesthetic and formal standards' while their purpose to satisfy the gaze of another culture, is shared with that of the souvenir or, as Graburn (1976) puts it, are 'produced by one group for the consumption of another'.

The most fitting way to understand such replicas is as souvenirs of a colonial past, in that, first, the historical moment of the collection of the original mask is an unrepeatable event and therefore is consistent with the idea that souvenirs are fragments of a one-off, fleeting experience of cultural 'Otherness'. Second, these marvellous works refer to an individual's experience of an exotic 'Otherness' that has been subsequently embraced by the collective identity of the Australian nation through the institution of a national museum. These works are, in effect, souvenirs of colonial Australia's engagement with the exotic 'Otherness' of the indigenous people of the Canadian West Coast. The exchange of this replica for the original is a correction of colonial plunder, while the replica status of the mask is identical to that of many Canadian West Coast souvenirs now offered by First Nations people to tourists, as a marker of their touristic experience of that culture.

To understand this further, one needs to consider how the Western consumption of material culture from non-Western cultures expanded the notions of what was worthy of collection, and how that impulse has been sustained in the collecting habits of contemporary tourists, museums and art galleries.

Institutional terms of display

As we have discovered, what was collected during the seminal period of Western tourism by those of Romantic sensibilities stood apart from the collections described previously as 'Naturalia' and 'Artificialia'. The primary purpose of the former was not that of public display but was intended for the personal enhancement of the experience. For example as Pearce argues:

> The enhancement of individual experience took a number of forms. The desire to extend sensation took some collectors to the exotic, and is in part the genesis of contemporary accumulations of Chinoiserie and 'primitive' material where, as we have seen, there is a link with popular sensationalism. The accumulation of exotic and artistic pieces went hand in hand with a highly developed self image and the desire to create a world within a world.... Objects which were already seen to be 'true relics' by reason of their 'real relationship' with past people and events were transformed by the Romantic eye into a sensation of knowing the past, of resurrecting the body of the past intact so that it might be experienced in the present.
>
> (Pearce 1995: 130–131)

Clearly, Pearce's understanding of the activity of souveniring is astute and her observation that the act of 'resurrecting the body of the past intact so that it might be experienced in the present' provides a telling description of the contemporary souvenir. It is today, as it was then, the desire to make that which is past and lost live again in the present. What compels contemporary tourists to collect souvenirs is the desire to recall the initial moment of experience. Pearce places Romantic collections outside the socially condoned museum framework, which has caused them to be located within the then-deviant world of collections gathered for personal enhancement, collections which 'extend sensation' and the construction of a 'world within a world'. This, as we have seen in Chapter 4, is consistent, in many ways, with fetishistic collecting and the condition of the contemporary tourist.

Following this hypothesis, it can be seen how the Romantic period expanded the initial categories of what was collected from two to three primary categories of collected objects, which Pearce (ibid.) has summarised as follows:

1 Naturalia: natural history samples, such as botanical specimens
2 Artificialia: Fine art objects and other representations
3 Romantic: exotic objects of 'primitive' and otherness

According to Pearce, the first two were displayed in the institutional forums of the museum and art gallery and the latter in the private home or through commercial display. These three categories can be used as a basis upon which to understand the souvenir object, although I will suggest a further refinement, which will have a bearing on the definition of the contemporary souvenir. First, however, I want to investigate the appeal of objects that rest within the above categories, as they existed during the early part of the last century. Pearce outlines three approaches or methods of collecting during that period. She describes these as 'the souvenir, the fetishistic and the systematic modes of collecting' (ibid.). It is the first two that I want to now scrutinise more closely, in the belief that an indelible relationship exits between them.

Souvenir collection is defined by Pearce as the way in which 'the individual creates a Romantic life history' (ibid.). She differentiates between fetishistic and souvenir collecting on the grounds that for the fetishist the 'objects are dominant and the collector responds to his obsessive need by gathering as many items as possible: here in contrast to souvenir collecting the objects are allowed to create the self' (ibid.). In making this broad distinction, between fetish objects and souvenirs, Pearce neglects many of the structural qualities of both objects, outlined in the previous chapter, that underpin their mutual production and consumption. Of particular importance is the substitutive role of both objects, their capacity to substantiate what Freud has termed 'a sensation of "eternity" ' in respect to the holiday period.

Equally, consideration needs to be given to their significance in creating and sustaining narrative. There is also the supernatural power of the material object to be considered – the power it carries to make that narrative believable. Above all, there is the surplus value found in both objects and their serial nature, which, as Steiner (1999) and others explain, remains dominant in the souvenir's production and consumption. This, as we have already discussed, is grounded in their activity as a fragment of the visited site and/or culture and is a flaw in Pearce's otherwise sound hypothesis, grounded, as it is, in the field of museum studies. She fails to consider the unique condition of the contemporary tourist and the fundamentally deviant nature of tourism. However, Pearce's text does provide a more than useful insight into the history of collecting. The purpose for the collection of 'objects and artefacts of cultural others' ranges historically from the scientific to the formally aesthetic. They are, as Clifford (1994) informs us, sorted 'as antiquities, exotic curiosities, orientalia, the remains of early man, and so on'. All of these categories of objects and artefacts have subsequently found their way into museum collections. As Clifford goes on to say:

> With the emergence of twentieth century modernism and anthropology, figures formerly called fetishes (to take just one class of object) became works of 'sculpture' or of material 'fetishes'. The distinction between the aesthetic and the anthropological was soon institutionally enforced. In art galleries non-Western objects were displayed for their formal and aesthetic qualities; in ethnographic museums they were represented in a cultural context.
>
> (Clifford 1994: 198)

I have already demonstrated how today the formal and aesthetic qualities of objects are blended with cultural contexts, as in the case of the Tasmanian Museum and Art Gallery exhibition, *Behind the Mask*. The corruption, or confusion, of art and artefact that occurred with the 'emergence of twentieth century modernism' and the corresponding democratisation of long distance travel is demonstrated and further complicated in the case of the famous Hopi–Tewa Indian potter of that period, Nampeyo.

In an enlightening essay, 'Fewkes and Nampeyo. Clarifying a Myth-Understanding', Traugott (1999: 7–20) presents four contradictory explanations regarding Nampeyo's artistic production and how her work has found its way into respected museums as coming from a much earlier period. Each explanation revolves around the artist's relationship with anthropologist, J. Walter Fewkes. The first is that Fewkes' assistant, Walter Hough, promoted Nampeyo and her work through early tourist brochures published by the Santa Fe Railway. These brochures sold over 42,000 copies and were photographically supported (ibid.: 8). This model is similar to the presentation of Tjapaltjarri's boomerang and many other Aboriginal art objects, where the typicality of the destination is established prior to the visit, so that the tourist knows what sort of artefact he or she may expect to find.

The second was a clinical anthropological version of the story, developed by Fewkes, that situated him as an expert on Hopi pottery and denigrated much Hopi pottery after the sixteenth century; that is, after colonial contact. Fewkes was able to capitalise on his archaeological finds, enhancing their value, while denying any benefit to the Hopi people (ibid.: 9). In this version of the story, one is able to recognise the nineteenth century anthropological desire for purity in 'Other' cultures, how the colonial appropriation of indigenous peoples' objects, empowers the colonial collector and favours the ethnographic value of the object at the expense of its aesthetic qualities.

The third version rests with Ruth Bunzel, who saw Nampeyo's work as the result of artistic genius. Traugott argues that while this model 'strived to empower the artistic sensibilities of Native people, it offered a simplistic explanation of a complex cross-cultural phenomenon' (ibid.). In this version one can see how the objects consumed as primitive art, adorned by a simple and reduced narrative, mirror the shallow and fragmentary experience of the souvenir narrative. The final model argues that it was the establishment of a trading post that prompted what has become known as the Sikyati revival (Townsend-Gault 1999).

It can be seen from the above models that nineteenth century anthropological theories for understanding indigenous art were at odds with the appreciation of similar objects from the field of fine art and, most importantly for our purposes, that economic conditions, in tandem with artistic development, underwrote Nampeyo's production. Like the work of Tjapaltjarri and Hunt, Nampeyo's artistic output straddled the field of ethnographic artefact, souvenir and fine art.

In the same volume, Townsend-Gault (1999) recounts a more recent tale of three indigenous men of the Canadian West Coast, fuelled by hotdogs, beer and dope, carving a mask in collaboration, that was subsequently sold to a dealer and which enabled the men to have a night out. The current resting places of Nampeyo's pottery and the collaboratively made mask, are, of course, somewhat different, but Nampeyo's pottery has had a 100-year's head start, while the conditions of trade and exchange are also somewhat different. However, the consumption patterns are similar.

A not dissimilar situation occurs in the case of the contemporary artefacts contained in the Tasmanian Museum and Art Gallery exhibition, *Behind the Mask*. For while not belittling the artistic achievement of Hunt's Seal Bowl, Echo Mask or Raven Mask, similar objects, like the collaboratively made mask, cited above, are to be found cluttering the walls of indigenous craft and souvenir shops in British Columbia. The same applies with examples like the Tjapaltjarri boomerang discovered in the jumble of souvenir shops in Alice Springs, because these are now just as likely to be found displayed in the contemporary museogallery system.

The institutional terms of display designate the cultural context, or miscontext of the anthropological artefact. Many contemporary souvenirs may be distinguished from such objects, in that a recontextualisation takes place prior to their display for exchange. This is brought about by the ingenuity of the artist, or recontextualisation by the retailer. In the latter case, the object is dependent upon the exhibition environment for its context and value. In the case of souvenir objects, that environment is not institutionally defined but is, instead, defined by commercial success. It is these objects, that often begin as utilitarian tools or ceremonial artefacts, that are later reinterpreted by embellishment and decoration as objects of fine art. They are artistic expressions of time and/or place and the Tjapaltjarri and Hunt examples typify this kind of tourist art.

An understanding of the relationship between ethnographic artefacts and contemporary souvenirs is crucial to the study of travel art and, as with the arguments informing the work attributed to Nampeyo, it is a complex issue. The following section considers this relationship by examining a suite of Aboriginal Australian artefacts.

Four Aboriginal shields

In the ethnographic collections store at the Tasmanian Museum and Art Gallery are four Aboriginal Shields, among many. The provenance of these objects is a little sketchy but records suggest that they were collected during the late nineteenth and the early to mid-twentieth century. Two are from Southeastern Australia and two from further north. As a suite of objects they serve to demonstrate the change in purpose of shields from combat and ceremonial tool to marker of people, place and culture, just like the boomerangs examined in Chapter 3.

The first two shields I want to examine were collected by H. S. Lewes, during the early part of the last century. Cat. No. M4266 (Plate 5.4) is a utilitarian shield, that is one that bears the marks of its traditional intention in combat and/or ceremony. This shield measures 50 cm in length and about 17 cm across the widest part of the convex front. The frontal surface has been divided into six, slightly out-of-square areas along the length of the artefact. These divisions are

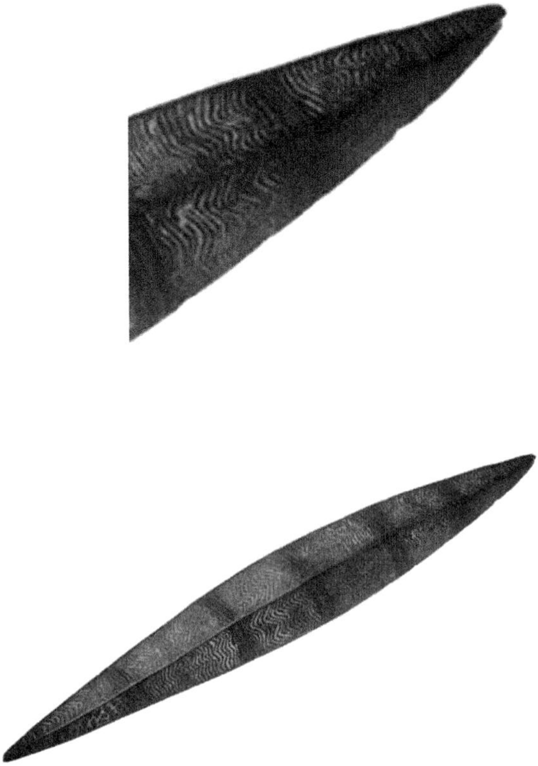

Plate 5.4 Aboriginal Parrying Shield, wood with incised relief, 66 cm. Collection: Tasmanian Museum and Art Gallery, Cat. No. M4266.

mirrored either side of the convex surface, providing a total of twelve discrete spaces. The latitudinal division has been obtained by 1 cm wide grooves, cut at roughly regular intervals. The surface of these dividing grooves is uneven, as if picked out with an irregular blade. The spaces between are filled with abstract cross-hatching for the most part, that is in keeping with the traditional design found on many Aboriginal artefacts from Southeast Australia of this period.[8] The irregular division of the shield's surface suggests an approximated partitioning of the surface according to Aboriginal convention and design principles, rather than the precise ruled measurements achieved by the use of a Western mathematical system and tools.

The second shield (Plate 5.5), from the same collection, is of similar size, weight and material. It is also divided into sections, like the first. In this artefact, the divisions appear to be more regular and mechanical in their execution. In this

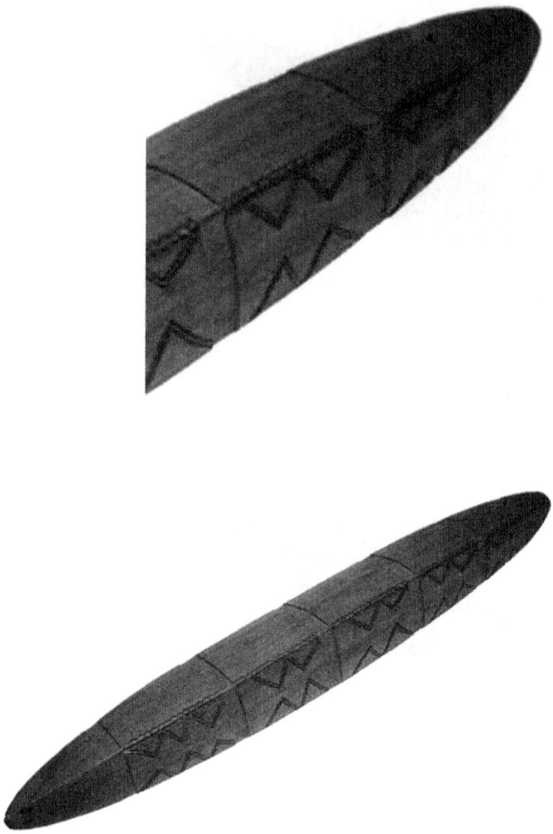

Plate 5.5 Aboriginal Parrying Shield, wood with incised relief. 66.5 cm. Collection: Tasmanian Museum and Art Gallery, Cat. No. M4267.

it is possible to discern a distinct difference between these two similar artefacts that would see the latter accommodated in Graburn's 'Traditional' or 'Functional Fine Art' category, due to the 'changes in technique'.

The tools used for carving are difficult to discern; they seem to range from stone cutting edges, to animal teeth, to introduced steel and glass. There are cleaner, sharper and more parallel edges in the second example. The wide cuts dividing the surface are all the same size and feature exact, straight edges that suggest that they have been made with the use of a steel tool of some sort. They appear to be either cut on the edges with a hacksaw or another type of saw blade, or marked with the edge of a knife used in the fashion of a chisel. The outlined relief surface is also flat whereas, in the first example, it was undulating as if picked out by a small irregular cutting tool. This also indicates the use of some kind of machined cutting edge like a chisel. The decorative patterning that occupies the divided spaces is similar to that in the first example, but in the second example this design is inscribed on only one side of the shield's length. This gives the shield the appearance of being unfinished. The absence of percussive indentations, of the sort that occur in combat, suggest that this shield has not been used in the conventional way. Furthermore, the cross-hatching along the one side of the second example is much deeper and more precise in execution than the inscription of the first example and again suggests the use of introduced tools and their application in the carving of traditional design.

A third shield (Plate 5.6) in the collection of the Tasmanian Museum and Art Gallery demonstrates an extension of the shield's purpose, from conventional use in combat and ceremony to that of a marker of people, place and culture in

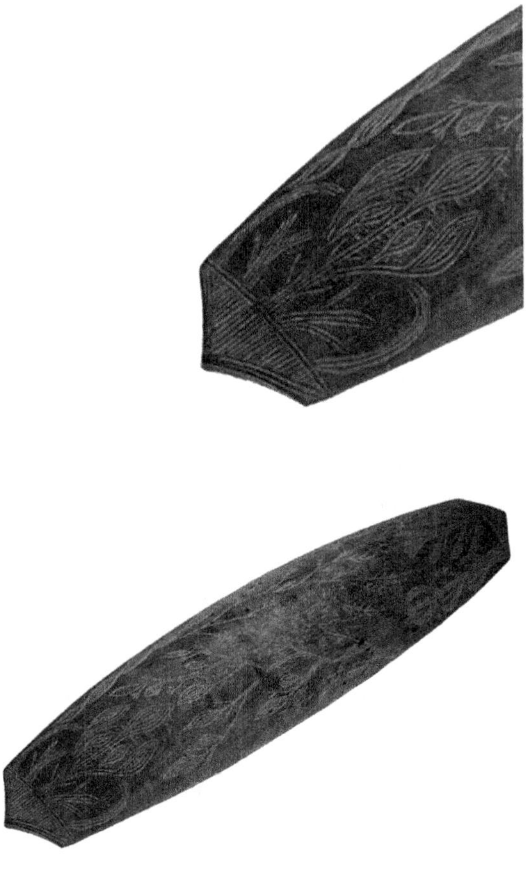

Plate 5.6 Aboriginal Parrying Shield, wood with incised relief, 58 cm. Collection: Tasmanian Museum and Art Gallery Cat. No. M4214.

the form of a souvenir. This shield is considerably lighter in weight and surface colour and features the development of a design that shifts away from the abstract incisions of the previous examples, to one describing the familiar flora of the region. Trees and shrubs are outlined on the surface, in close proximity but not intertwining. The orientation of this pattern is such that the trees and shrubs are grounded at both ends of the artefact, while the central area shows two branching stems growing in opposite directions. At the two narrow ends of the shield a tree and a palm, or grass-tree like shrub are described. The trees continue into the broad central area of the artefact, one veering to the left, the other the right. At no time do the branches intertwine. There is a development from the abstract shuttle designs common to the earlier Aboriginal artefacts and the presence of a figurative pattern is more in keeping with the European tradition of representing place. The fact that this artefact is unstable in providing a top or bottom (but insists on being viewed on the vertical axis) seems to demonstrate an underlying decorative design principle that is faithful to the abstract patterning of the previous two examples, but fixes the consumer as colonial European.

This shield, like the second example, is most likely of post-contact origin and made specifically for the colonial collector. As with the second example, the method of production shows signs of the employment of introduced tools that occurred very quickly after contact. The most interesting and telling feature of this third example is the development of a realistic figurative motif, occurring at and after contact, that utilised the carving and incising skill developed under the application of traditional design. This is evidenced not only in the confused gravity of this artefact, but also by the division of the surface into two distinct areas and the continuous linear motif. A further reference to traditional design is found in a singular shuttle design that embellishes one edge of this fascinating crossover artefact. This shuttle motif is clearly the influence from which the floral design has developed.

The final example from this collection (Plate 5.7) is an even more flimsy shield that is further removed from traditional use. The wide grain of this timber suggests some fast growing shrub or root. The handle on the reverse is impossible to grip in a useful manner and the design on the front is a naïve pokerwork landscape that runs horizontally the length of the shield. This causes the artefact to be viewed in opposition to its traditional angle of view, as established in the previous examples. The purpose of this shield is clearly to provide a canvas for the figurative depiction of landscape in the Western style. This artefact from Yuendemu bears no history of use as a fighting or ceremonial shield.

At first glance this artefact appears as a crude example of early pokerwork and figurative landscape. It is not unlike Namatjira's spear thrower, cited in Chapter 3 (Plate 3.6), but it lacks the high degree of skill in its execution. The outline of a deep gorge is centrally located, with a large tree filling the geological void. The tree branches into two at the top and is bounded either side by two large hummocks, while to the left is a third, smaller or more distant hill. It is in these hills that a three dimensional plane may be detected. In what at first appear

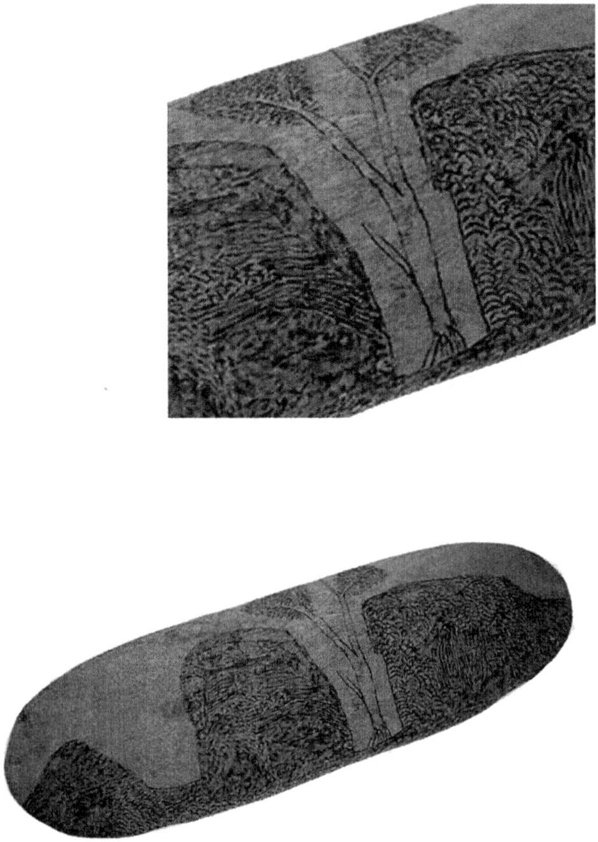

Plate 5.7 Aboriginal Parrying Shield, wood with pokerwork detail, 60 cm. Collection: Tasmanian Museum and Art Gallery, Cat. No. M6897.

to be randomly burnished curves infilling the outline, we can, on close inspection, discern an attempt to depict pathways, watercourses and vegetated areas.

Above all, what can be seen in this final example is the complete transition from a traditional tool of combat and ceremony to one of artistic canvas for the representation of people and place, probably for consumption by the colonial culture. But parrying shields form only one part of the ceremonial or combat kit that is completed by the nula-nula or club. A study of contemporary artefacts of this type will serve to further clarify both the activity of indigenous art and artefacts dragged into the souvenir trade and their relationship to artefacts displayed in a museogallery context.

The strength of the Koori[9] line: souvenir nula-nulas (killing sticks or battle clubs) and other tools of life from Southeast Australia

So far, I have examined the iconic sculptural form of the boomerang in Chapter 3 and the lesser known parrying shield in this chapter, and barely touched on the decorative, figurative line drawing traditions of Aboriginal Australia and its application in the production of souvenirs. This style of decoration has a long history in the representation of the traditional hunter-gatherer lifestyle, particularly among the Koori of Southeast Australia.

Koori is the collective term that refers to the indigenous people of the Southeast Australian mainland. Its use within the art world occurred in 1984 with the exhibition *Koori Art 84*, which brought together a group of Aboriginal artists from various backgrounds. This group contained a number of artists 'who made the journey from the tourist trade to the galleries' (Neale 2000: 268).

Three of the preceding shields originate from the Southeastern quarter of Australia and two display the use of Western cutting tools, while another clearly shows an early attempt at pokerwork design with a naïve landscape inscribed in the surface. Pokerwork is a unique art form among Aboriginal people and particularly given to the decorative embellishment of wooden tools. It is a clear example of a postcolonial art form, initially relying on heated fencing wire for its execution. In this respect it is hugely ironic that the creatures and mode of production most commonly illustrated and decorated by this method are those that resist the initial purpose of the fencing wire. Its main feature, with regard to this research, however, is its capacity to extend the traditional line figuration of Koori Australia, its employment in the re-presentation of aspects of traditional hunter-gatherer life styles and its operation within the field of tourist art and souvenirs.

Undertaking field research along the South Coast of New South Wales, I was searching for similar artefacts to those examined above within the range of Aboriginal souvenir art. Recent shields were not to be found, but the other half of the kit, in the form of nula-nulas or clubs, were plentiful.

The following artefacts are traditional battle clubs carved from authentic material, while their shape shows some alteration. Plate 5.8 shows a pair of Red-gum nula-nulas, collected from the Umbarra Aboriginal Cultural Centre on the Far South Coast of New South Wales. These clubs are geographically complementary to the first two shields cited above (Plates 5.4 and 5.5) but, in the clubs, the addition of figurative imagery occurs and there is a displacement of the familiar crosshatched design to a supporting decorative role. Figurative representations are common to the indigenous tribes of the South Coast of New South Wales, if not the traditional decoration for battle clubs, while the pokerwork method of decoration developed among Aboriginal people during the mid to late colonial era.

In the detail there is a clear attempt by the artist to refer to the traditional hunter-gatherer ways of his people, together with the important material culture

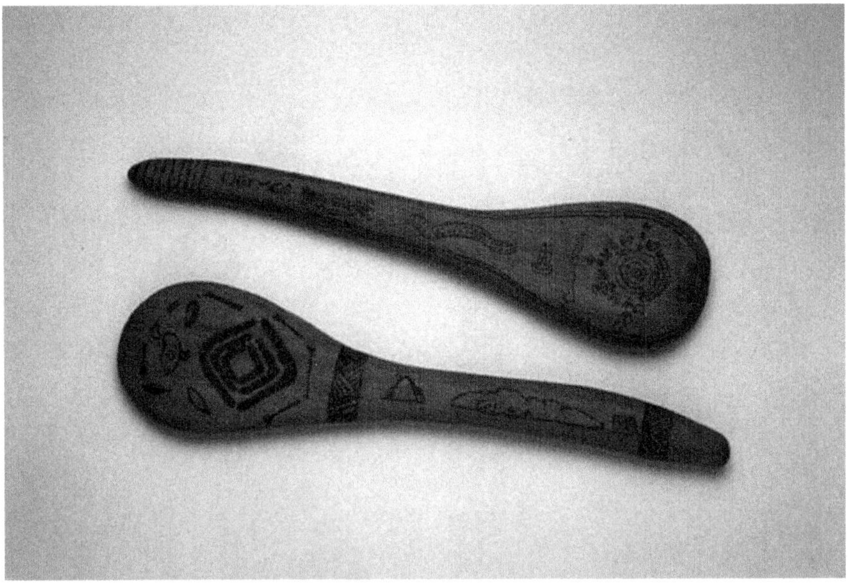

Plate 5.8 M. Naylor, *Tools of Life*, 2001, a pair of nula-nulas, Red Gum with pokerwork detail, 41.5 cm. Private collection.

and fauna of that lifestyle. This is apparent on the broad blade of the club where a shield, reminiscent of the shape of the first two shield examples featured above, is inscribed; a swamp hen, a coolamon, a woomera and three fishing spears are also represented. The desire to express the sense of people and place is further underscored by the inscribed text, 'Tools for life', and the landscape representation of an important sacred site labelled 'Gulaga'. There are also two bands of crosshatch design around the end of the handles that compare favourably with the decoration on the first two shields.

This desire to represent the tools and technology of the Aboriginal people of Southeast Australia is also evident in Kevin Mason's work, *A set of tools*, contained in the recent exhibition *Keeping Culture: Aboriginal Art to Keeping Places and Cultural Centres*, organised by the National Gallery of Australia, 2000. In this suite of works Mason has produced four artworks that represent some of the tools of life depicted on one of Naylor's nula-nulas. In his work, Mason's preference is for the clean natural beauty of the wood which, together with the smooth carved forms, he finds more aesthetically pleasing and authentic in the rekindling of ancient Aboriginal technology. However, like Naylor, he is keen to mark the object as a Koori design and says that: 'Sometimes I put a little design on the shield or boomerang, a Koorie design' (Mason 2000: 18). But Mason feels that although his 'brother used to do pokerwork onto boomerangs', the 'woods are so pretty' that they don't need it (ibid.). This decision may be

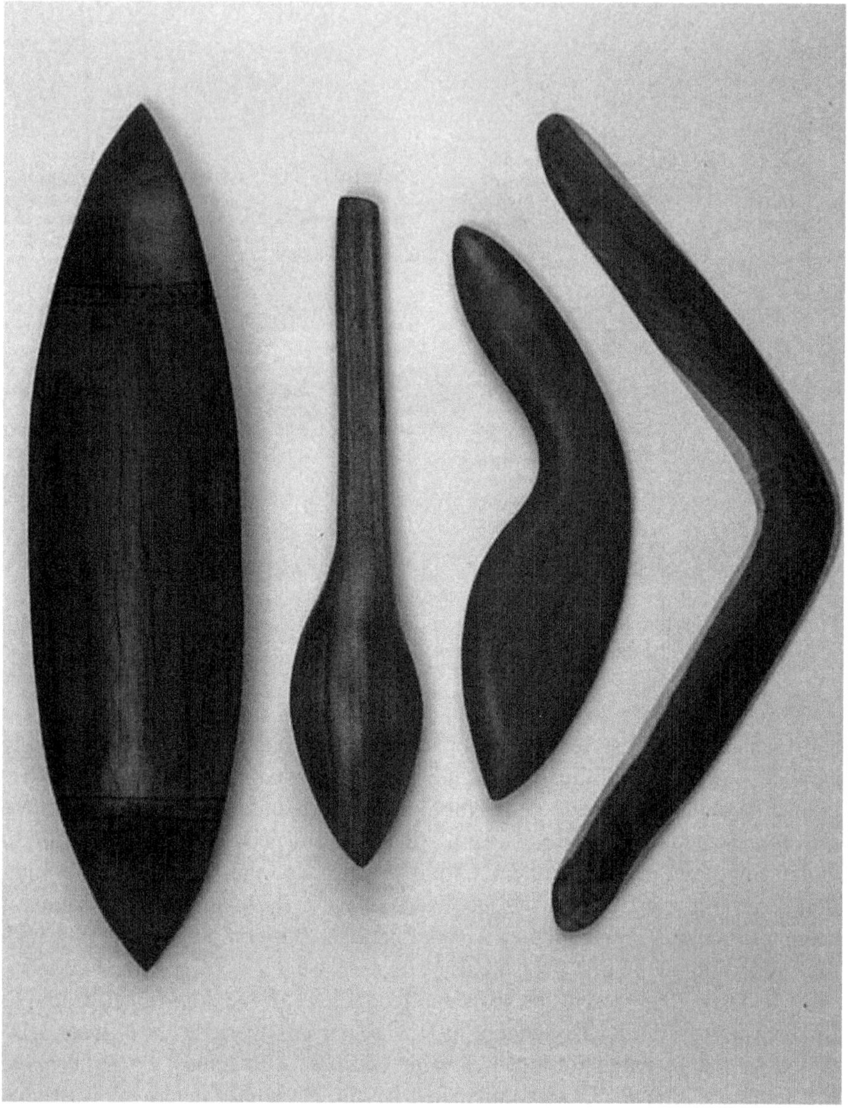

Plate 5.9 Kevin Mason, *A set of tools*, 1999, Monaro people, carved and incised wood. Collection: National Gallery of Australia.

seen to separate Mason's artistic work from the souvenir art of Naylor, but Mason's introduction to the Western appreciation of his art is founded on the production of souvenir objects and developed through that market. As Mason says, 'With the tools, I started about three years ago making artefacts, for petty cash' (ibid.). He then hawked them around to a number of commercial outlets in tourist precincts like the Rocks in Sydney, and various local markets and cultural centres (ibid.). What can be seen in the work of Mason and Naylor is a concern to document the traditional lifestyle and material culture of Southeastern Aboriginal Australia.

The intention to catalogue the material culture of the Southeastern region of Australia has been a priority among the Aboriginal people of this area since colonisation, as too has an engagement with the tourist industry. In the work of nineteenth century Aboriginal artist, Barak, there are not only friezes depicting the activity of Aboriginal people during the mid to late nineteenth century, in which the use of various tools is depicted, but also, in Plate 5.10, a catalogue of those tools.

Barak, like Naylor and Mason, lived in a Western society on the then reserve of Coranderrk and, as Sayers (1994: 13) informs us, his intention was to illustrate the traditional ways of his people. While Barak is today recognised as one of the great Aboriginal artists of that period he, like Mason, Naylor and Namatjira also produced souvenir artefacts and his 'practice as an artist was part of the tourist market component of Coranderrk's economy' (ibid.: 22).

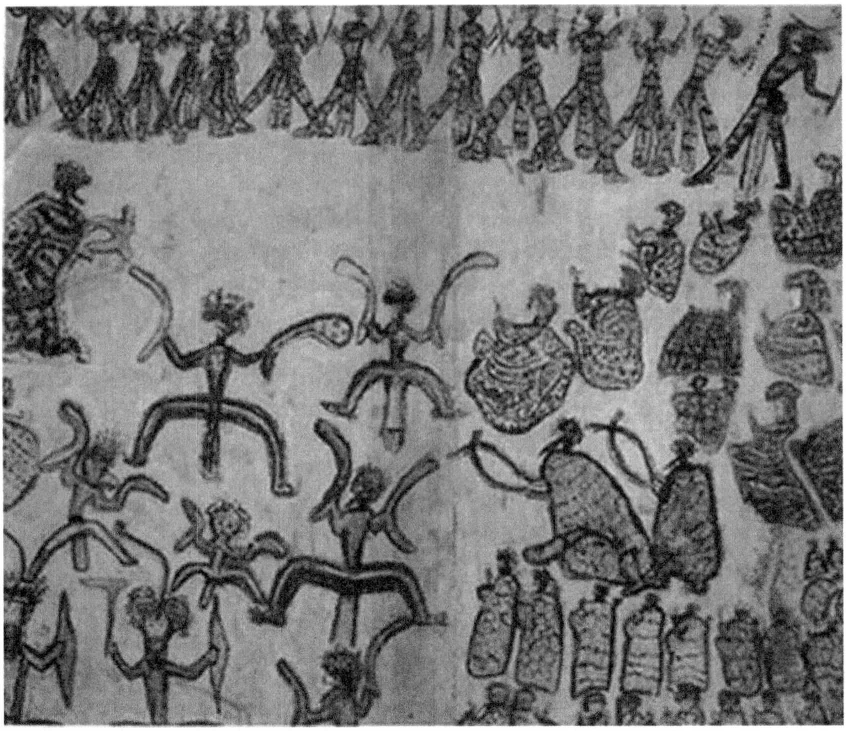

Plate 5.10 Barak, *Ceremony*, ochres, pencil, pre-1914, 58.5 × 70.2 cm. Collection: Staatliches Museum für Volkerkunde Dresden.

A similar preoccupation with representing traditional ways is also seen in the example in Plate 5.11. This was collected, during the same field research period, from the Giriwa Aboriginal Cultural Centre at Ulladulla. Like the earlier examples, it is carved from local timber that was traditionally used for this purpose. But the unusual shape of this club marks it as a rare souvenir. Known as a lil-lil, this rare style of club is thought to be exclusive to 'Aborigines living in the upper reaches of the Murray River and its tributaries' (Cooper 1981: 93), some distance from the location of my research. Its production and collection in the Ulladulla area on the South Coast of New South Wales may be due to two factors: first, that it is the result of travel and trade within Aboriginal cultures; and second, that the rare historic example (Plate 5.12) may have been sighted by the artist in some form or another.

The nineteenth century example features 'a raised linear design' on the club head that is said to depict the tribal land of the owner within the two patterns (ibid.). This is typical of the linear patterns that characterise the Aboriginal art of Southeastern Australia and particularly that applied to wooden artefacts. As Cooper points out, however, 'there appear to be two central coexisting functions of traditional visual art in south-eastern Australia'. One is concerned with 'mythical religious and social customs; the other with the maintenance of individual and group identity' (ibid.: 92). Within these two functions there existed an abstract form such as that cited above and the figurative style that appears to be more prevalent but not exclusive to rock faces. It is the second of these concerns – the 'maintenance of individual and group identity' – that comes to the fore in the production of souvenir art. In the example cited here (Plate 5.11), this communication to outsiders, or tourists, is expressed in a figurative style.

This lil-lil from Mingu speaks of the traditional life style of hunting through its burnished or pokerwork detail. This example has no cross-hatching. Instead, the maker favours a figurative frieze that refers to the tool itself within the hunting scene. This figurative style of expression, traditional to the indigenous groups of that area, is also found in the work of another famous Aboriginal artist of the nineteenth century, Mickey of Ulladulla (Plate 5.13). It is clear, from a study of Mickey's work, that the style and strength of line has been continued in the depiction on both surfaces of the lil-lil from the contemporary artist Mingu.

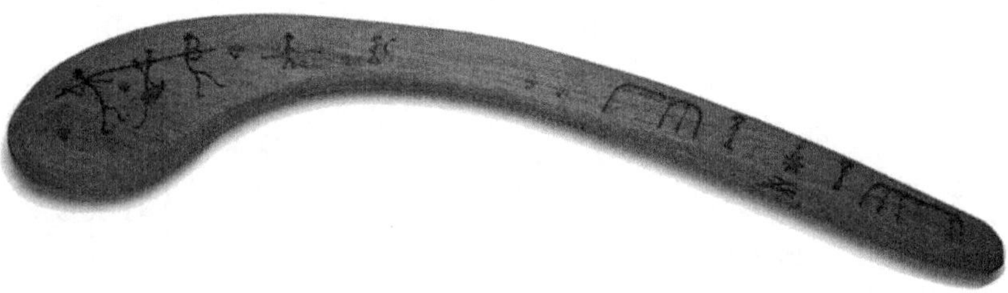

Plate 5.11 Mingu, *Lil-lil*, 2001, Red Gum with pokerwork detail, 70 × 11 × 2.5 cm. Ulladulla, New South Wales Australia. Private collection.

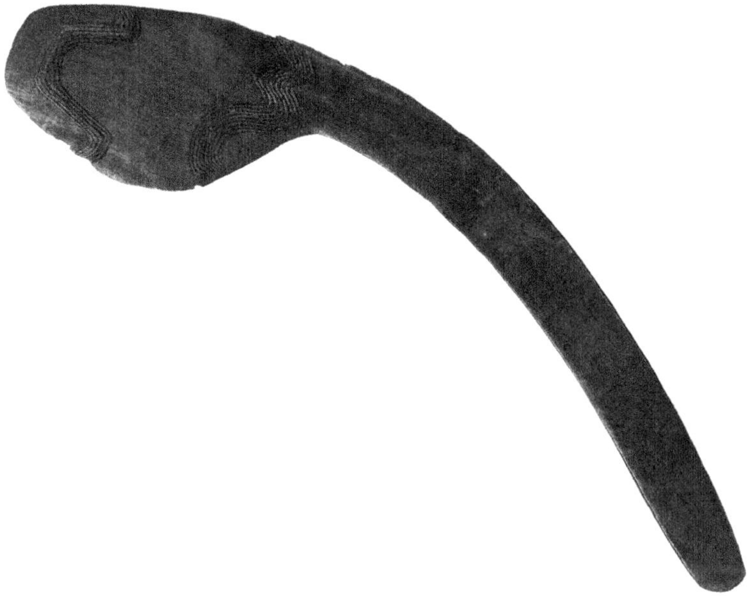

Plate 5.12 Lil-lil club with incised design representing the country of the maker, early nineteenth century, Ovens and Broken River regions, wood. Collection: National Museum of Victoria.

It is the subject matter of the respective artists that provides an interesting point. Mickey of Ulladulla's intention was, in part, to document the impact of colonialism on the area around Ulladulla, while today a sensitive reading of his work might understand it also as a map of the land and the natural resources the people relied upon. On the other hand, the project depicted in Mingu's club is clearly intended to describe the traditional lifestyle of the indigenous people to contemporary tourists and in this Mingu shares a common motive with Barak who depicts a similar shaped club in his catalogue of Aboriginal material culture. (Plate 5.10)[10]

Mingu's figures are rendered in a minimalist and simple stick form and, by and large, the only variation is in scale – for the purpose of describing adult and child figures. In their artistic style, Mingu's figures bear a closer relationship to the work of Mickey of Ulladulla. Mickey's figures extend to the representation of the female and the settler and this is the extent of his detail. The fact that Mingu is working out of the Giriwa Cultural Centre at Ulladulla, where a number of Mickey's works are represented in reproduction, would seem to affirm the artist's familiarity with Mickey's work.

In its composition, medium and rendering of three-dimensional space, however, Mingu's work shares much more stylistically with Tommy McRae, another Koori artist of the nineteenth century. While Barak utilised traditional

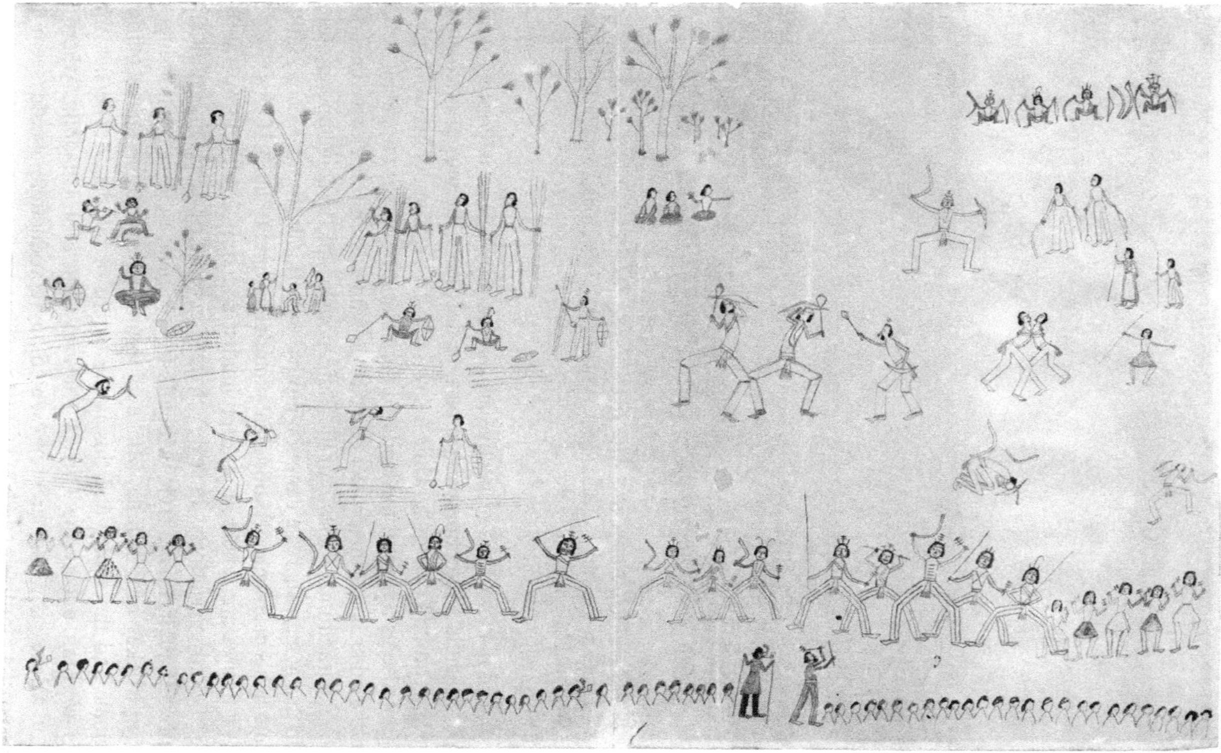

Plate 5.13 Mickey of Ulladulla Yuin/Dhurga peoples 1825 Australia – 1891 not titled (Corroboree) *c.*1888 pencil, coloured pencil, black ink and brush printed image 12.4 × 18.4 cm. Collection: National Gallery of Australia, Canberra. Purchased 1991.

and introduced colour mediums and Mickey of Ulladulla created works with pencil, coloured pencil, gouache and watercolour, McRae's art is almost exclusively executed in pen and ink. In this dominant monochrome body of work there is a style of figurative representation from the nineteenth century that lends itself to a favourable comparison with the colour limitations of pokerwork. McRae's figures are more fully developed than Mingu's, his Aboriginal figures most effectively represented in dark, fully shaded silhouette.

In the untitled image (Plate 5.14), the artist has depicted similar subject matter to that found in Mingu's lil-lil (Plate 5.11). In both scenes sticks are used to carry the prey and both incorporate the involvement of children. The scene represented on Mingu's lil-lil extends the narrative to include the camp of the returning hunters. In this instance, the prey of the hunters is different but McRae depicts the hunting of emu in other work.

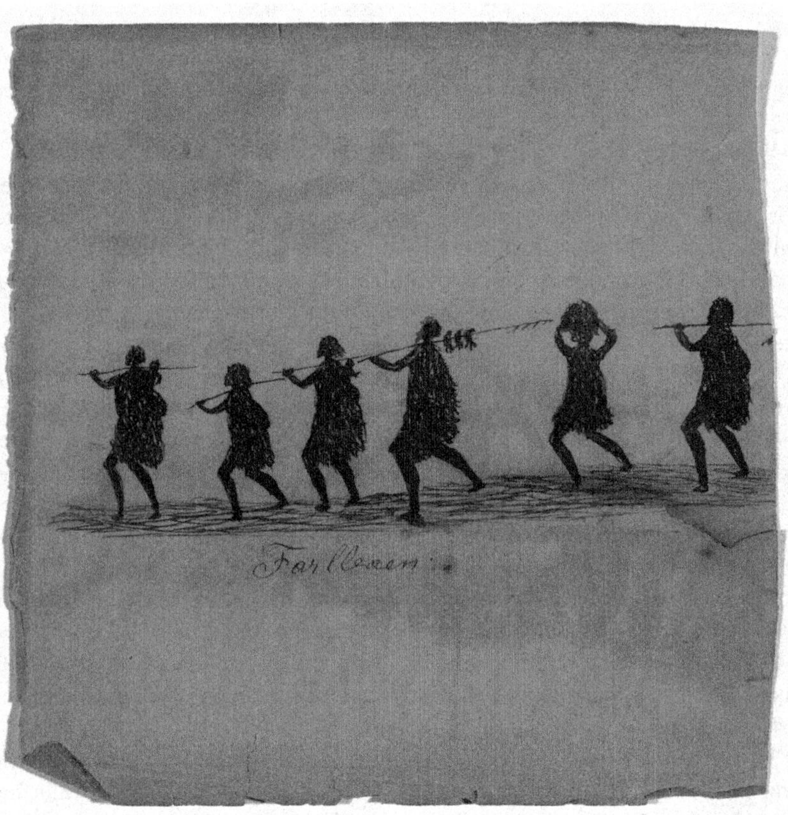

Plate 5.14 Tommy McRae Kwatkwat people 1840/1844 Australia – 1901 Farlbaen (?) c.1890s pen and iron-gall ink sheet 23.8 × 36 cm. Collection: National Gallery of Australia, Canberra. Purchased 1994.

It is in the level of detail in the grounding of the figures within an illusionary three-dimensional space that these two artists have most in common. Although Barak's images lack depth and, with the exception of coastal scenes, Mickey of Ulladulla's are largely flat, McRae grounds his figures in what Sayers (1994: 14) calls a 'furry rope of lines', as seen in Plate 5.14. The employment of this technique is also found in the hunting scene on Mingu's lil-lil (Plate 5.11). Here, the artist has applied a speckling to the ground along the lower length of the artefact, which is enhanced with a faint shading of the ground that runs parallel to the grain of the timber. This effect is most apparent at the point where the club head gives way to the shaft. A similar technique, using shorter lines, is also used to define the camp shelters, while a speckling is utilised again to ground the snake design on the reverse of the artefact.

This speckling effect is also found in two further examples of Mingu's work. First, on another club, for which I can find no historical precedent for its shape, the artist has used the technique to enhance the natural flow of the grain and, in doing so, provides a grounding for the figures and the illusion of three-dimensional space for a clutch of fleeing emus. It is in the final example from Mingu – an untitled depiction of a traditional camp burnished onto a small Masonite board (Plate 5.15) – that the artist's composition skills, together with the speckling technique, are more fully realised.

With this rendition of a traditional Aboriginal camp, Mingu confirms that the figurative detail is the foremost priority and that the preceding artefacts are of most value in their role as canvases for the representation of Aboriginal history and the hunter-gatherer lifestyle. Given its size and monochrome format, this small image is composed with a great deal of spatial depth. The foreground is rendered closest to the viewer on the right of the picture, in the form of a broken tree with a large goanna climbing its trunk. In the lizard's markings and the relative height of its depiction on the trunk, there is a strong similarity to the patterning found in the ceremonial and sacred art of the Aboriginal people of Southeast Australia, in that the markings that detail the body of the lizard are formed from an arrangement of small, slightly ovoid dots, producing three chevron shapes. According to Cooper (1994: 98–99), markings like this were used to indicate 'ceremonial grounds or as monuments to deceased headmen'. Depending on their importance, these dendroglyphs were 'scratched or carved into the bark of the tree … or incised deep into the heartwood and thus made more permanent'. The burnishing of a relief image into timber is a quicker way of achieving the same traditional effect, while the inscription of the lizard in this image provides a link between the ritual and utilitarian art of indigenous Southeast Australia.

This tree is no simplistic rendition either: it is given length through vertical scratching and some speckles and there appears to be a burl on the right hand side of the trunk. A well placed limb functions to contain the eye within the central portion of the image and points to a figure on a rocky overhang. The figure on the outcrop is posed on one leg, resting upon a spear, a pose typical of many sixties souvenirs of Aboriginal Australia. The rock itself, marked in deep

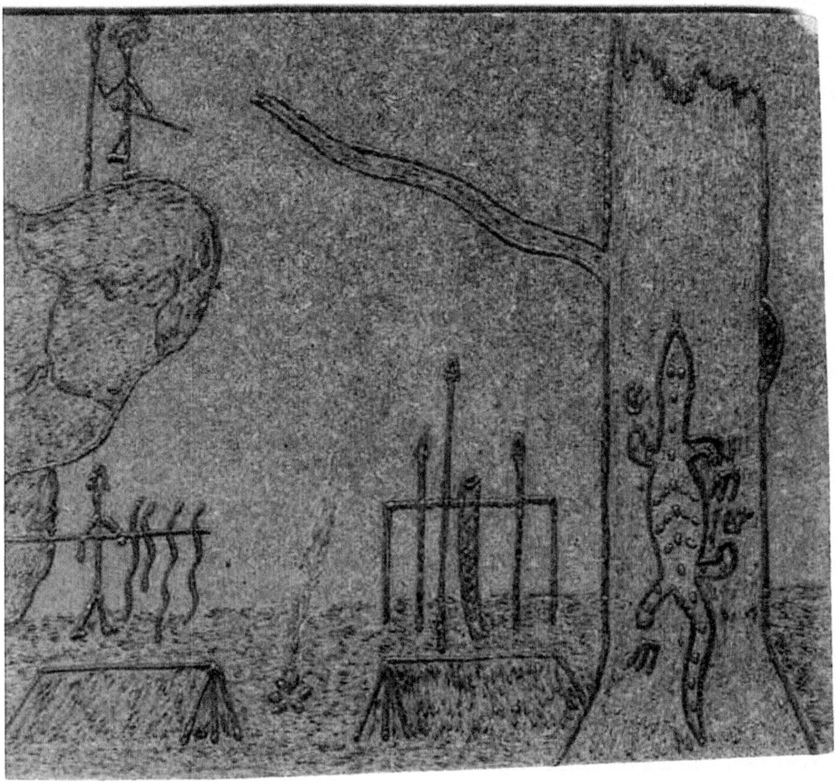

Plate 5.15 Mingu, *Untitled camp scene*, 2001, pokerwork on Masonite, 17 × 20 cm. Private collection.

burnished outline, is given fissured detail by fainter lines and texture through the application of scratching and speckling. The middle ground of this image is concerned with the camp. It features two tent-like shelters and a fire, nearest the viewer, that gives way to a figure returning from hunting, with four snakes. There is also a frame against which are stacked three slender spears and what appears to be a didgeridoo, upon which a crosshatch design has been marked. The inclusion of the didgeridoo is an oddity in this scene since, like the design of the lil-lil, it is alien to the local traditional culture and, as such, testifies to the travel of Aboriginal material culture across tribal boundaries. In this instance, this influence may be ascribed to other Aboriginal artists from Northern Australia found to be working out of the Giriwa Cultural Centre in Ulladulla.

In the preceding examples there is a clear relationship between fine art and tourist art. They show how the subject matter of traditional modes of production and the desire to catalogue traditional tools and other aspects of that life style are prominent in both forms of art. They also demonstrate how the style of late nineteenth century Koori art has provided a method of representation that has been continued in the souvenir art of that culture. In the case of Alice Springs artist, Tjapaltjarri, the ability of the artist to work in both spheres is clear, while Mason is quite alert to the similarity of his work to tourist art, suggesting that decorative embellishment through pokerwork is the point of separation.

What I have not addressed in the analysis of the above artefacts is their function as miniatures. Size and portability are defining qualities of most souvenirs, although not all souvenirs are necessarily of reduced scale. Nevertheless, as we have found previously, in narrative terms, all souvenirs are miniatures, for they invoke stories that expand upon the subject of the souvenir. For example, the priority component of Mingu's lil-lil (a full-scale artefact) is the depicted hunting scene which, in narrative terms, depicts only half of the story – the return from hunting. It is, thus, a fragment and of reduced scale. Tjapaltjarri's painting and the markings on the nineteenth century lil-lil equate to scaled maps of the land.

In concluding this chapter, I want to look at a number of examples that demonstrate the idea that all souvenirs are miniatures. To achieve this I will cite souvenir artefacts from the Western and non-Western past showing how the museogallery system is complicit in the final stage of magnification and how it fulfils the needs of the tourist gaze.

All souvenirs are miniatures

So far in this chapter I have dealt almost exclusively with souvenirs of exotic 'Other' cultures; most are redundant utilitarian artefacts, residues from modes of production that are no longer viable, or at least are under pressure. As I have just shown, moribund artefacts are often invested with the representation of heritage, either through artistic enhancement or concepts of antiquity. Indeed, heritage is the key to the souvenired object, for it is through the distant past that one is able to more comfortably locate difference and 'Otherness' and detect clues to what makes a particular place and culture unique. This applies to past periods of Western history as much as the history and presence of exotic non-Western cultures. In this respect there is no culture, ancient or modern, Western or non-Western, that is immune to souveniring. All that is required is the concept that the artefact represents a place and culture that is other than that of the collector.

In her text, Pearce (1995: 25) exemplifies the expansive capacity of moribund tools to invoke big stories, using the example of a Rabbet Plane, a carpenter's tool made for the purpose of manufacturing decorative wooden mouldings. She explains how this object was produced in about 1910 and saw service up until the Second World War. After that, it fell into disuse and Pearce suggests that at this time it probably fell into what she refers to as a passive collection; that is, stored with other bits and pieces that might be of some use, some day. This she describes as its second life form, arguing that '[s]omewhere around this time it will have become an object of interest to those who were beginning deliberately to gather material relating to dying crafts' (ibid.: 26). This is clearly a fetishistic collection, in that firstly it is directly derived from the earlier passive collection and secondly that, as a fragment of the 'dying crafts' it enables the collector to build a more complete notion of that craft. Following this period of collecting, in which the artefact has moved from private to domestic display, the author asserts that, 'the next and final step is into the collection of a respected and probably public, museum, where the sacredness of the collections becomes a kind of immortality' (ibid.).

This example features three transitions in the life of the Rabbet Plane that correlate quite clearly to the collecting process and narrative transition of Graburn's examples that pertain directly to non-Western artefacts, as cited in Chapter 3. Here the object has existed in passive and private collections and has finally undergone a change from utilitarian tool to antique object with heritage reference and value, and has passed into a revered public collection. Taking the object's passive state as the conventional fetish, in that the accompanying narrative is unorganised and non-expansive, it is possible to detect, in these three existences of the one object, a clear parallel to the transition of the fetish object.[11] The object's secondary state sees it move into the private domain as an 'object of interest to those who were beginning deliberately to gather material relating to dying crafts' and finally into the public collection of a 'respected and probably public, museum' (ibid.: 25).

Once ensconced in the public realm of the museum, such objects and artefacts, from Western and non-Western cultures, fall under the expansive purview of Museum Studies and Material Culture, as we ask why such objects are collected. According to Pearce (1991: 7), the first analytical study to isolate this question and in so doing present a specific theory relating to the consumption of souvenirs is Stewart's *On Longing* (1984), in which she writes:

> We might say that the capacity of objects to serve as traces of authentic experience is, in fact, exemplified by the souvenir. The souvenir distinguishes experiences. We do not need or desire souvenirs of events that are repeatable. Rather we need and desire souvenirs of events that are reportable, events that whose materiality has escaped us, events that thereby exist only through the invention of narrative. Through narrative the souvenir substitutes a context of perpetual consumption.
>
> (Ibid.: 135)

Stewart refers to the experience of the site or event that is invested in and rematerialises as the object. She writes that '[t]he experience of the object lies outside of the body's experience – it is saturated with meaning that will never be fully revealed to us' (ibid.: 133). Much of this meaning has been inscribed by the maker and, as with Tjapaltjarri's boomerang, Hunt's Seal Bowl or any of the Aboriginal artefacts examined so far, much of its meaning will never be revealed to the collector without further inquiry and study. This is the activity of the souvenir, where the experience of the object, or rather the site or event, invokes the composition of the collector's narrative. A narrative that is saturated into, or perhaps inscribed onto, the surface of the souvenir, and occurs over the top of, or alongside, the narrative of the maker. This process of inscription empowers the collector with the ability to recall the experience to others through an expansive narrative invoked by the object.

Stewart suggests, however, that this narrative is always incomplete. This is especially the case when the object is remote from Western culture and is generated from a non-Western narrative and history. Instead, it relies upon the collector's personal experience to develop a meaning and to interpret the use of the object or decorative enhancement. In this way, a small portable object or artefact is used as the material centre from which this dislocated, fanciful and idealistic narrative radiates. As Pearce (1991: 32) puts it: '[t]hey are objects which form a starting point for a personal narrative and which demonstrate the truth of a story'. It is a story that, like many travellers' tales, is always larger than life.

Stewart is acutely aware of the importance of size and portability and how, as a fragment of the site or event, the miniature operates in this system of memory and nostalgia. For Stewart, the body is the ultimate form by which experience is scaled. She argues (1984: 133) that '[w]hen the body is the primary mode of perceiving scale, exaggeration must take place in relation to the balance of measurement offered as the body extends into the space of immediate experience'.

An example of the importance of scale that correlates very closely to Stewart's own example of a wood basket (ibid.: 144) – now reduced in scale to suit the demands of the souvenir trade – could be seen in the rich *Behind the Mask* exhibition at the Tasmanian Museum and Art Gallery. Here, in close proximity to Hunt's Seal Bowl and artefacts from the Wilkes collection, were a number of indigenous Alaskan artefacts from the Tasmanian Museum and Art Gallery's own collection. These included a whaler's hat, a fish skin basket and an exquisitely woven baleen basket, with a polar bear finial carved from seal or whalebone.

The text accompanying this exquisite basket (Plate 5.16) states that it is a miniature of the type of basket used to store 'food and other household items'. The reduced size of this object demonstrates its production as a prototype souvenir, and the simplification of the narrative from that of use and fit within the culture of origin – the ethnographic criteria – to one signifying the experience of exotic 'Otherness'. This small woven basket, in its reduced form, is no longer capable of the utility of the original, upon which it is modelled. It renders it vulnerable to a miscontextualisation that is remedied by the supporting text. In other words, the basket, like the fridge magnet boomerang (Plate 3.13), fails to speak the truth without the supporting text. This text refers to the original's use and thus frames the object as an ethnographic artefact, while the persistence of the ethnographic contextualisation obscures the appreciation of its formal and aesthetic qualities. The souvenir narrative of this artefact, existing only in the spoken word, is now lost. It survives only in the museum's anecdotal records of the artefact's provenance. In this particular case, the record declares that it came to Tasmania as a keepsake, collected by a crewman of a Tasmanian whaling fleet operating in the Bering Sea at the beginning of the last century.[12]

This basket is without doubt a miniature, but souvenirs defined as keepsakes, that is objects or artefacts collected from a visited site and installed by the

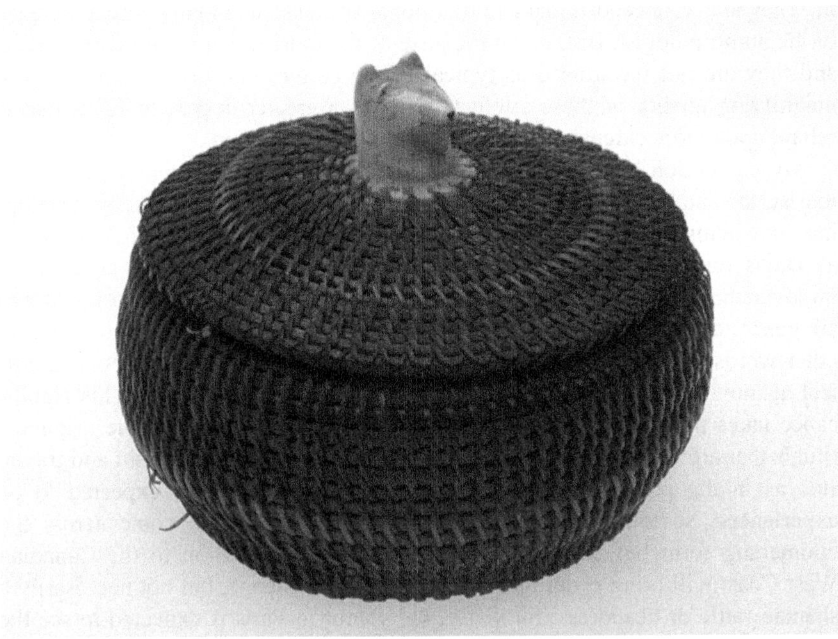

Plate 5.16 Baleen basket with carved ivory finial, Alaska, early 19th century, 17 × 12.4 cm. Collection: Tasmanian Museum and Art Gallery, Cat. No. 5848.

collector in their home, are always miniatures whether of reduced scale or not. As Stewart suggests, they rely upon a playful exaggeration of scale. This is due, at least in part, to the need for such things to be portable; that is, suitcase size.[13] The latent trick of the souvenir is to recall what I have termed the 'largesse' of the original and to act as props within the greater narrative. It is true that many souvenirs are of exact or a similar scale to the original, such as the indigenous Australian and Canadian artefacts shown above, or the prints of famous paintings sold in national, state and other major galleries and museums around the world, but some contain superior qualities of magnification, while in others this quality is limited.

This has to do with the iconic status of the souvenir in question. In the boomerang examples previously cited, all of the boomerangs possess a high degree of 'largesse', in that the form alone is instantly recognisable as the iconic Aboriginal tool. The same may be said about the cedar masks featured in the *Behind the Mask* exhibition, while Tjapaltjarri's painting, *Possum dreaming*, is iconographic in its dot painting style. In contrast to these souvenir artefacts of intense magnification are all of the nula-nulas and shields from Aboriginal Australia and the shaman rattles, headdresses and Alaskan artefacts. Their site and culture of origin is not instantaneously attributable or recognised by the tourist, and in that respect such artefacts are impoverished, for they are, in Steiner's (1999: 94–96) terms, deviations from the tourist's canon of authenticity, originals that do not fit. They are, at once, original and traditional artefacts, and many attract the gaze of the anthropologist. But, under the gaze of the tourist, there is no iconic status and they are not recognised as typical of the culture that produced them. The magnifying quality of these artefacts requires a greater degree of focus that is reliant upon more extensive engagement and documentation.

My contention here is that in the hands of, or rather under the gaze of the tourist, the souvenir copy actually enhances the aura of the original by developing, enhancing and underscoring the iconographic status of the original. For if, as Davis (cited Lurry 1997: 78) suggests, 'an object without an anecdote is impoverished', then the ensuing anecdotes that revolve about the original and are generated by the souvenir copy can only enhance the aura of the original. In other words, as Davis concludes, '[c]irculating images of such objects is a critical acknowledgment that those objects have significance' (ibid.). This significance takes the form of new or extended rituals associated with the originals; rituals that are no longer based on religion but upon those of tourism and travel. Just as in the pre-modern world, where certain rituals were expected to be experienced, so today a visitor to Australia may expect to come across the boomerang form but not a nula-nula.[14] Likewise, a vacation to the Canadian West Coast will bring cedar masks into the tourist's scope, but not necessarily a shaman rattle or headdress. Similarly, the visitor to Paris is expected to see the Eiffel Tower, the subject of Stewart's inquiry into the miniature, in which she demonstrates how the exaggeration in scale, based upon the scale of the body, takes place through the collection of a model (Stewart 1984: 136). But what Stewart does not explore is the 'largesse' of the model, which causes it to represent not just Paris but the entire nation.

This notion of 'largesse' runs contrary to the emptying of the aura that is attributed to Benjamin's thesis on mass produced art. As I have noted previously, Benjamin's thesis rests, in the first instance, upon the artwork's dislocation from its ritual basis as a result of mechanical reproduction. This process, Benjamin argues, liberates the work from its ritual source and makes the work available to the masses. But, according to Benjamin, in doing so it denigrates the aura or authentic status of the original (1969: 224). However, Benjamin's thesis was directed to the work of art and does not consider the specific condition of tourism and the material culture of tourism. Therefore, in closing this chapter I want to apply this notion of 'largesse' to the work of art in the Western context and see how the unique gaze of the tourist affects the aura of Western art works.

Some material forms, artistic periods, styles and movements are given to this notion of 'largesse' more than others. In terms of Western art history, large paintings, such as John Constable's twelve-foot canvasses or the frescoes of Michelangelo, are plainly restricted from this practice and their reduced scale in miniature souvenir form is obvious. An excellent example of the less deceitful miniature – in that real scale can be, and is, offered in the souvenir – is discovered in the work of Van Gogh. As souvenirs, the slick reproductions of Van Gogh's work, as posters and textured canvasses, owe much of their popularity to their commercially desirable poster size format. The 'largesse' afforded these real scale copies is furnished by the conditions in which the original is experienced; that is, a combination of the grandness of the gallery or museum, the security in place, the accompanying crowd and the exotic perception of the city or town in which the original is viewed. These contemporary environmental features of the artwork represent an exclusive space that distances the viewer from the work and invokes the wish to record the experience through the souvenir. In this respect the original work of art is as fixed in its location as the scenic spectacle or monument, what Rojek (1997: 58), reading Benjamin, refers to as the 'unique manifestation of distance' that defines the aura of the original. For just as a glance at a miniature boomerang conjures up the experience of Australia, a glance at the copy of a Van Gogh masterpiece conjures the experience of the original in its culturally expected and 'authentic' site. Here, even, the real size souvenir has the capacity to exaggerate scale through narrative. In this deceptive exaggeration of scale is found the invocation of narrative, as an anecdote of the holiday, that affords some credence to the souvenir copy – what Stewart (1984: 135) expresses as a context of perpetual consumption 'achieved through narrative'. This, in turn, contributes to the preservation of the aura of the original.

For MacCannell the dislocation of the 'aura' from its ritual base is more extreme. He argues that the 'aura' of the artefact or object exists only in the reproduction. Beginning from the standpoint that artists and not societies produce art, MacCannell (1976) argues that:

> [s]ociety for its part, can only produce the importance, 'reality' or 'originality' of a work of art by piling up representations alongside. Benjamin believed that the reproduction of the work of art is produced because the work has a socially based 'aura' about it, the 'aura' being a residue of its origins in a primordial ritual.
>
> (MacCannell 1976: 47)

MacCannell then suggests that, reflecting on the conditions of tourism:

> Benjamin should have reversed his terms. The work becomes 'authentic' only after the first copy of it is produced. The reproductions are the aura, and the ritual, far from being the point of origin, derives from the relationship between the original object and its socially constructed importance.
>
> (Ibid.: 47–48, author's emphasis)

In other words, society authorises the artefact or object – the aspiring artwork – as a work of art. It does this by constructing a framework that includes the modern secular rituals of authority, through which the work is consumed as a sacred object or artefact. Conventionally, this framework exists in the structures of the museogallery system and other institutions involved in the arts. In the case of tourist art, that authority is largely devolved to the ephemeral community of tourists, who negotiate it through the phenomenon of free trade, enhanced by the exaggerated consumption habits peculiar to tourism.

MacCannell's argument relies on the claim that societies do not create art, or rather the original artefact, and that is a debatable claim. In order to understand why this is, I want to distinguish between 'originality' and 'aura'. If an original object is without a sacred status and aura until it is copied, is it art or simply a mundane artefact, a work of art in waiting? In MacCannell's inversion of Benjamin's thesis, the work is authenticated only after the copy or representation is produced. In this case the reproduction pays homage to the original, or sensation of the original, and in that discourse rests the aura, which in turn authorises the original artefact as a work of art.

MacCannell's thesis is relatively inconclusive in this regard and my reading of it confuses matters further. I agree that the 'aura' is manifest in the copy and enhanced through subsequent reproductions, and that the museogallery structures – buildings, security and ensuing anecdotes – that surround the work make up a significant component of the contemporary ritual of viewing art, or, rather, original artefacts. But I contend that art is, at least in part, socially constructed and defined and that this contributes significantly to the production of the original artefact.

This can be pursued further by examining MacCannell's extension of his argument to tourist attractions. Tourist attractions, especially those with a core attraction of landscape and natural beauty, are firstly appreciated in terms of the found object. As the effect these sites have on the viewer becomes popular, they are curated and organised by legislation that preserves such sites and declares them as national parks and other public spaces. This works in the following way: someone discovers a view, communes with it and is affected by it, they tell someone else and so on. Without the articulation of an anecdote about the experience, many sites of natural beauty and art works remain unknown. Now, as the artwork or site becomes popular and attracts more and more visitors, certain measures are taken to protect the object/artefact from its own popularity. Barriers, such as gilded ropes, encroachment alarms, glass panels and legislation set boundaries around the work or site and prescribe suitable behaviour within its proximity or confines. It is a boundary that is not necessarily part of the work or site, but one that is incorporated into the anecdote about the work or tourist narrative and as such inflates the aura, the 'largesse' that surrounds tourist attractions and works of art. In this respect, even the souvenir of authentic scale has the power to exaggerate its meaning and therefore operates as a miniature: a poster of a Van Gogh masterpiece represents the original work, the museum or gallery, the city where the work is located and the country of that city.

The expression or language of such objects and artefacts, of which 'largesse' is a measurable component, is configured to address the peculiar conditions of tourism. I will explore this and Stewart's binary classification of souvenirs in the following chapter, where I will present a new theory by which to analyse souvenirs, based on interpreting the language of such objects and artefacts according to what has been discovered so far.

6 The language of souvenirs

Three discrete groups – the Sampled, Crafted and Representative

Introduction

In this chapter, I will expand upon Stewart's binary classification of souvenirs as 'Sampled' and 'Representative' and establish a new category of the 'Crafted' souvenir. To achieve this I will introduce one ideal souvenir from each category that will serve as a typical example, from which the variation of ensuing souvenir objects and artefacts will later be assessed. I will then describe five souvenir attributes that are present, to some degree, in the expression of all souvenirs. They are:

a Medium
b Maker's mark
c Relational
d Invitational
e Iconofetish

This analysis then leads to a method that expresses the descriptive data of individual souvenir artefacts, so that the patterns of the language may be analysed and implemented in the construction of a design theory for the production of successful souvenirs.

These criteria will be shown graphically as axis points that assess the degree of presence or absence of each expressive feature in the individual groups. Following this, I will present a range of examples, gathered in the course of this research, from various parts of Australia that demonstrate how atypical souvenirs may be plotted between the three key groups. These will include indigenous examples, many cited previously, which will be contrasted to settler souvenirs. In doing this I will demonstrate the fundamental activity and expression, or language, that is common to all souvenirs. As Stewart says, 'the souvenir must remain impoverished and partial so that it can be supplemented by a narrative discourse, a narrative discourse which articulates the play of desire' (1984: 136).

To recap Stewart's definition, she categorizes souvenirs as either 'Sampled' objects or 'Representative' artefacts. She defines Sampled objects as souvenirs of individual experience. They are real samples from the actual site and are not available as general consumer goods (ibid.). Sampled objects consist of objects that are collected directly by the tourist, with no intervention or mediation by the host culture. These objects are, in Stewart's terms, the most 'impoverished and partial' (ibid.); in their purest form, literally samples of the environment. They take the shape of sea shells or pebbles, wild flowers dried and pressed, or animal remains. This type of souvenir collecting finds its history in those collections gathered by the scientific company of early explorers and conforms to what, we have discovered, Pearce calls 'systematic collection' (1995: 32) in that the imperative was to relate the exotic sample to the known botanical system.

Stewart's second category, the Representative, is defined as those 'souvenirs of exterior sights ... which most often are representations and are purchasable' (Stewart 1984: 138). Here she places all other souvenirs; objects that may properly be called artefacts, in that they are produced from human mediation and interpretation. This class of souvenir includes postcards, wilderness posters, calendars and other re-presentations of the site. It also embraces crafted objects, such as Stewart's own example of a miniature basket (ibid.), and other crafted souvenirs like clay pots, Aboriginal coolamons, didgeridoos and boomerangs, Huon pine trinkets, convict and colonial artefacts. It is the purpose of this research to provide reasons why the latter category should be further divided into the Representative and a new category, which I have defined as the 'Crafted'.

Leaving in place Stewart's Sampled grouping, the revised Representative category takes account of the mass production of souvenirs, made from non-native or generic media, such as postcards. These are distinct from crafted artefacts, in that souvenirs in the Crafted category are reliant upon native materials and local craft traditions, and frequently retain some utilitarian reference. In their ideal form, these three categories of souvenirs and their attributes are summarised in Table 6.1.

This framework favours the artefact's operation as a souvenir, rather than the museogallery categories of ethnographic artefact or work of art, that is consistent with Pearce's (1995) pre-Romantic classification of collected objects as 'Naturalia and Artificialia'[1] from which, it seems, Stewart's categories are derived. It therefore engages with the Romantic sensibilities of collecting; a period commensurate with the advent of contemporary tourism, in which collecting took a 'demotic turn' (ibid.).

Table 6.1 The three primary categories of souvenir, with ideal examples and attributes

	Sampled category e.g. sea shell	*Crafted category e.g. authored Huon pine bowl*	*Representative category e.g. landscape postcard*
Medium	of the site, unmediated	of the site, mediated	unassociated, generic
Maker's Mark	absent	present	dominant
Relational	place	place and people	place and/or people
Invitational	open	ajar	closed
Iconofetish	personal	domestic	public

A further strength of this expanded typology is that it permits the analysis of Western and non-Western artefacts within the same framework. This is more expansive than Graburn's typology, because, while Graburn (1976: 4) alluded to Western craft in his analysis as folk art,[2] the scope of his typology is not inclusive of souvenirs of the Western past.[3] However, as with Graburn's typology, there are some souvenirs that are difficult to place within the three main categories I have set out. This will become apparent as this chapter develops.

Ideal objects/artefacts are used to establish the new typology of souvenirs that, in turn, will elicit a visual expression of the individual souvenir's language and further indicate the souvenir potential of objects and artefacts hitherto unaffected by the tourist industry. This visual expression is formed of graphic patterns that are constituted from five principal attributes and occur, to varying degrees, in all souvenirs. It is the play between these attributes that gives rise to the pattern of expression that is related to the ideal types charted in Table 6.1.

I want to begin by qualifying the details of each attribute that, like the vowels of language or the primary colours of the artist's palette, form the cornerstones of souvenir expression. In the following typology, I will identify the degree of the attribute's activity in each of the three discrete classes of souvenirs, which distinguishes them from one another. The presence of each attribute is assessed using a scale between one (1) and ten (10). Following this, I shall present a number of souvenirs of each type and chart their distinguishing attributes, showing how they vary in their expression but retain the basic patterns outlined in the ideal or typical souvenirs.

Souvenir attributes

Medium

What material constitutes the object/artefact and what is the importance of this material in its activity as a souvenir?

The term 'medium' is self-explanatory and refers to the raw and/or mediated state of the material from which the artefact is made. Consistent with Stewart's division based on the economics of collection, I have used this fundamental feature to initially determine between the Sampled and the other two categories. By isolating the *Medium* axis it is possible to see how the Sampled souvenir is produced of raw, natural material from the visited site, without the intervention of the host culture. The Sampled souvenir is therefore reliant upon the tourist's recognition of its capacity to signify the experience of the site (Stewart 1984: 136). On the other hand, the Crafted souvenir is of the same material but is interpreted through the craft of the host culture. At the other end of the scale, the Representative souvenir carries no marker of the visited site in its medium. The most important feature of Sampled souvenirs is, therefore, their presence as genuine fragments of the experienced site. In the light of this, I have allotted a value scale from ten (10) to one (1) along this axis beginning with the Sampled

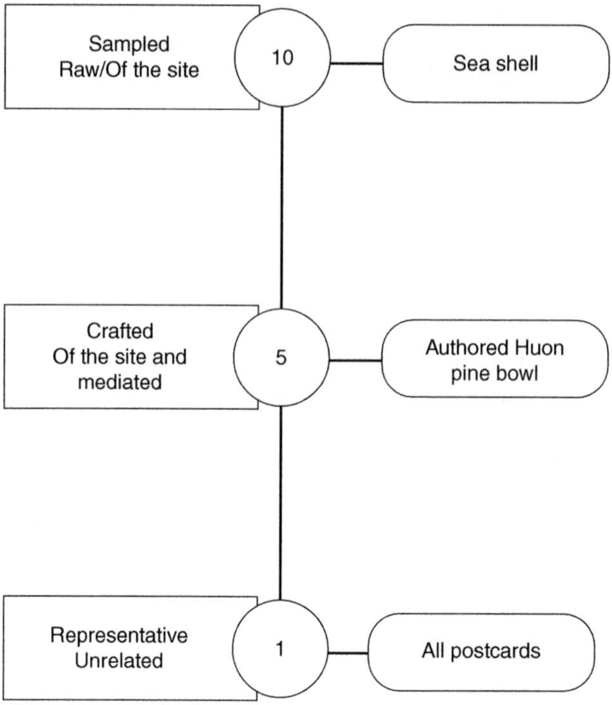

Figure 6.1 Medium axis showing ideal souvenir types.

category at ten (10). This reflects the overriding importance of the endemic medium in the Sampled souvenir. It then progresses to the Crafted group at the median point with a value of five (5), recognising the raw materials' augmentation through craft and its contribution to the activity of the artefact as a souvenir. Then, finally, to the Representative category with a value of one (1) that is not dependent on an endemic medium to refer to the visited site. This reverse scale of assessment from ten (10) to one (1) beginning with the Sampled category is not constant for each attribute. The only other axis in which it is found is the *Invitational*, as will be shown shortly.

Maker's mark

What level of human intervention has the object/artefact undergone and how important is it to its function as a souvenir?

The *Maker's mark* axis refers to the authorship of the maker and measures the degree to which it is present. The sea shell is without a maker, other than the specifics of the environment from which it is collected, so is rated at one (1). The

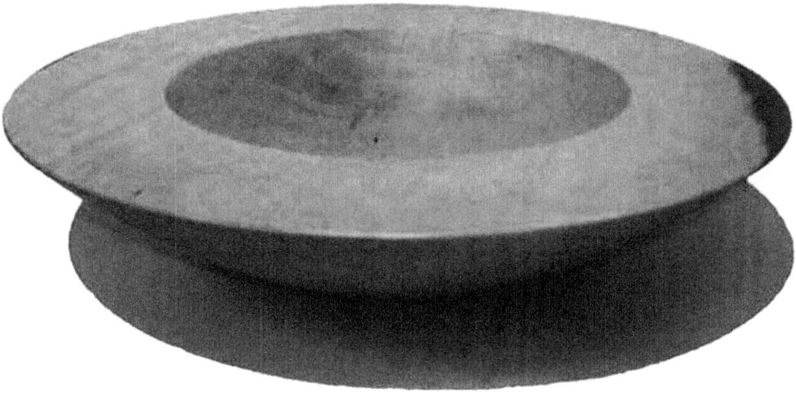

Plate 6.1 Peter Meure, *Huon pine bowl*, undated, 27 cm. Private collection.

signed Huon pine bowl (Plate 6.1), like many other minor species timber souvenirs, often carries the maker's mark on the underside. In this way, the artist's attribution is present but not dominant and therefore, like most Crafted souvenirs of that type, attracts a rating of five (5). The Landscape postcard, like the work of art, most often features the photographer's signature in a prominent position (Plate 6.3) and so is rated at ten (10). However, this is not the case with all postcards, as the more generic varieties of postcards (Plate 6.2) are often without authorship. These fall into the same sphere as the ubiquitous, mass-produced mugs with national flags printed upon them, that are produced far away from the site they purport to represent and attract a rating of one (1) along this axis, in line with the sea shell. It is the rating of their other attributes, such as the preceding *Medium* axis, that set them apart from the sea shell example.

This axis becomes rather cluttered with souvenirs that rest between the three key points and include, for instance, unattributed Huon pine souvenirs, like the many lathe-turned minor species timber fruit objects (Plate 6.7), honey dippers or cheese sets, for sale in various souvenir outlets. Unlike the exampled bowl, these souvenirs do not carry the craftsperson's signature. They are, instead, attributed collectively to the company that produced them, if at all, but importantly that company is located within or near the site of reference. Due to this collective authorship, such souvenirs are plotted near the Sampled end of the scale, in that they are more reliant on the distinctive medium for their souvenir activity and rest between the sea shell and the exampled Huon pine bowl.

At this point, it is possible to see how the Crafted souvenir signifies a touristic engagement with the environment and heritage of the visited site and, most importantly, the people of that site. It can be seen, in the example of the unsigned Huon pine souvenir, that the Sampled aspect of the souvenir relates to the specific environment of the site and that this persists in the Crafted artefact.

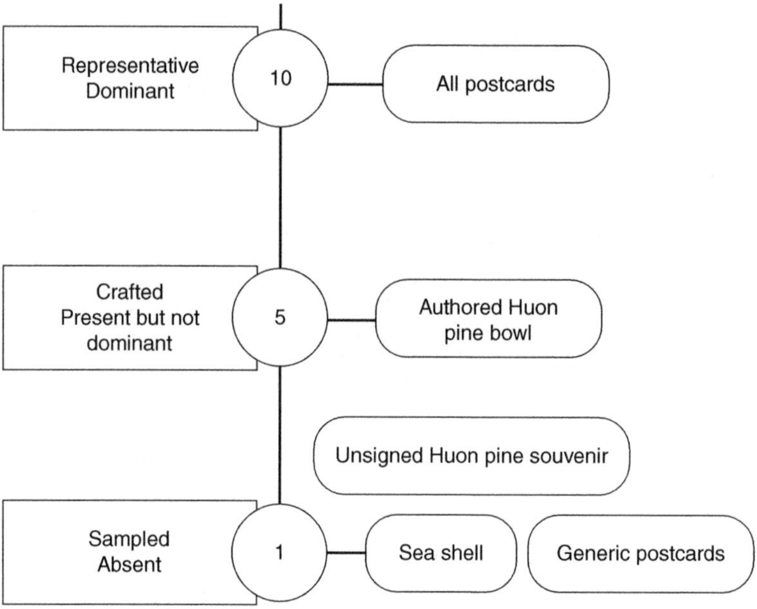

Figure 6.2 Maker's mark axis showing ideal and atypical souvenirs.

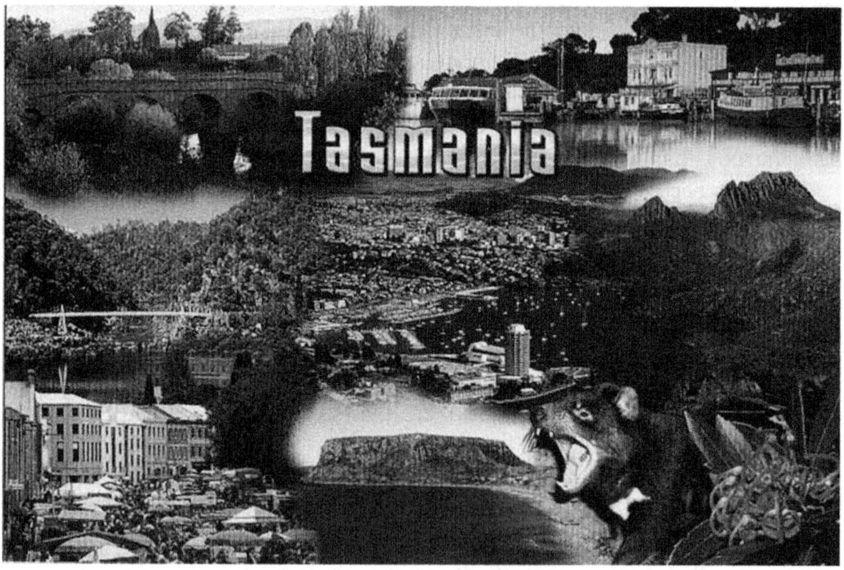

Plate 6.2 Nu-colour-vu, *Views of Tasmania*, 2002, postcard, 12 × 17 cm. Private collection.

Relational

What does the object/artefact relate to?

The *Relational* axis of the souvenir refers to the underlying motive behind its collection. As a narrative component this axis seeks to define the thematic base of the object or artefact, framed as a souvenir. This feature gauges the relationship between the tourist and the site. Some souvenirs relate the tourist's experience of the site alone, while others speak of the people that inhabit that site. This axis assesses that relationship and begins with those restricted to references of the environmental specifics of the place, rated as one (1); then, sliding up to those that relate to people and place, rated at five (5); and, finally, people and/or place, rated at ten (10).

This axis addresses the feature or features of the visited site that are embedded in the souvenir. In the ideal examples it can be seen that the sea shell's reference is confined to the place of its collection. This is due to its raw nature, in that it has not been mediated by the people of that site. In this case it is not invested with any narrative of human heritage and is reliant upon the collector for its meaning.

In contrast, the ideal Crafted souvenir always consists of a raw material extracted from the site but is mediated by the artists/crafts people of the site. This fixes the relational feature of this category of souvenirs as one of people and place. These first two groups of souvenirs therefore attract values of one (1) and five (5) respectively.

The *Relational* axis is completed by the Representative category to which I have allotted a value of ten (10). As we have seen, this category of souvenir is produced from a generic medium that is not drawn from the site and is typified by the postcard. Unlike the Sampled group, it is not restricted to referencing place alone, nor does it insist on a people and place reference, governed by medium and craft. The Representative souvenir is perhaps the most flexible souvenir on this axis and has the capacity to relate to people and/or place due, in most cases, to its reliance on imagery alone.

The *Relational* axis, illustrated in Figure 6.3, is also complicated by souvenirs that range along its length. For instance, the landscape postcard, while clearly falling within the Representative category of souvenirs, due to its lack of endemic medium, may equally be situated closer to the Crafted category, in that the style of photography has been developed in and around the visited site. However, it will never meet the fundamental quality of the Crafted souvenir, based, as it is, upon the insistence of specific local material.

In the instance of the Dombrovskis (1945–1996) style of landscape photography (Plate 6.3), we have a fine example of these atypical Representative souvenirs. The name Dombrovskis is uniquely associated with the Tasmanian wilderness and since his notoriety, achieved with images of the Franklin River during the early 1980s and his untimely death some years later, many erstwhile photographic artists have followed in his footsteps and style.[4] Postcards and

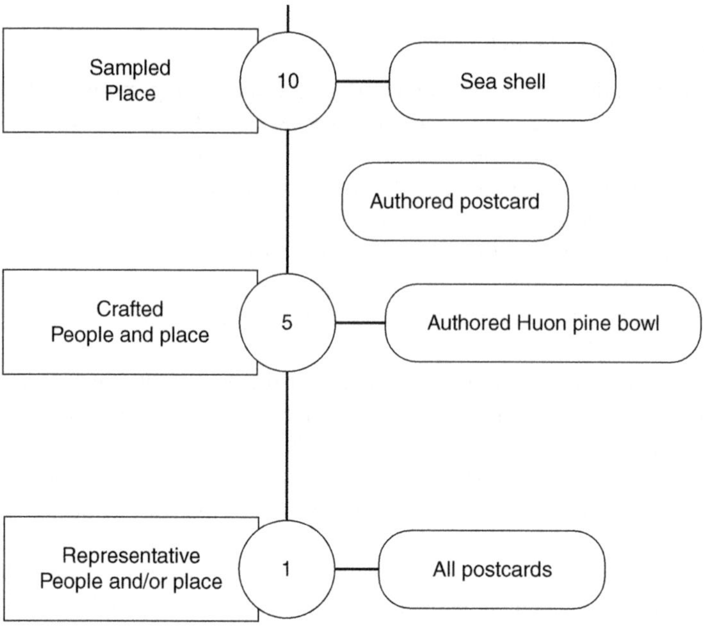

Figure 6.3 Relational axis showing ideal and atypical souvenirs.

other photographic medium souvenirs of a Dombrovskian style now compete with the more generic postcards, such as *Views of Tasmania* (Plate 6.2). However, the Dombrovskian postcard always carries the signature of the artist and so alludes to a crafted photographic engagement with the site. Therefore, through its demonstration of a local craftsperson engaging with the site, it should be plotted closer to the Crafted category along this axis. This demonstrates the flexibility of this group of souvenirs, in that they may relate to people and/or place depending on the subject of the image.

Invitational

What is the object/artefact's capacity to absorb the tourist's narrative?

This is the second of two reverse scales of assessment. The *Invitational* axis assesses the way the narrative of the souvenir is progressed. It refers to and favours the souvenir's capacity to accept the collector's narrative of experience and therefore assesses the completeness of the souvenir's narrative prior to collection. For instance, the sea shell contains no anecdotal narrative of the site, so invites the collector to supply its meaning as a souvenir. The sea shell's souvenir narrative is therefore open, its invitational qualities are high and it is allotted a value of ten (10). The Crafted example, on the other hand, carries a value of

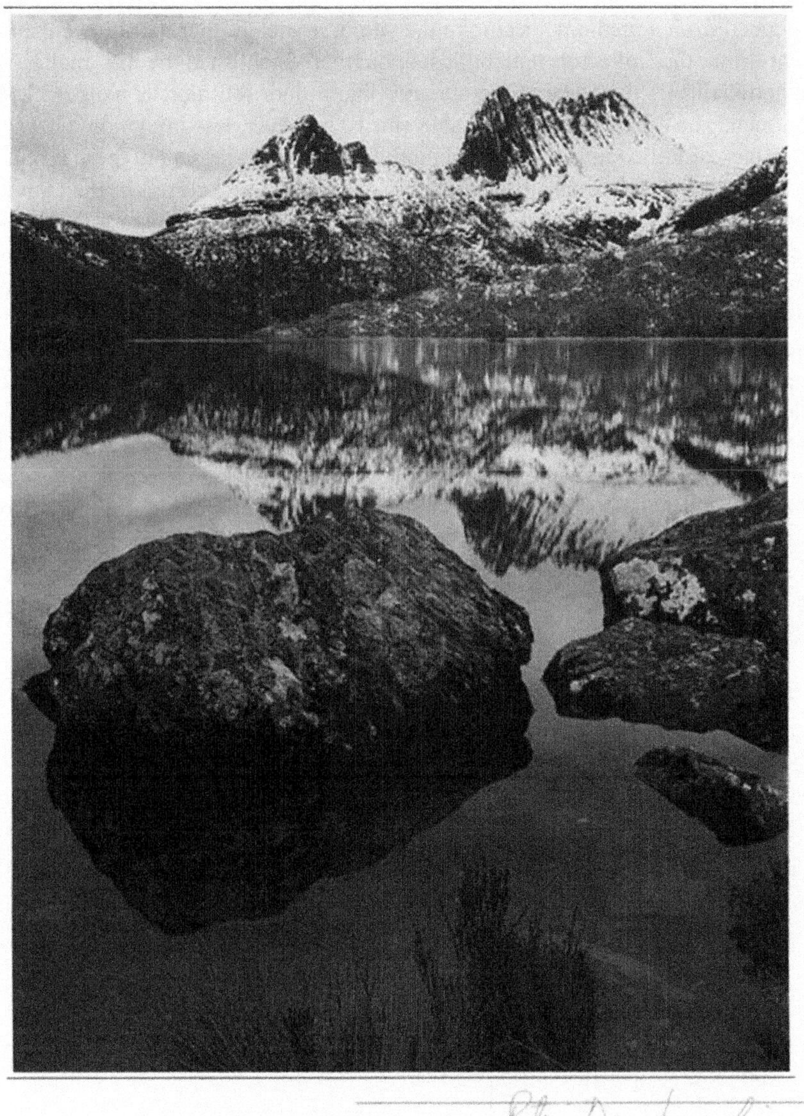

Plate 6.3 Peter Dombrovskis, *Cradle Mountain And Dove Lake*, 2001, greeting card, 19 × 13.7 cm. Private collection.

five (5). Due to its mediated state it has been interpreted by the maker and a souvenir narrative set in train. But, by retaining some utility in its form and being produced from a medium specific to the site, it invites further narrative enhancement from the collector that builds upon that established by the maker. Its invitationality is therefore moderate and, like a door left ajar, is neither closed nor open. The ornamental Crafted souvenir is, however, less invitational because of its lack of utility and so is plotted more toward the Representative category.

The Representative group of souvenirs are, moreover, closed in their invitational capacity and are allotted a value of one (1), reflecting the closed and completeness of their narrative. These souvenirs are clear in the site they represent through the images of well-known features of the visited site. For instance, the postcard featuring views of Tasmania (Plate 6.2) is overtly labelled and is unequivocal about the site it represents. It is therefore full and explicit in its testimony of people and/or place and requires no augmentation from the collector. The same may be said of other postcards or printed matter, such as a postcard of Sydney harbour, featuring the Harbour Bridge and Opera House. An image of Uluṟu also attracts the same value, as does a Dombrovskian postcard of *Cradle Mountain* (Plate 6.3). These Representative souvenirs are all high in the volume of their narrative content, which is made complete by the producer. These types of souvenir leave the viewer in no doubt as to what the souvenir represents and do not insist on the collector to contribute to their narrative.[5] They are consequently low in their invitational capacity.

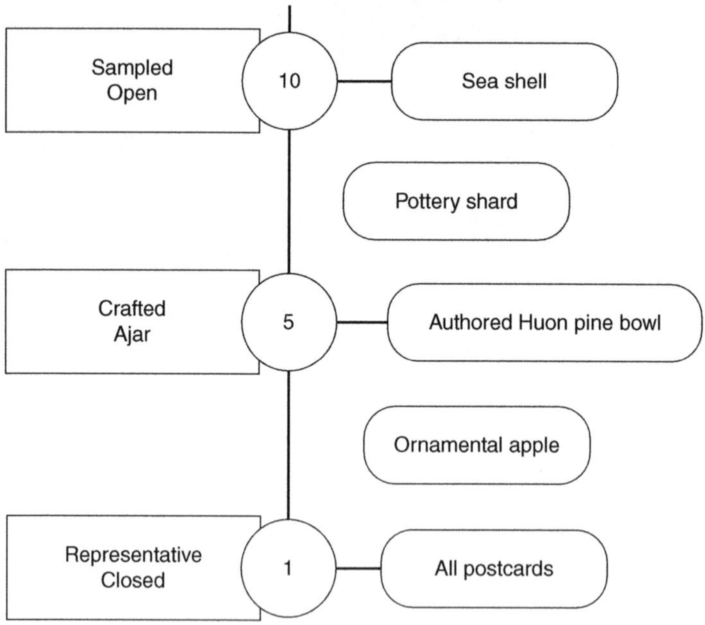

Figure 6.4 Invitational axis showing ideal and atypical souvenirs.

If we contrast the built-in fullness of the postcard to the exampled sea shell it can be seen that the nature of the sea shell's narrative is far from obvious and relies upon the collector's explanation. That is, the artefact does not indicate its site of collection in itself; rather, it is in Stewart's terms (1984: 136) 'impoverished'. In this respect, the fullness of the narrative occurs post-collection, through the expansive development of the fetishistic narrative that is at the core of the tourist's attraction to the fragment.

These Sampled objects are generally, but not always, made of a material that is endemic to the site. Ceramic fragments are an anomalous example of this, in that the material may come from afar and is also crafted. However, the manner in which these souvenirs are collected, that is as found objects, sees these fragments plotted more toward the Sampled than the Crafted category. This degree of narrative completeness can be best tracked through the above diagram in which I have isolated the *Invitational* axis, along which the invitational capacity of individual souvenirs of various types has been plotted.

Iconofetish

Where does the inherent narrative of the object/artefact reside?

The last of these narrative components explores the *Iconofetish* nature of the souvenir and is a further refinement of the souvenir's intrinsic narrative quality. This narrative feature has been examined closely in Chapter 4, dealing with the fetish, in which I addressed and reassessed the notion that the conventional narrative of the fetish is closed and circular. The argument has been made in Chapter 4 that the qualities of the fetish embodied in the souvenir do not make its narrative potential closed and circular; rather the souvenir's narrative potential is of an expansive nature. The *Iconofetish* axis seeks to plot the development of this quality in each class of souvenir.

This attribute gauges the degree of 'largesse' (my term) to be found in the souvenir; that is the iconographic reception of the artefact. This refers more clearly to the complex content of the narrative, while the *Relational* axis is concerned with the narrative in its simple reference to place, people and place, and people and/or place. This attribute is concerned with the sacred quality and value of the souvenir's features; as authorised, or not, through the collective gaze of the tourist and host community. It is concerned with the socio-historical nature of the narrative rather than the bald forms to which the souvenir refers. As Panofsky (1972: 3) writes, '[i]conography is that branch of the history of art which concerns itself with the subject matter or meaning of works of art, as opposed to their form'. In terms of tourism, form is largely discounted in favour of meaning, that is the meaning that the tourist can attach to the object/artefact, which is the subject of iconography.

This iconic status is most prevalent in the Representative category of souvenirs, especially the photographic type. For instance, postcards almost always feature subject matter read as iconic and in turn produce an iconic image, such as the aforementioned Sydney Harbour Bridge, Uluru or Cradle Mountain. This is due to their extremely high heritage value and untouchable status. The intrinsic meaning bound up in heritage is discovered by 'ascertain[ing] those underlying principles which reveal the basic attitude of a nation, a period, a class, a religious or philosophical persuasion … condensed into one work' (ibid.: 7) and to sample those sites in the terms described by Stewart (1984: 136) would be a sacrilegious act, although it does happen. Certain styles of Representative souvenir also tend to carry an iconographic quality that is less tangible. The Dombrovskian style of landscape photography is one example; so, too, is Central Desert dot painting in which the style of the image, rather than the image itself, is understood as typical and distinctive of the site (see Plate 5.2).[6] It may be argued that all tourist destinations contain at least one iconic feature, though it may often be intangible (such as the sunshine associated with the state of Queensland).

Following the theory of the fetish proposed in Chapter 4, in which the fetish is structured in a way that permits its leakage from the deeply personal and furtive sphere of collecting and display into the domestic and then public space, the *Iconofetish* axis plots and gauges the quality of this allure in the souvenir. It seeks to discover the fetishistic and iconic appeal inherent, to some degree, in the activity of all souvenir objects and artefacts and assesses it through its mode and site of display.[7]

There is quite clearly nothing iconic about a sea shell gathered from the beach, unless it is a specific type for which the site is recognised. In a case such as this, the specific sea shell is likely to be found in the Crafted and Representative category of souvenir as well. Coral from the Great Barrier Reef is a good example of a popular sampled souvenir, furtively gathered by tourists, which is also collected as a raw material for crafting jewellery.[8] The red sand of the Central Australian Desert may also be viewed in this way, and I will examine this particular sampled icon later in this chapter.

Moreover the iconic, in relation to the souvenir's narrative content, refers to the level of the public's broad reception of the artefact, demonstrated through its mode of display. This can be gauged by the 'largesse' that is afforded the site of representation; that is, the site's notoriety or fame within the public perception, which has much to do with the communal value afforded the site or object that the souvenir represents. I have demonstrated this diagrammatically in Chapter 4 and, in Figures 4.1 and 4.2, have plotted the development of the narrative from the fetish, showing how the once-fetishistic narrative may evolve from the personal to the domestic and finally to the public sphere where a communal value is accorded the object. This may be ascertained through the environment in which the artefact or object is curated and reflects the popularity of the site or object. This, in turn, has the effect of distancing the tourist from the iconic feature, which prohibits the collection of Sampled and Crafted artefacts and promotes the production of Representative souvenirs. Souvenirs of iconic sites, events and objects may be discovered in each class of souvenir, but the Representative category is the most preferred. By isolating this axis (Figure 6.5), it can be seen how the *Iconofetish* features of our ideal souvenirs may be mapped.

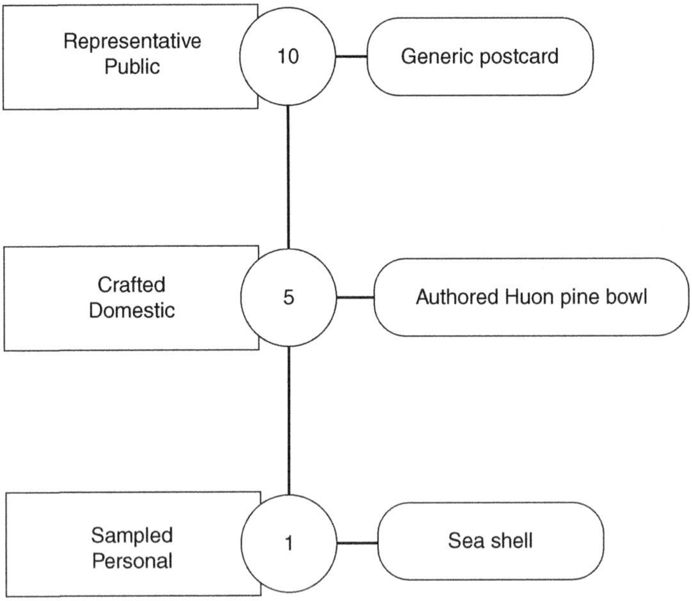

Figure 6.5 Iconofetish axis showing ideal souvenirs.

The expressive patterns of souvenirs

In this section I want to draw together these five axis points in order to graphically express the language of example objects as souvenirs by the area covered and pattern described. In the following graphic summaries of the visual language of individual souvenirs, I have categorised souvenir objects and artefacts into the three discreet groups.

Where I have shown two or more souvenirs in the one graph and the expressive patterns do not obscure one another I have shaded the areas delineated by the visual language of the souvenirs. However, when the expressive patterns are similar and one pattern obscures the other I have dispensed with the shading and shown these patterns in linear form.

These graphs are not meant to prove that one souvenir language is superior to another. They are provided only to show the pattern of the individual souvenir's expressive language and its relationship to that of other souvenirs.

Beginning with the ideal examples, it is possible to see in Figure 6.6 how the strength of the typical Sampled souvenir rests along the *Medium* and *Invitational* axes. The Crafted souvenir is typified by an equal spread along each axis (Figure 6.7), while the area covered by the Representative example (Figure 6.8) is dominated by the *Relational* and *Iconofetish* attributes. It is these patterns that I now want to explore and in doing so, clearly distinguish the tone of expression that is particular to each group.

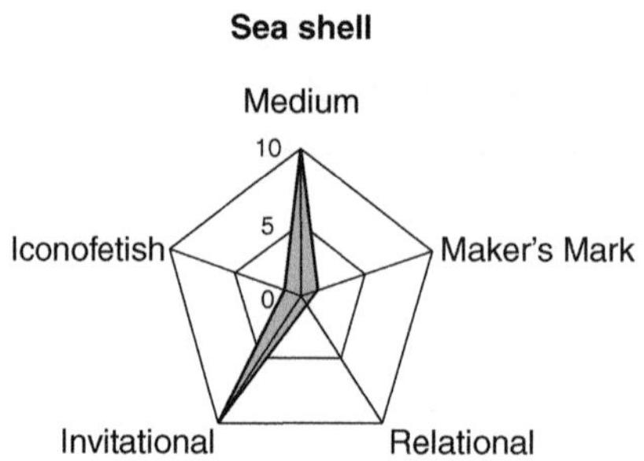

Figure 6.6 The pattern of the ideal Sampled souvenir expression.

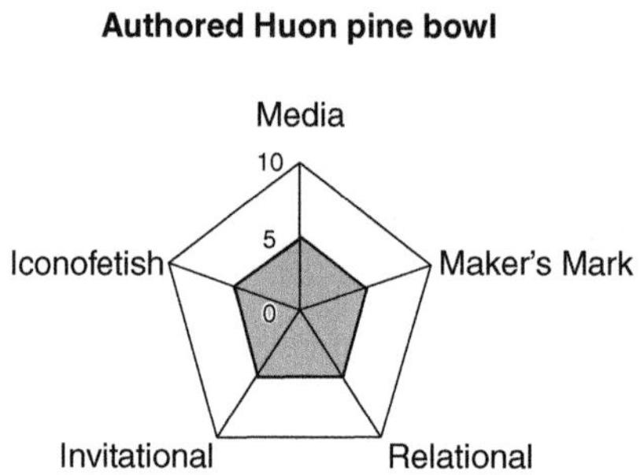

Figure 6.7 The pattern of the ideal Crafted souvenir expression.

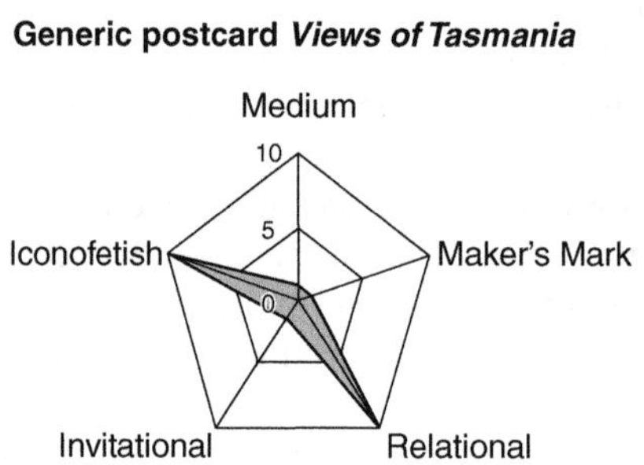

Figure 6.8 The pattern of the ideal Representative souvenir expression.

In the preceding detail of the common attributes of the souvenir I have presented ideal examples of each category. I have also pointed toward certain souvenirs that refuse to be contained within each discrete group. Having outlined the three ideal types of souvenir I will now examine particular atypical souvenirs in relation to this typology to determine its usefulness as a tool of analysis and design. I will compare these irregular examples with the ideal examples using the structural criteria established above and graphically plot their active souvenir properties. This structural analysis will then be applied to souvenirs gathered during the course of this research.

Sampled souvenirs

The Sampled souvenir is the most stable of the three categories and, as stated, is, by and large, consistent with that outlined previously by Stewart, and with what Pearce terms 'Naturalia'.[9] However, as with most attempts to categorise objects, there are always some found objects that evade categorisation. For example, while Sampled souvenirs are best summarised as flora and fauna and mineral samples, collected directly from their natural environment, the premise for their containment in this category rests primarily with the fact that they are endemic, collected directly by the tourist and are unmediated by the resident culture of that environment through craft. Such a tight definition would, however, exclude artefacts made by people from the Sampled range and this would be erroneous. It is, therefore, necessary to include fragments of human endeavour, such as the aforementioned shards of china, glass and other such humanly produced litter that has since been harboured and worked on by the environment, just as one might also include ancient stone artefacts and shells illicitly collected from an Aboriginal midden. The defining factor, in respect to this type of Sampled souvenir, is that these irregular souvenirs of human mediation are not in their original form, but most often are fragments that bring to mind the objects' original form and intended utility and/or associated lifestyle. This type of souvenir is also consistent with others from this category, in that it is not acquired through commercial exchange. As I have shown, it is upon this basis that Stewart (1984: 138–139) seems to arrive at her initial classifications. These souvenirs may be situated within the schematic as follows:

What needs to be understood here is that, under this system of classification, an object or artefact, particularly a fragment produced for any purpose other than as a souvenir, rests above the Crafted point. Furthermore, if its collection was achieved outside the capitalist economic exchange system it is plotted closer to the Sampled category.

In this respect it is beneficial to engage a more complex scheme and to invoke Levi-Strauss's triangular configuration of raw-smoked-boiled.[10] Utilising the stable sea shell, the two irregular examples cited in Figure 6.9 and introducing a third, in the form of a midden shell, their classification may be expressed as follows.

Taking the sea shell as the purest form of the Sampled souvenir, it would equate to Levi-Strauss's raw state, the midden shell to smoked, and the pottery shard to cooked. This is based on the level of human intent with regard to the object's natural or mediated state. For instance the sea shell, collected from a beach, being naturally formed, worked by tidal action and carrying no human history, remains in a raw state. The midden shell, however, bears a human history that is formed of unintended or incidental consequences. That is, there is no intentional craft bound in the artefact, but rather incidental human deposition in the creation of a souvenired site, while the pottery shard and stone artefact do

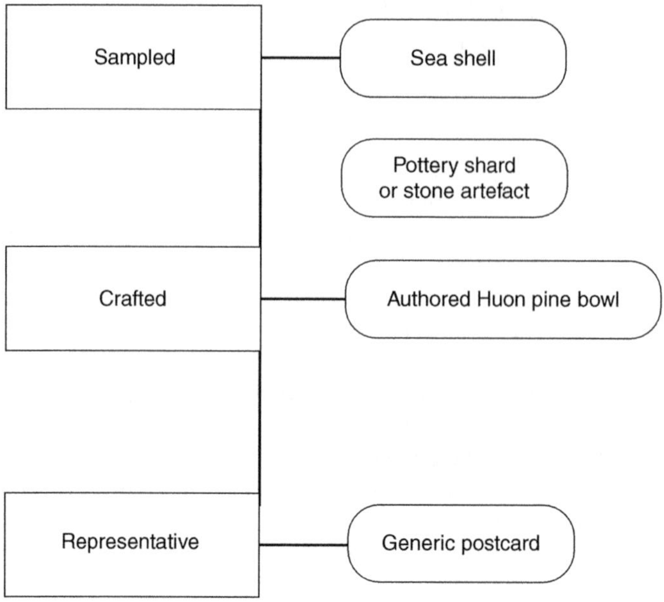

Figure 6.9 Three category axis showing variation of atypical Sampled souvenirs.

carry a history of craft and so relate to Levi-Strauss's 'boiled' or cooked category. The individual characteristics of these souvenirs are detailed in the following assessment and graphically summarised in Figure 6.10.

Midden shell

Medium: (10)
The midden shell rates ten along this axis as this feature is integral to the object's function as a souvenir.

Maker's mark: (2)
Along this axis it rates a two as this is incidental and not crafted as an individual object.

Relational: (3)
Along this axis its rates a three as the artefact refers to an exotic people and place in a very distant historical sense rather than current.

Invitational: (8)
The inherent narrative is faint and further distanced from the collector by being one of exotic 'Otherness'. However, this is reliant upon the collector, so is largely open to the inscription of the collector's own narrative. Therefore it attracts a rating of eight along this axis.

Iconofetish: (1)
Lastly, the artefact is not iconic of the site and is likely to be displayed in a personal setting, so is rated at one along this axis.

Stone artefact or pottery shard

Medium: (10)
This is integral to the object's function as a souvenir.

Maker's mark: (3)
This is crafted, but very broadly collective and historically distant.

Relational: (4)
The artefact refers to people and place, but is historical rather than current.

Invitational: (7)
The artefact invites the collector's narrative, which is only. faintly coloured by the mediated state of the artefact.

Iconofetish: (1)
The artefact is not iconographic of the site and is likely to be displayed in a personal setting.

In the above assessments I have reflected the varying nature of the artefacts' attributes by assessing the relevant attributes midway between the Sampled and Crafted categories.

I have illustrated this placement in Figure 6.10 showing the degree of the attribute's presence, where the area covered by each souvenir may be contrasted to show their expressions as souvenirs.

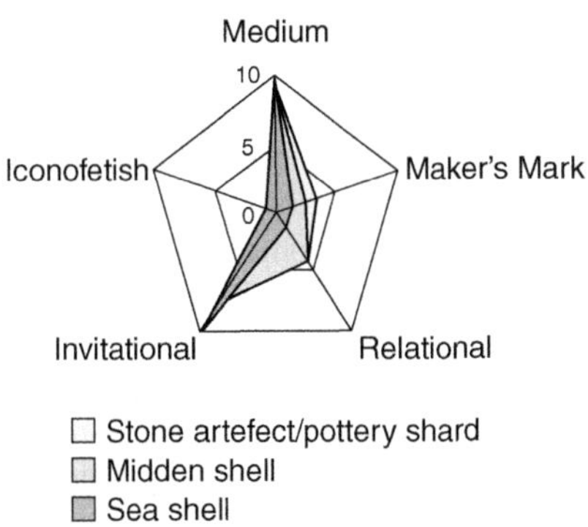

Figure 6.10 Graphic summary of the variation found in the expression of three types of Sampled souvenir.

It can be seen here how the graphic expression of the stone artefact and pottery shard is almost identical to that of the midden shell and how the marginal human engagement with those artefacts impinges on their invitationality. It is also apparent that, in relating to people and place, these artefacts, framed as souvenirs, operate across a slightly different surface to the sea shell with its solitary reference to place. But above all it is evident how the medium of each example is the binding feature that situates the tone of each souvenir's expression in the Sampled category.

This form of collecting – sampling – is, as I have stated, driven by scientific inquiry. It is typified by the collection of pressed flowers, butterflies, fossils or gemstones, in which the scientific imperative is applied; that is, a desire to gather and order and, in so doing, come to know the site of collection. As souvenirs, these objects appeal to children and young adults because they cost nothing.[11] They were also common among what might be termed early eco-tourists who, embarking on, say, a protracted bushwalk, would gather numerous flora samples like an amateur naturalist, just as a child might gather a collection of shells from the beach.

In common with all souveniring, the practice of sampling is based upon a discourse of difference. Sampled souvenirs are gathered by a method that is more closely related to a foraging mode of existence, which further distinguishes the Sampled souvenir from the other categories. This form of souveniring emphasises the historical grounding of souvenir collecting, based on the colonial collection of samples from exotic places and 'Other' cultures. It also raises the spectre of the colonial sampling of other races. More germane to the mission of this project is the contemporary tourist's engagement with foraging as a method of souveniring. The sampling of the visited site, through the collection of sea shells and pebbles, situates the tourist outside of his or her normal mode of production as no other form of souveniring does. As tourism is characterised by unbridled consumption and little to no production, so this form of souveniring offers to the tourist the consumption of objects at no expense. It is a situation that takes no account of class or status and, as such, is most faithful to the levelling character of tourism itself.[12]

Due to its unregulated nature, this method of souveniring has an erosive effect on the environment, in that there is an impact on finite sites. As a result of this, the management authorities of many such sites have had to take remedial action to protect the integrity of the site. This, in itself, has placed a distance between the site and the tourist that has been overcome in part by the camera, with its unique ability to bring things closer and preserve the moment. This relationship between the Sampled souvenir and the photograph is foreshadowed by Stewart (1984: 138), who draws our attention to the fact that both the pressed flower collection and the photographic image preserve the subject for later interrogation, which suggests that some souvenirs need to be located directly between the Sampled and the Representative categories – something that I will explore further when I detail examples of Representative souvenirs. But before that I now want examine the new Crafted category.

Crafted souvenirs

Crafted souvenirs are, perhaps, the most familiar of the three categories and it is surprising that their unique attributes have not been recognised prior to this project. The distinguishing character of these souvenirs is demonstrated by the relationship that is developed between the tourist and the culture of the visited site. These artefacts are produced by artists and craftspeople who have, in turn, consumed the site's history and environment and subsequently represented it to the tourist. In their finest examples, the craftspeople have produced artefacts that are unique to the maker's environment. They often take the form of utilitarian goods or moribund tools of past and/or endangered lifestyles that refer to the visited culture's historical significance and heritage.

There are few other materials that lend themselves so well to the fabrication of Crafted souvenirs than wood. In previous chapters I have illustrated, through a number of examples, how wooden artefacts of non-Western cultures lend themselves to a commodification process that sees them become souvenirs. I have also shown that, through the agency of anthropologists, missionaries and other colonial travellers, those artefacts are, in most instances, the first items of material culture to be appropriated into the genuine souvenir trade.[13]

In order to cement in place this new Crafted category of souvenir, I will now explore and demonstrate how this same raw material is also utilised for the same purpose by Western or settler crafts people. I will then identify the common activity of the Western and non-Western, or settler and indigenous souvenir. To do this it is necessary to first outline exactly what it is about wood that makes it such a viable material for the production of Crafted souvenirs.

The initial appeal of wood is to be found on its surface. At its lustrous best, finished and oiled, wood assaults the eye with a flourish of poetry bound in the swirl of its grain. The rhythmic punctuation of knots, emotive star bursts and figurative suggestion, take the eye on a kaleidoscopic journey of shifting form and unspoken tales. Within the grain one can find an elaborate topographical sketch; the folding and compressed pattern of the earth's crust; mountain ranges, ravines and fault lines. Coastal contours and human and animal figures are also common features, detected by the eye in the abstract flourish of the grain. In short, the setting and figures of anecdotal tales and great epics lurk within the grain for the imagination to bring to life. View the grain on the horizontal and an imaginary landscape is available, flip it to the vertical and the human form may appear. There are few people that have not seen mischievous or familiar faces in the surface of a polished wood panel, just as many recognise similar images in passing clouds. It is the judgement and skill of the craftsperson that evokes these forms for the pleasurable consumption of the tourist.

Beneath that which is conjured up by the imagination there is a real and verifiable history embedded within the grain. Wood speaks its age and place of origin, of the climates endured through its lifetime, marking drought and flood in its growth. It may even talk of the subterranean conditions into which, as a tree, it stabbed its roots; conditions that, like a bend set by constant wind, are reflected in the turn of the grain and evolved growth habit. I have shown in Chapter 3 how the growth habit of the Mulga tree lends itself to boomerang making. These characteristics are not always formed solely by climatic and geological conditions but are often enhanced by the symbiotic interaction of other flora and fauna. The highly valued Black Heart Sassafras from Tasmania is one such example, where the natural hue of the timber is enhanced by the dark stain of specific micro-bacteria, while didgeridoo production is promoted through the action of termites. It is characteristics such as these which refer to the place and conditions of growth that, in turn, establishes certain timbers as unique to the visited site and enhances their value, particularly as a marker of place.

Grain pattern and surface are, without doubt, the primary allure of timber objects, but what lies beneath, or beyond, the surface is equally important. For unlike many other materials that have been utilised in the production of souvenirs, the form of wood is constant. If we take clay as a comparison, it is evident that without the intervention of the human hand and imagination clay is simply mud. It is human intervention that gives it form. Indeed, the biblical narrative cites clay as the raw material from which the human form was created by the hand of God. Long before the invention of the Christian creation myth, the imagination engaged with the form of trees. Many archetypes of Mother Nature and other early earth deities, such as the Green Man, are extrapolated from the form of a living tree, while their power is plotted on the tree's growth structure and habit.[14]

It may be argued that the authors of the creation story opted for clay as a metaphor because it had no specific form. The choice of wood, as the metaphoric substance, was unlikely because it already existed in arboreal form, complete with the characteristics of grain, spring, hardness, growth habits and a pre-Christian history in which human form featured large. Clay, on the other hand, requires human investigation to discover and promote many of its qualities.

Both clay and wood vary according to environmental conditions. The hue of clay alters according to the parent rock upon which it lies, while the sediments of ancient life forms imbue the clay with its initial character. But these qualities are, as I have said, largely dormant until the craftsperson begins to play and explore.

Wood, too, is formed out of different environmental conditions, the obvious manifestation being the deciduous forests of the Northern Hemisphere temperate ranges, contrasted to the narrow leaved, coniferous forest of the Northern Polar Regions. Tropical areas offer other arboreal qualities and the continent of Australia has developed its own species with unique characteristics. On a micro-scale, the species of tree also vary and produce timbers that are particular to small, unique geographic regions. I have already lauded the unique qualities of Huon pine, for example, and will return to it shortly.

It is these differences that attracted the eye of early explorers and, latterly, have come under the gaze of the tourist as markers of place. Joseph Banks recorded and sampled the flora and fauna of Australia long before any investigation was undertaken into the geological structure of the Australian continent. In short, the flora and fauna of a site serve as the starting point for the recording of difference. Such is the immediacy of that which proliferates on the surface of the land that difference is more readily identifiable and is used to measure the visited site against that which is known. This is the function of the Sampled souvenir object that is sustained and enhanced by the Crafted souvenir artefact. For, like Banks and other colonial explorers, the tourist's understanding of the new and exotic begins with that which readily denotes difference. He or she will seek not simply an artefact of the visited site, but one that offers a depth of reference, that begins with the material of which the souvenir is constituted and is enhanced by the knowledge, artistry and craft traditions of the resident culture. The minor species timber crafts of Tasmania offer just such a depth of difference, in that objects carved of Huon pine, Sassafras, Myrtle and Blackwood are specific to Tasmania, no matter what they are made into under the hand of the craftsperson.

Blackwood was the first of these timbers to be adopted into the manufacture of souvenirs relating to Tasmania. The R. Shott & Son Collection from the Queen Victoria Museum in Launceston is a case in point.[15] Dating from the early 1900s this collection is comprised mostly of crafted Blackwood artefacts, including kangaroo effigies, and other mantlepiece trinkets (Plate 6.12). This collection shows how the proprietor of a family umbrella-making enterprise recognised the aesthetic qualities of Blackwood and diversified the business into what Hamilton (1984: 8) records as the earliest production of minor species timber souvenirs in Tasmania.[16] In the Shott collection it is possible to see how animal plates and the boomerang motif of Aboriginal Australia provided the inspiration for these early souvenirs. In this way Tasmania is marked as different through its specific tree species, while the use of the boomerang motif integrates it as part of greater Australia, an activity consistent with Graburn's notion of integration and differentiation as the key functions of the souvenir.[17] These early souvenirs provided the groundwork for others to follow. Today the crafts of carving and woodturning, producing eminently portable and durable timber souvenirs, are common to most small towns and hamlets along the many Tasmanian tourist tracks and art and craft galleries that exist throughout the state.

Carved animal figures

The range of goods produced by these decentralised artisans is as varied as the skill and imagination that is applied to a raw chunk of wood. Animal figures are a popular choice; some are carved by hand, others are turned on the lathe, some are miniature or suitcase size, others are crate size. In many cases they demonstrate the craftsperson's desire to produce art with little concern regarding the commercial consumption of the work. An example of this is Chris Selby's *Frill Neck Lizard* sculpture (Plate 6.4). The subject of this sculptural piece is an oversized frill neck lizard, carved from a single chunk of Huon pine, inlaid with ivory. In this timber statue we have present the exotic fauna of arid Central Australia teamed with the exotic flora of the Tasmanian temperate rainforest. Like the boomerang-embellished models from the Shott collection this sculpture differentiates and integrates Tasmania as a unique part of Australia, yet on a much larger scale.

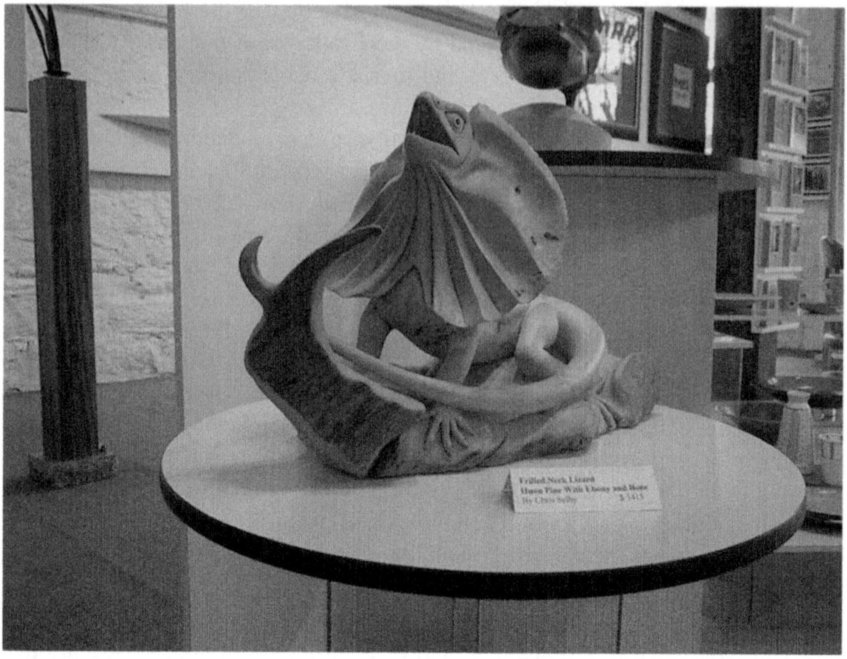

Plate 6.4 Chris Selby, *Frill Neck Lizard*, 2001, Huon pine and ivory, variable dimensions. Collection of the artist.

Tourism is so well developed today that artworks with high price tags, such as Selby's *Frill Neck Lizard* sculpture, are often consumed by well-heeled tourists as extravagant souvenirs. Like Tjapaltjarri's dot painting (Plate 5.2), cited in Chapter 5, these less portable and more expensive works of art cannot today be discounted from the souvenir market. However, the bulk of souvenir artefacts, hewn from Tasmanian minor species timbers, are turned on the wood lathe and made to specifications that fit the demands of the average tourist and his or her more modest budget and baggage allowance.

As with the early period of Aboriginal tourist art and souvenir production, price is largely dictated by the size and quality of work, with size being the overriding factor.[18] In the Crafted souvenirs on offer from settler craftspeople these extremes are demonstrated by the range of small lathe-turned vessels and animal figurines, such as the bookmark *Tasmanian Marsupial Mouse* (Plate 6.5), which offers a similar souvenir expression to the larger *Frill Neck Lizard* sculpture, but is much more portable and reasonably priced.

This variation in the price and size of crafted artefacts may be examined further through a parallel study of the range of contemporary Aboriginal souvenirs known collectively as pu<u>n</u>u, the carved and pokerworked animal figures from Aboriginal artists and craftpeople of Central Australia (Plate 6.6).

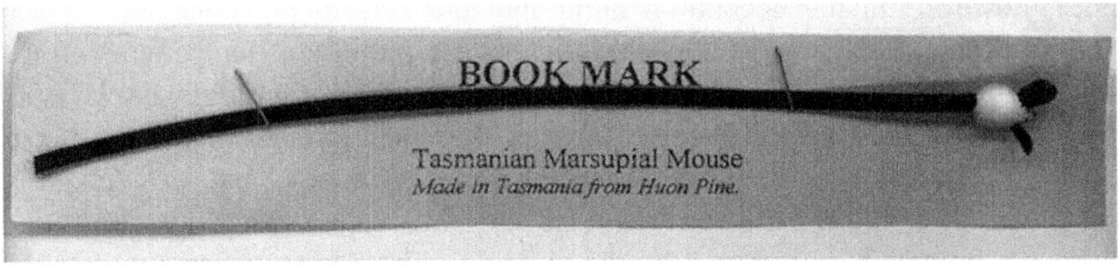

Plate 6.5 Bookmark *Tasmanian Marsupial Mouse*, 2001, Huon pine and leather, 18 × 1 cm. Private collection.

Among the decorative souvenir crafts of Aboriginal people, one of the most accessible and successful is pu<u>n</u>u. These sculpted animal figurines are hewn from the soft root of the River Red Gum or Malley and range in size and quality (see Plate 3.5).[19] At their largest they stand as massive life-sized Perentie lizards, immaculately carved and detailed. Many of the finest examples are collected by state and national galleries and are exhibited internationally at contemporary galleries in Europe and America (Isaacs 1992: 46–53).[20]

As a traditional craft, pu<u>n</u>u is of post-contact origin. This is most obvious in the pokerworked detail burnished onto the surface by strands of hot fencing wire. As we have seen in Chapters 3 and 5, this method of decoration is also used to great effect in the embellishment of traditional objects like boomerangs, nula-nulas, and coolamons (wooden bowls made from the same wooden material

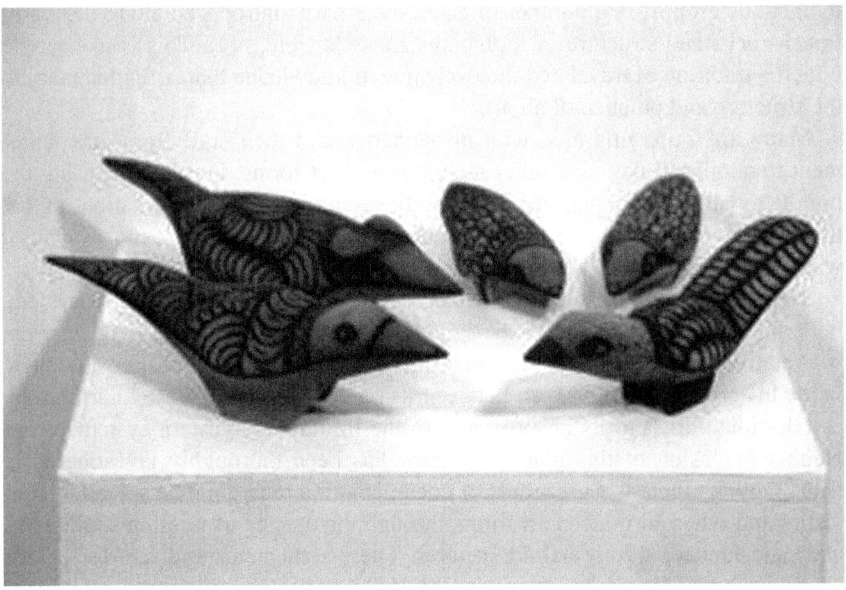

Plate 6.6 Maruku artists, Pu<u>n</u>u bird figurines, 2010, wood with pokerwork detail, various dimensions.

as puṉu and used for various activities in traditional daily life). There is a difference, however, in the decoration burnt into the surface of coolamons, which feature designs based on traditional stories, as the purpose of the patterns on the puṉu figurines is to describe the individual animal and is not so tightly drawn from traditional design. Isaacs (1992: 114), writes that puṉu 'are not mere tourist souvenirs, manufactured purely for their commercial usefulness' but are 'delightful renditions of animals, particularly reptiles and birds whose every movement and habit are intimately understood by the maker.... The designs often simulate the natural markings of the animal'. The hybrid development of this art form, applied to traditional objects and puṉu figurines, has, in part, restricted its appreciation within fine art circles, as that market for many years insisted on notions of purity in Aboriginal art. According to Isaacs (ibid.: 44), 'Desert people have been making their traditional weapons and utensils for thousands of years, but the technique of carving animals and incising them with burnt wire decoration is much more recent' and suggests that it was a familiarity with 'the effect of red hot wire as a decorative technique through branding cattle' (while working as stockmen) that introduced the art of pokerwork to Aboriginal people. Other art forms to suffer from this craft categorisation were Batik-making and Hermannsburg watercolours. This is unfortunate and resulted in limited study of these art forms, many of which preceded the flurry of interest in Aboriginal art during the 1970s.

The introduction and development of puṉu and other introduced arts across Aboriginal communities occurred initially through the agency of mission settlements and subsequently through the travel of the Aboriginal artists and craftspeople. So that, while a Western structured introduction took place among some indigenous groups, in a number of cases the art was introduced along the traditional tracks and structure of a nomadic lifestyle (ibid.: 44). This is in keeping with the tradition of travel and the exchange of knowledge that is fundamental to the structure and practice of all art.

Many art forms migrated with missionaries and their staff from one settlement to another. Like most other mediums and art forms, introduced during the middle to late colonial period, puṉu may be seen as an art of assimilation, in that the motive of the missionaries was to introduce Aboriginal people to a system of waged labour.[21]

This motive, of commodification and enculturation into the capitalist system, underpins the introduction of Aboriginal art to the Western gaze. Beneath what is a relatively recent history, there rests an interesting blank space, like a hyphen, in the history of Aboriginal art; between its perception in the Western art market as traditional art, and its absorption into the traditional Western system of art. Neither extension of this glaring paradox has been thoroughly investigated to date, although there is a great deal of documentation regarding the spread of souvenirs and other introduced art forms through the agency of mission settlements and state-funded, Aboriginal arts centres. These settlements and centres include Hermannsberg, Ernabella, Maruku and other well-known centres in Central Australia. Maruku, near Uluṟu has developed into one of the largest and most successful outlets for Aboriginal art and craft.

Similarly, the exploration and utilisation of specific Australian timbers by settler artists and craftspeople may be viewed as a form of material assimilation. In the recognition of the special qualities of endemic timbers, such as Huon pine, the souvenir maker has become more integrated with the natural environment in which he or she lives. Just as many indigenous Australians were assimilated through the economic changes brought about by colonialism through art and craft, so it can be seen how, in the case of the bookmark *Tasmanian Marsupial Mouse* (Plate 6.5), the producer underwrites the reference to Tasmania (that is implicit in the raw material) by labelling his product after a member of the unique Australian fauna. This demonstrates the maker's knowledge of Australian fauna and provides the tourist with a small sample piece of Tasmania, while introducing them to a rare and unique creature. The fact that this identity is not contained in the abstracted object itself is a failing in this particular souvenir that is overcome, to some degree, by the label. This shortcoming is allayed in the case of the *Frill Neck Lizard* (Plate 6.4) by the quality of the work that is realistic in form, but exaggerated in scale, and is a more well-known, familiar and visible creature to tourists.

While both the bookmark mouse and the pu<u>n</u>u figurines operate in the same arena, referring to the exotic flora and fauna of their respective sites, there are a number of differences that set them apart. These exist primarily in the processes of production. The pu<u>n</u>u figurines are hand carved and their form is enhanced with the pokerwork detail, while the bookmark mice are produced repetitively on the wood lathe. The result of this is mice of uniform shape with a unique surface inherent to the material that is largely lost in the scale of the work. On the other hand, the pu<u>n</u>u figurines are of singular but regular form, with an approximated uniformity applied to the surface through the pokerwork detail. The Huon pine, from which the bookmark mice are made, is accorded greater value than the lathed form of that souvenir. It is this Sampled attribute of the artefact that underwrites its function as a souvenir. For the pu<u>n</u>u figurines, on the other hand, it is the Aboriginal craft and form displayed in the artefacts that endorses their operation as souvenirs. The souvenir attributes of these artefacts, large and small are assessed and summarised as follows:

Chris Selby, Frill Neck Lizard, *2001, Huon pine and ivory, variable dimensions (Plate 6.4)*

Medium: (10)
Framed as a souvenir, this sculpture attracts a ten rating on this axis due to its latent presence as a large sample of Huon pine, which precedes its form. For the collector is not only buying a majestic carving of an iconic Australian animal but also, primarily, a significant piece of Tasmania.

Maker's mark: (7)
I have rated the expression of this artefact along this axis at seven, on the grounds that the artist's name is present and contributes to the work's marketing. However it is not dominant and does not compete with, or eclipse the appreciation of the work in its own right.

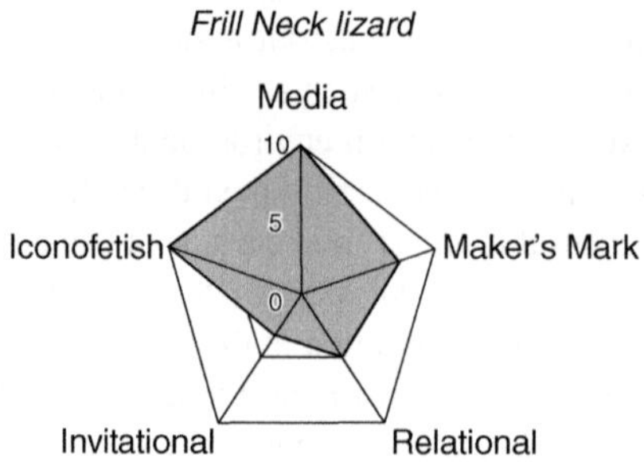

Figure 6.11 Graphic summary of the souvenir expression of Chris Selby's *Frill Neck Lizard*, 2001, Huon pine and ivory, variable dimensions.

Relational: (4)
This axis gauges the flexibility of the souvenir's relational properties and refers to place, people and place, and people and/or place. This souvenir relates to two distinct Australian sites: the Southwest of Tasmania through its medium and the Central Desert through its subject. The fact that the object is mediated through carving speaks of the presence and craft of people and is commensurate with a five rating in line with the ideal Crafted souvenir. However, the reference to two discrete sites weights the souvenir closer to a reference of place.

Invitational: (3)
This souvenir attracts a three rating along this axis due to its directional qualities. It directs the narrative to Southwest Tasmania, through its medium, and to the Central Australian Desert, through its form. It frames the subsequent touristic narrative around those sites. As a decorative piece, it does not invite physical interaction, which further restricts the tourist's narrative and places the emphasis on the narrative invested by the maker. This confines the opportunity for the tourist to develop an experiential story around the work, as it may be recognised for what it is without much interpretation from the collector.

Iconofetish: (10)
This work attracts a maximum ten rating along this axis, due to its medium and subject matter. Huon pine is an icon of Tasmanian flora and the most sought after, minor species timber; the frill neck lizard is singularly associated with Central Australia. On both counts it emphatically proclaims Australia and is recognised as such by the tourist. It therefore exists in the public perception as a marker of Australia.

Topsy Tjulita, Lizard, *wood with pokerwork detail (Plate 3.5)*

Medium: (4)
The wood from which this work is carved is a generic timber from the Central Desert, probably Malley. The type of wood varies depending upon which part of

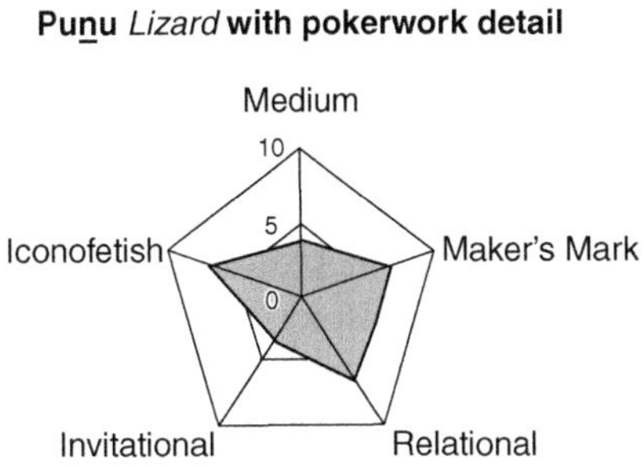

Figure 6.12 Graphic summary of the souvenir expression of Topsy Tjulita's *Lizard*, undated, wood with pokerwork detail.

the vast area the artist comes from. It has no reputation for specific properties other than being soft and easy to carve, so is reliant upon the artist's interpretation. It therefore attracts a four rating that reflects the endemic nature of the timber but also its lack of tight specificity.

Maker's mark: (7)
This rating is commensurate with that of the *Frill Neck Lizard* for the same reasons. That is, the artist's name is present but not dominant.

Relational: (6)
This souvenir attracts a rating of six on this axis, as it demonstrates a flexibility in its inherent reference. The subject matter and, moreover, the style of the work speak clearly of Aboriginal people in their place. That is, a part of Australia where the tourist expects to encounter Aboriginal people, in something approaching traditional conditions. This is not eclipsed by the over riding double reference to place alone that is found in the *Frill Neck Lizard* sculpture.

Invitational: (3)
This rating of three is largely commensurate with the above in that it prescribes a tourist narrative, in this instance to the Central Australian Desert and Aboriginal Australia. It is also decorative, so restricts the tourist's interaction to the imaginative.

Iconofetish: (7)
The subject matter of this souvenir is recognisable as a creature of exotic 'Otherness' as, too, is the decorative style. However, neither speaks of the site the souvenir represents with the volume of the frill neck lizard form or Central Desert dot painting style. Its reference is therefore less recognisable by the tourist and is rated accordingly.

Bookmark Tasmanian Marsupial Mouse*, 2001, Huon pine and leather, 18 × 1 cm (Plate 6.5)*

Medium: (8)
The medium of this souvenir is important, but is augmented by its form which refers to a rare form of the Australian fauna and further by its utility. This interpretation partially eclipses its operation as a sample and causes it to be located slightly closer to the Crafted category of souvenir. However the scale of this artefact limits this appreciation and suggests its main activity as a souvenir is moreover that of the sample and is rated accordingly at eight.

Maker's mark: (3)
The maker's mark is collective and is not included as part of the work but only in its packaging and is therefore disposable. It does not contribute to the marketing of the souvenir in the way the title does, so in all respects slides toward the Sampled category and is rated accordingly at three to reflect the collective mark of production.

Relational: (7)
The relational qualities of this souvenir are flexible. It refers to a specific place through its medium and people through its craft and utility. It is, on one level, a piece of Huon pine. It is also an abstracted figure of a marsupial mouse, which takes some explaining, and also a bookmark. Together these features refer to people and place, or people and/or place, and so this artefact attracts a rating of seven to reflect the flexibility of the potential narrative.

Invitational: (7)
The invitationality of this souvenir rests strongly with the collector. Its form is so abstracted that the tourist is invited to explain it. As a result of its scale, its medium is also difficult to distinguish and so requires a narrative. These qualities render the invitationality of the souvenir between open and ajar, but it is closed slightly by its utility as a bookmark.

Iconofetish: (5)
This rating of five is consistent with the stable Crafted souvenir, in that it is reliant upon the personal narrative of the collector to elaborate its meaning and

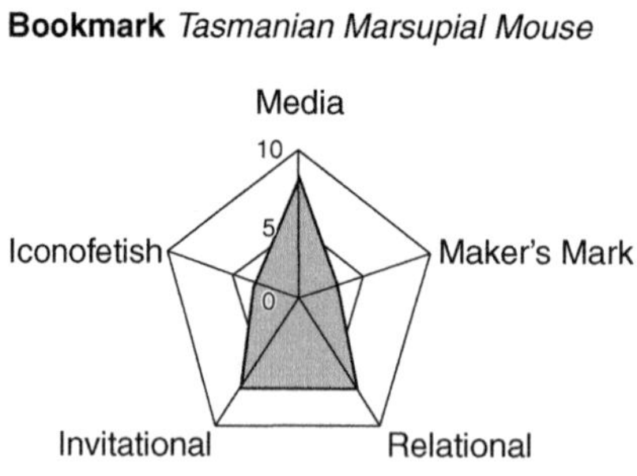

Figure 6.13 Graphic summary of souvenir expression of bookmark *Tasmanian Marsupial Mouse*.

iconofetishistic features. That is, the souvenir does not speak for itself, in the way the *Frill Neck Lizard* sculpture does, but requires the collector to complete the narrative that is invoked by the maker. This narrative partnership, therefore, rests between the personal and domestic domain.

Maruku artists, Pu<u>n</u>u bird figurines, wood with pokerwork detail, variable dimensions (Plate 6.6)

Medium: (3)
As with the larger pu<u>n</u>u figure the medium is specific only in that it is endemic to the vast site of origin, but it carries no particular qualities that distinguish it from other timbers of that area. This distinguishes them from the bookmark *Tasmanian Marsupial Mouse* and causes these artefacts to be located more toward the Representative group of souvenirs, and so attract a rating of three.

Maker's mark: (3)
It is collective in that it is of Aboriginal craft. It may therefore be considered a sample of the craft of the Aboriginal people of the vast Central Desert region. There is no name or company name attached to these artefacts.

Relational: (7)
This rating of seven is largely commensurate with the bookmark *Tasmanian Marsupial Mouse*, with the exception of utility, but this is replaced by the pokerwork detail of these figurines. Thus the subject refers to place alone while the pokerwork detail refers to the people of that place. These references may contribute to the narrative separately or together, but are likely to taken as one.

Invitational: (5)
The invitational qualities of these souvenirs rest largely in their Aboriginal origin and craft. The inherent narrative of these souvenirs ceases at that point and is continued by the collector. Unlike the larger pu<u>n</u>u figure, these smaller versions are more playful and invite use as a toy. The subsequent narrative is therefore framed by the maker, but not directed, and so may be understood as ajar and is rated at five.

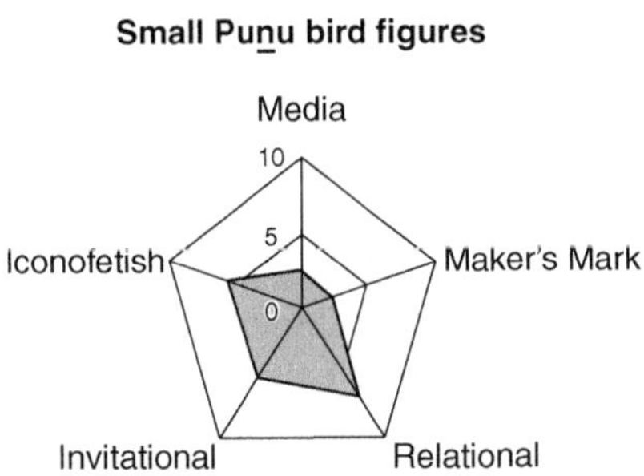

Figure 6.14 Graphic summary of souvenir expression of small pu<u>n</u>u bird figures.

Iconofetish: (6)
This rating is commensurate with the larger pu<u>n</u>u carving, but these smaller examples are more diverse in Australia and more visible in metropolitan souvenir outlets. They therefore follow a similar path to the ubiquitous boomerang and have some claim to be iconic of Aboriginal Australia. They are first sighted in the public commercial space, and so they attract some rating as an icon but, as this is largely related to the commercial site of display and has not transcended to other arenas (as the boomerang has) the rating is not so high (6). Unlike the larger pu<u>n</u>u sculpture, the value of this small artefact is not authorised by the respected institutions of museogallery system.

From the graphic analysis of these crafted animal figure souvenirs, the variation between each souvenir can be seen to change according to the individual attribute values listed above, although all operate in roughly the same field of expression.

The main variation in the graphs exists in the *Frill Neck Lizard* sculpture, which features a twofold iconic reference through its medium and subject matter. It can be seen how the importance of the medium also drags the bookmark mouse into this area, while the variable and less known medium of the pu<u>n</u>u figures see this angle blunted. This is redressed by the pokerwork detail that is considered a traditional Aboriginal art form, and so provides a meeting point through craft for these two objects. However, the maker's mark recedes in its presence from the two large works to the smaller souvenirs, which is a common, but not constant, distinction between the souvenir and the work of art. What each artefact has in common is its crafted nature. This is clearly defined in the Figures 6.12 to 6.15, in which each artefact registers a significant rating along all axes points and, in so doing, veers toward the median pattern delineated by the ideal Crafted souvenir.

Minor species carved wooden vessels

The timber souvenirs featured above are, in the main, ornamental and operate at economically diverse ends of the souvenir market. I now want to extend this study of crafted wooden souvenirs to an examination of more functional timber souvenirs, from the low to middle price range, and then to plot their variation from carved animal figure souvenirs.

The advantage of woodturning rests in the speed of production and the fact that, like the bookmark *Tasmanian Marsupial Mouse* (Plate 6.5), an almost immediate result is obtained from the smooth finish of the lathed artefact. But, as I have already suggested, the design values of these Crafted souvenirs stretches beyond the producer's need to manufacture a quantity of similar goods in order to make a dollar. It involves a sophisticated referencing system based on the artist/craftsperson's imaginative interpretation of tradition and heritage.

The multiple references to place, outlined in the examples of the bookmark *Tasmanian Marsupial Mouse* and pu<u>n</u>u figurines (Plate 6.6), are extended in the production of artefacts that foster an association with food.

The most common souvenir objects of this kind, produced by settler craftpeople in Tasmania, are constituted from Huon pine and other minor species

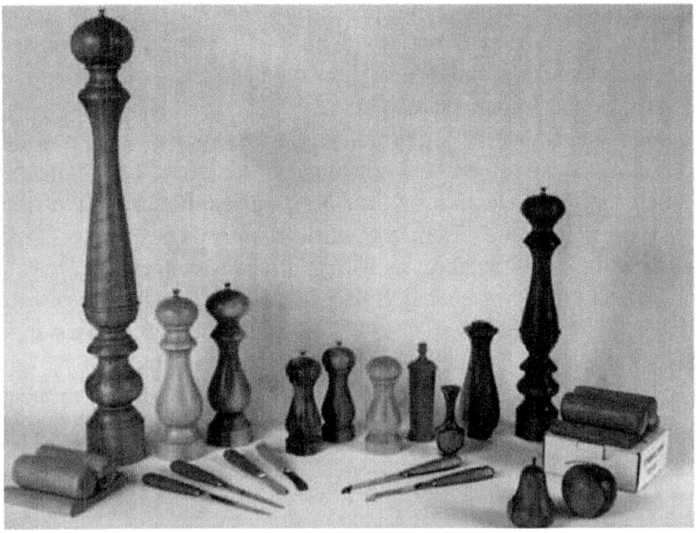

Plate 6.7 Assorted lathe turned artefacts, undated, various dimensions.

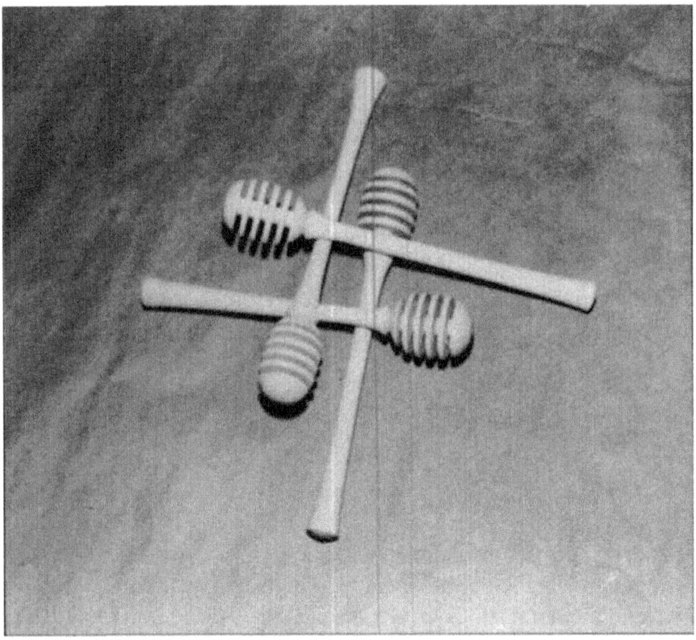

Plate 6.8 Mark Webb, *Honey Dippers*, undated, Huon pine, 12 × 3.5 cm.

timbers. They take the form of fruit bowls, at the middle to top end of the market, and honey dippers and other trinkets (Plates 6.7 and 6.8), catering to the more modest budget. This association with food, built into their form, capitalises on the perception of Tasmania as the clean, green state and assists in sustaining that image long after the tourist has returned home.

There is a complex mechanism of suggestion at play here that extends beyond the fact that both artefacts are given to production on the lathe. It needs to be remembered that the serial production of fruit bowls or similar vessels of the same dimensions and plane, even from the same minor species timber, will return a unique vessel in every instance, as far as surface is concerned. This is, as previously noted, due to the individual grain pattern found in the raw blocks of wood. In this the wood turner has an advantage that our earlier comparison – the potter – does not. But it is in the choice of end product that the craftsperson cements layers of meaning and reference to Tasmania.To that end, honey dippers (Plate 6.8) and other small minor species souvenirs (Plate 6.7) may be assessed within this typology as follows:

Artists unknown, assorted lathe turned artefacts, minor species timbers, variable dimensions (Plate 6.7)

Medium: (8)
As with most other souvenirs of this type, its medium is its dominating feature and, as such, it is perceived more as a sample of the exotic timber, through its medium and by extension a sample of the site of origin, than through its utilitarian form.

Maker's mark: (3)
This is absent, but we know it had a maker, as it is crafted. From this we may interpret a collective maker, which indicates the reduced importance of the maker's mark. So the rating here is reduced in favour of its operation as a sample of the exotic timber.

Relational: (5)
This souvenir refers to people and place through its utility and medium respectively. This attracts a rating that is commensurate with the ideal Crafted souvenir.

Invitational: (5)
This rating is also in line with the ideal Crafted souvenir, in that the narrative is set in place by the maker and completed by the tourist.

Iconofetish: (5)
Once again this artefact attracts a five rating in line with the ideal Crafted souvenir, in that the medium is an icon of the site, while the utility of the object sees its sphere of display in the domestic environment.

Fruit and other natural foods, such as honey, have long been associated with good health and well-being. The rejuvenation of both physical and psychological

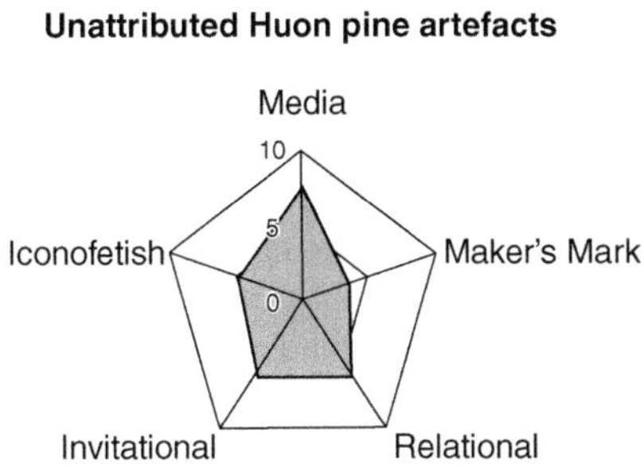

Figure 6.15 Souvenir expression of unattributed Huon pine artefacts.

health is fundamental to the development of the holiday and tourism (Shields 1991: 73; Urry 1990: 5–17), and to a large degree it is still the purpose of 'getting away'. Today tourist literature still engages with the idea of rest, relaxation and rejuvenation; a survey of most tourist literature will demonstrate this enduring theme. Tasmania is promoted along those lines through the power of its scenery, the allure of a relaxing life style and fine and natural foods. Historically, Tasmania was recognised as the 'Apple Isle', and still is, not withstanding the decline in the apple industry during the 1960s–70s. This continuing association demonstrates how heritage can fix people and place in time. Other examples of this museumification of cultures exist in the presentation of Tasmania's convict past and the misguided perception of Aboriginal people as primitive, hunter-gatherers. These generalisations are not always positive or welcome, but are an enduring and popular theme in the framing of people and places as tourist destinations. Those reservations aside, the association of health and well-being, attributed to food products from Tasmania, is suggested and framed by the vessel into which the fruit is placed, making the association indelible in the eye and mind of the tourist through this simple invitational narrative. The honey dipper, in particular, extends this play even further by reminding the tourist of the unique Leatherwood honey, produced from the endemic Leatherwood species that proliferates on the edge of the Tasmanian temperate rainforest. This refers to a flavour specific to Tasmania, with all its health giving associations, that is produced from a plant inhabiting an area that is, itself, a major tourist drawcard. This, in turn, is dispensed from a utensil made from the state's most famous minor species timber. The reference structure here is fourfold and includes medium, place, utility and heritage-based imagery.

In both the honey dippers (Plate 6.8) and the lathe-turned, minor species bowl (Plate 6.1) examples, the strength of reference exists through their interactivity. This interactive component draws the consumer into the narrative that is set in train by the maker. Unlike ornamental or photographic souvenirs that rely on the eye to engage and stimulate the imagination into remembering the visit, the fruit bowl and the honey dipper invite the consumer to enter the narrative through touch and use. This invitational character of the narrative may also be applied to Aboriginal souvenirs and explains the success of the returning type boomerang and the didgeridoo, in that they provide the tourist with an experience of the place and culture that extends beyond the visual. It is this corporeal engagement with the artefact that deepens the experience and authenticates the tourist's encounter. If the tourist can return home and not only show what he or she has gathered from their encounter with an exotic site and culture but can actually demonstrate the artefact's use, then the depth of his or her experience is likely to be perceived as deeper and more knowing. Such artefacts provide a deeper sense of understanding, fit and even ownership of the site – what Pearce has expressed as 'power and knowledge'.[22] This tactile mode of engagement and resultant power and knowledge may be extended further in the case of what has recently been framed as 'creative tourism' (Richards 2011), whereby tourists engage more fully with the visited culture, learning the crafts of the visited culture and, in effect, producing their own souvenirs.

It is regrettable that Aboriginal artefacts involved in food production, preparation and presentation are not viewed in the same way by tourists. I suspect that this has much to do with the fact that most tourists are from developed Western societies and need to integrate the experience, via the souvenir, within their own society. This may be achieved with the honey dipper and fruit bowl, as both suggest a use with familiar foodstuffs and thus integrate and differentiate the visited site as knowable yet unique. A digging stick is a little more difficult to integrate on its own terms, so it operates as a decorative souvenir instead.

Like the digging stick, the most successful Aboriginal souvenirs (such as the boomerang, spear thrower and coolamon) are the tools of hunter-gatherers. Their appeal to tourists attests, quite clearly, to MacCannell's (1992: 2) suggestion that tourists seek a primitive and primordial engagement with the visited site and/or culture, albeit an engagement that is controlled by the tourist through various means of retreat. This engagement is invented, deepened or sustained, in this instance, through the collection of hunter-gatherer artefacts. This is problematic for indigenous people the world over. It is of vast benefit in monetary terms and assists in the preservation of heritage and traditional ways, but, at the same time, the double-edged sword of integration and differentiation also museumifies the people, place and culture it represents by overlooking the diversity of the people and treating them as unindividuated groups. Moreover, this problem of integrating Aboriginal artefacts associated with food also rests in the absence of health and well-being associated with Aboriginal people.

There is some use of Aboriginal wooden vessels, collectively referred to by the European term 'coolamons', as fruit bowls. Many of these artefacts, however, like many boomerangs and spear throwers, are embellished with pokerwork and/or painted designs (see Plate 3.3). Due to this they are appreciated for their decorative rather than their utilitarian qualities. This sees such artefacts located more toward the Representative category, at the expense of their Sampled and Crafted qualities, and reduces their invitationality. I have assessed Nangala's decorated *Coolamon* (Plate 3.3) below and in Figure 6.16 contrasted its souvenir potential to the ideal Crafted example, shown through Meure's *Huon pine bowl* (Plate 6.1).

Mary Rose Nangala, Coolamon, *2000, acrylic paint on wood with pokerwork detail on reverse 63 × 18 cm (Plate 3.3)*

Medium: (4)
The weight and dimensions of this artefact testify to its authentic material, being soft, light and easy to shape with rudimentary tools. All the surfaces are decorated; the front, with a painted design typical of the Central Australian Desert region, and the reverse with an equally typical pokerwork effect. This excessive decoration suggests that the underlying material, probably Redgum root, is of little importance. As a result, this artefact is situated toward the Representative category and attracts a rating of four. It would be located nearer the Representative category of souvenir if not for the dot painted surface that may be considered a sample of the visual style of expression peculiar to the people of the site.

Maker's mark: (3)
The name attached to this work refers to the painted detail only. So it may be assumed that the coolamon itself was collectively produced. This suggests that the artefact may have some history of traditional use, in the activity of food collecting, especially given its light weight and ease of fit in the crook of the arm. The pokerwork effect, on the reverse, is without an individual author so may be considered to be of collective manufacture, in accordance with the undifferentiated mode of production, traditional to many pre-capitalist societies.

Assuming that two out of three production processes are collective, with only the most recent and noticeable painted detail attributed to the artist, the maker's mark may be considered less dominant than that of the ideal Crafted example and so attracts a rating of three.

Relational: (5)
This artefact clearly relates to people and place, given that the form and both decorative effects are recognised as particular to the people of the Central Australian Desert region. The rating is then identical to that of the ideal Crafted souvenir at five.

Invitational: (2)
The invitational attributes of this artefact are muted by the painted surface that is not suitable for food collection or presentation. The decoration is also, by and large, impenetrable without some understanding of Aboriginal iconography. This artefact has transcended its use as a tool for gathering food and now favours its surface as a canvas for the traditional dot painting design. The invitationality of this artefact is largely closed, almost completed by the painter. We know from its form what it was used for and, from its form and decoration, where it is from. The only speculation for the collector is in the meaning of the painting. It therefore may be assessed as almost closed, and attracts a rating of two.

Iconofetish: (7)
The iconofetish rating of this artefact is high, due mainly to the typical style of the painted surface, which is supported by the pokerwork effect on the reverse and the artefact's form. All these are associated singularly with the Aboriginal people of the Central Australian Desert and are to be found displayed in the public sphere. The rating of this artefact, on this axis, is seven, due mainly to the public perception of the dot painting style as typical of all Aboriginal people.

By bringing these artefacts together and expressing them graphically, it is possible to see the variation in their language, or souvenir expression. This variation is brought about by the decorative design in the coolamon, in contrast to the invitationality of the Huon pine vessel, induced by its utility. Moreover, we can see from the graph below that the souvenir language of the painted coolamon describes a pattern that rests somewhere between the Crafted and Representative categories.

There is, as may be seen from the above assessments, much variation in the expressional tone of woodcraft souvenirs, the extremes of which are highlighted when food-related vessels from different cultures are compared. As a result, it is necessary to scratch deeper into the surface of the exampled, authored Huon pine vessel and to contrast this ideal Crafted souvenir with other minor species souvenirs.

These Crafted souvenirs are, in Graburn's terms, summarised as 'the art of one culture produced for the consumption of another'.[23] The key to the production of this type of souvenir is, first, that the purpose of their production is the satisfaction of the touristic consumer and to achieve this they must invite engagement from the tourist. While conceived and developed by the maker, they must leave a space for the inscription of the tourist's own narrative of fleeting experience, side by side with the intimate narrative of place expressed by the maker. In other words, they offer a glimpse of the site that promises to project more of the site through the tourist's appended narrative. This may be understood as an imagined surplus value.[24]

From the above examples it can be concluded that minor species timber souvenirs are a complex form of souvenir and that their simple form belies their

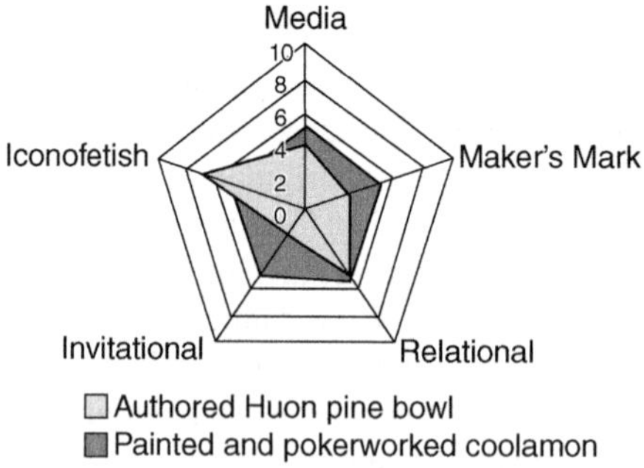

Figure 6.16 Variation between vessels of Aboriginal and Settler Crafted souvenirs.

complex activity and meaning as souvenirs. Furthermore, they provide a good example of the difficulties faced when attempting to categorise souvenirs.

This difficulty arises from the skilled and imaginative enhancement of the unique medium. Like many other timber souvenirs, Huon pine souvenirs are given to mass production and, in that sense, they can be theorised according to Steiner's notion of seriality.[25] But, as Steiner (1999: 98) suggests, mass-produced timber souvenirs are only 'almost identical'. They are, in actuality, one-offs as no grain pattern is the same. Due to this, the tourist has the opportunity to engage in some aesthetic discretion and to select, say, a Huon pine honey dipper, vessel, or some other artefact that either pleases the eye with its grain, sculptural form or both, or best testifies to the nature of its medium. This small but significant detail is enhanced further in the case of larger crafted wooden souvenirs, where the detail of the grain becomes more apparent. What the tourist engages with here is not so much the skill of the maker but the aesthetic of the raw material and, in so doing, the tourist is purchasing a Sampled souvenir. This variation, from the Crafted toward the Sampled is more apparent at the lower end of the timber souvenir market. In the case of the small, lathe-turned Huon pine souvenir, meaning has, as I have shown previously, been reduced to that of the Sampled souvenir, in that it is simply a piece of Huon pine, while its unique grain pattern, form and use is largely insignificant. This shift of the Crafted souvenir toward the Sampled category is not necessarily a fixed feature of small minor species souvenirs, as the following example demonstrates.

Austin Penney crafts a range of delicate spoons from a variety of Tasmanian minor species timbers. Each of these elegant spoons is unique, while their use as spoons is marginal. They are, moreover, ornamental in the way that a collection of metal teaspoons from any well-known tourist site is but, as spoons, they address that time-honoured tourist pastime of spoon collecting and, in so doing, speak of a fetish that is well-known among tourists. Here the elegant form of each spoon is paramount and the skill of the craftsman is a key factor in their appeal. These artefacts are not simply a piece of rare timber but carry with them the engagement and skill of the craftsman. Unlike the former, lathe-turned examples, these souvenirs retain a greater degree of their Sampled attributes, in that the length and angle of the stem is dictated by the raw piece of timber from which they are formed. This feature might cause these spoons to be located toward the Sampled category were it not for the carver's finessing of the stem, gouging of the bowl and, finally, the placement of his signature on the reverse of each stem. These spoons are therefore, according to the following assessment, located at the centre of the Crafted category.

Austin Penney, Carved spoons, *2002, minor species timbers, variable dimensions, collection of the artist (Plate 6.9)*

Medium: (5)
The medium is important in these souvenirs but equally so is their hand-carved form together with the presence of the maker's mark, which balances the importance of the medium to a degree.

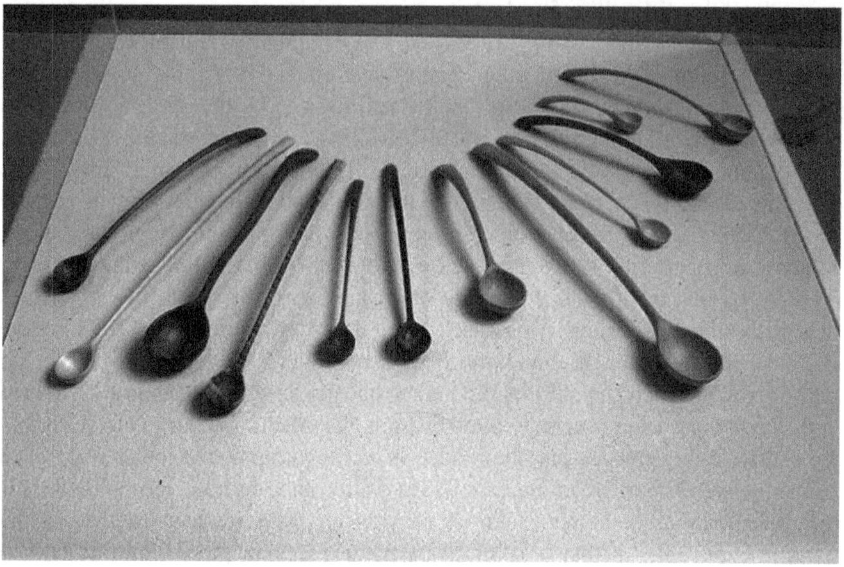

Plate 6.9 Austin Penney, *Carved spoons*, 2002, minor species timbers, various dimensions. Collection of the artist.

Maker's mark: (7)
This is present on the reverse of these artefacts and, relative to the scale of the artefacts and hand-carved method of production which lends some degree of dominance.

Relational: (5)
These artefacts clearly relate to people and place through their form and medium respectively.

Invitational: (5)
This is in line with other ideal Crafted souvenirs, in that the narrative is left open by the maker and completed by the collector.

Iconofetish: (9)
These artefacts attract a high rating here, firstly through their medium and then through their form. The spoon form is an iconic souvenir in general and the medium is iconic of the site. While its domain is the domestic, it is easily recognised for what it is.

Once again, by drawing these minor species timber artefacts together and expressing them graphically (Figure 6.17), the variation in their operation as souvenirs can be seen. It shows how the honey dipper, as a consequence of not being signed by the maker, relies more heavily on its medium and diverges from

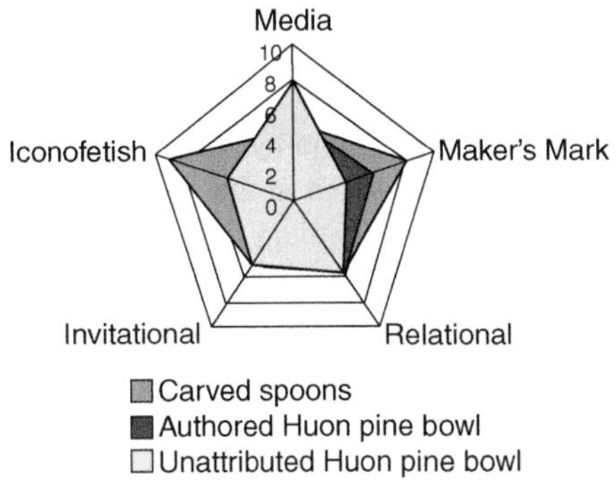

Figure 6.17 Variation between utilitarian, minor species timber souvenirs.

the typical Crafted souvenir, which is represented here by the attributed Huon pine vessel. It also shows how the carved spoons embrace a broader area of souvenir activity as a result of their form and the increased presence, relative to scale, of the maker's mark.

For my final example from this Crafted category I want to look at a lathe-turned wood souvenir from Far North Queensland. This artefact introduces a further complication, in that the wood it is produced from is not endemic to the region or, for that matter, Australia.[26]

The mango tree was introduced to Australia's tropical region for its fruit. Since its introduction it has escaped the plantations and may be seen in urban and country parks, on roadsides and occasionally in wilderness areas. The timber from this tree has no historical or natural base in the timber-getting heritage of Far North Queensland. The timber-getting tradition in Far North Queensland was initially based around the cedar forests. Due to over-cutting and the declaration of the Daintree World Heritage Area in the mid 1980s, this resource has become scarce. Faced with this shortage of traditional timber, the woodcrafts people of the area were compelled to develop a new timber source that was typical of the area and would catch the eye of the tourist.

In its natural state, mango wood is a dull, rather boring, timber, bereft of character. However, subjected to a spalting process, the wood develops some fine figurative swirls that contrast well with the dull featureless grain. Spalting is a process that introduces a micro-organism into the log, which is then allowed to develop; it is part of the natural process of rot and occurs in other timbers across Australia, one, of particular note, is Black Heart Sassafras from Tasmania. What makes spalted mango wood special is the attempt to manage the process and to gauge the amount of spalting required before the timber turns to mush. To do this, the craftsperson must know the site of production intimately, in a way that goes beyond the gathering of specific timber from the forest. To achieve the required degree of spalting, the craftsperson must read and manage the environmental conditions, estimating the right level of humidity to produce the desired effect. This treatment of the timber, then, becomes part of the crafting process and contributes to the narrative that the craftsperson invests in the artefact. In turn, the tourist carries this narrative away and thickens it through his or her own narrative.

The variation of this last example from the ideal Crafted example is apparent because the medium is not indigenous. It is thus plotted in the third category: the Representative. However, spalted mango wood is a medium that is extracted from the environment that it represents, and this is further underscored by the spalting process, which is a direct result of conditions specific to the tropical environment of Far North Queensland. These characteristics, therefore, secure souvenir artefacts produced from it within the Crafted category, in line with the following assessment:

Graham Davis, Spalted Mango Wood Vessel, *2002, 17 × 13 cm (Plate 6.10)*

Medium: (8)
It is difficult to plot this artefact on this axis as, even though the medium is perceived as coming from the site that the vessel purports to represent, it is not

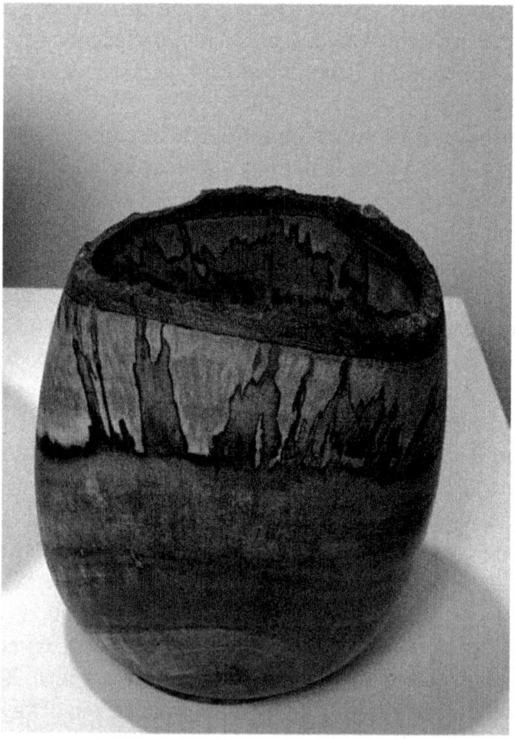

Plate 6.10 Graham Davis, *Spalted Mango Wood Vessel*, 2002, 17 × 13 cm. Private collection.

indigenous to that site. The public perception of the mango as belonging to the site is enhanced because the fruit the tree yields is so typically a product of Queensland and its climate. Climate is used to enhance the indigenous nature of the medium and so the object attracts a high rating to reflect this partnership.

Maker's mark: (4)
This is collective and not inherent in the object but, like the bookmark *Tasmanian Marsupial Mouse*, appears on the label. It therefore attracts a rating of four and is located slightly toward the Sampled category.

Relational: (6)
This artefact refers clearly to people and place through the fact that it is a crafted artefact and so attracts a five rating. However, the addition of the spalted pattern enhances its reference to place, in particular the climate of that place, therefore its insistence on people and place (understood through the local medium and traditional craft practice) is liberated somewhat in favour of people and/or place. For it may be read as a crafted artefact or as a representation of the place and climate of that place alone.

Invitational: (5)
The invitational qualities of this souvenir are commensurate with the typical Crafted souvenir in that its medium is broadly perceived as being of the site, while its crafted form offers a utility with which the collector may engage.

Iconofetish: (4)
This timber is not broadly recognised as an icon of the site, while the fruit from the tree is. In its enhancement through climate, it may have some claim but that is reliant upon the tourist narrative and so causes it to be located toward the private domain and attracts a rating of four.

If we then express the language of this spalted mango wood vessel graphically (Figure 6.18), and contrast it to timber souvenirs constituted from endemic

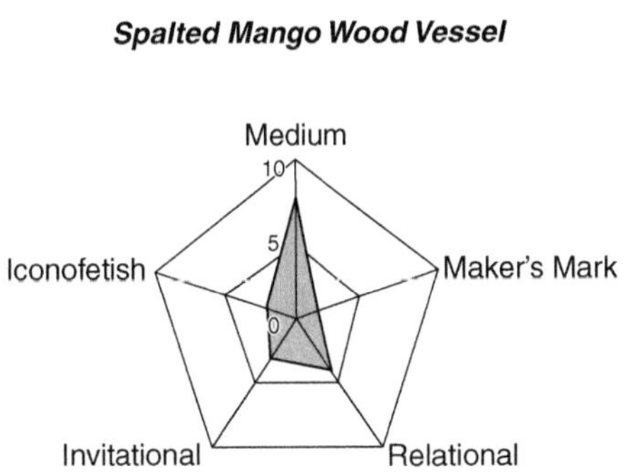

Figure 6.18 Souvenir expression of the spalted Mango wood vessel.

timbers (Figure 6.1), it is possible to see the variation in their souvenir potential. In the light of this variation, and that of the earlier examples, it is clear that this category requires some further investigation. This may be achieved firstly by examining the production process.

A binary division of hand-made and machine-made might break it down in the first instance and serve to differentiate between the examples of the lathe-turned minor species souvenirs and Penney's predominantly hand-made spoons, but it is of little use for the current example. As we have seen, the lathe-turned souvenirs from Far North Queensland and Tasmania can be distinguished according to the indigenous nature of their raw medium, but that would leave spalted mango wood vessels in the Representative category. It is in the definition of the third category, the Representative, that the answer may be discovered.

Representative souvenirs

The third discrete category of souvenir is initially separated from the previous two according to the medium from which it is produced. Unlike the Crafted souvenir, the Representative souvenir takes nothing from the environment that it represents other than image and allusion. Its physical form is characterised by generic media.

Representative souvenirs are typified by the photographic medium and, particularly, by such artefacts as postcards, greeting cards and calendars. Printmakers engage in the production of this type of souvenir, as do ceramicists, glass artists and metal smiths. Like the Crafted souvenirs of the previous category, the success of Representative souvenirs rests upon their perceived and recognisable association with the visited site and culture of that site. This is most often achieved through the composition, colour manipulation and other pictorial structures and processes associated with the picturesque. That is, the image is manipulated to best effect a view or views that entice the tourist. In this way, such images present a pristine and ideal image that both comforts and attracts the tourist. Less desirable aspects such as litter and unsightly buildings are excluded from the picture postcard image. Unlike Crafted souvenirs, this type of souvenir is dominated by the two-dimensional form and, because of this, they are, moreover, ornamental rather than utilitarian in their reference, which has the effect of diminishing their invitational qualities.

One exception to the dominance of two-dimensional artefacts within this category is the cast souvenir, such as ceramic or metal objects. These artefacts may well fit within the Crafted category in that their raw material, or parts of the material, may be derived from the environment to which they refer. This is particularly the case with specialist clays and glazes or techniques that may be specific to the resident culture of the site.[27] However, this is increasingly rare and the process of their production – being cast from a negative mould, in identical multiples – sees such objects allied to the photographic process. These souvenirs then fall more clearly within the Representative category, along with the stable example from this group (Figure 6.8).

A good example of a three-dimensional Representative souvenir is found in Penny Smith's suite of ceramic boxes entitled *Australian Aspects*, in which the artist has combined her ceramic craft with the photographic medium (Plate 6.11). Here the artist has placed an image on the lid of each vessel that is enhanced through the textured surface. This suite of works refers to a number of diverse Australian landscape features. As vessels they also retain a strong invitational aspect through use, which surpasses that of the postcard. The souvenir qualities of Smith's work may be assessed as follows:

Penny Smith, Australian Aspects, *2000, slip cast lidded stoneware boxes, glazed inside, photographic decal, 6 × 11.5 cm (Plate 6.11)*

Medium: (1)
Generic medium with no specific link to the site.

Maker's mark: (5)
Present, but not dominant.

Relational: (7)
Its first line of reference is place, in that the photographic decal and title refer to an unpopulated Australian landscape. But the nature of the souvenir is clearly

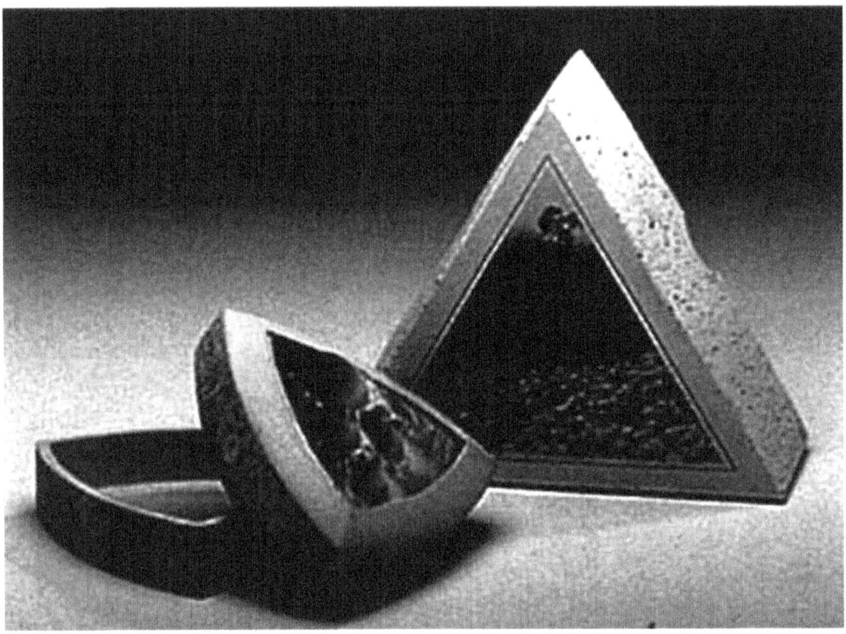

Plate 6.11 Penny Smith, *Australian Aspects,* 2002, slip cast lidded stoneware boxes, glazed inside, photographic decal, 11.5 × 6 cm. Collection of the artist.

crafted, so the artefact demonstrates a flexible reference to place, people and/or place in that priority and attracts a rating that reflects this flexibility.

Invitational: (5)
In its depiction of an unpeopled landscape, this souvenir offers collectors the opportunity to imaginatively place themselves in the site and so complete the narrative invoked by the maker. In other words, the tourist may be induced to recount a narrative to do with a solitary experience of any of the landscapes depicted in this suite of works. It is the type of narrative that might otherwise be attached to a sea shell or pebble and is typical of the sampled souvenir. This is enhanced by the utility of the artefact as a vessel and brings into play the tactile qualities of the artefact that are prominent in the relief surface of the lid. Mimicking the wind-blown patterns of the desert sand, the rocky shoreline of picturesque rivers and other environmental textures and themes, these uniquely shaped ceramic boxes, abstracted from Tasmania's triangular form, offer a great range of narrative beginnings. The door in this respect is ajar, despite the lack of an endemic medium, and so attracts a rating in line with the typical Crafted souvenir.

Iconofetish: (3)
There is nothing iconographic of the site inherent in this souvenir. This is due to its broad reference to the Australian landscape. Neither is there a typical style of ceramic design or particular clay or glaze technique that is recognised as distinctively Tasmanian. As a result, these ceramic boxes tend toward the Sampled end of the scale and their narrative authority exists in the fetishistic realm of the personal or private domain rather than in the public, so attracts a rating of three.

Representations of people and/or place are emblazoned on many crafted artefacts, which serve to enhance the power of the souvenir. A number of artefacts from the previously cited R. Shott & Son collection were enhanced in this way. A matchbox cover, set of candlestick holders and, particularly, the *Map of Tasmania* picture frame (Plate 6.12) are excellent examples. Made from Tasmanian Blackwood, the matchbox cover and candlestick holders are appended with a small, silver-plated map of Tasmania that denotes the place of origin. This amendment still occurs today, but was necessary during the period in which these souvenirs were made, as the quality of Tasmanian minor species timbers was much less renowned then. In many ways this amendment also imposes the souvenir function upon the artefacts.

The central feature of this souvenir (Plate 6.12) is a round photographic image, framed in the centre of the Blackwood map of Tasmania. This image refines the referred site from Tasmania and Tasmanian flora, evident in the artefact's form and medium, to the specific town of Launceston in the north of the state. Like a three-stage zoom of the camera, the invitational openness of the narrative is graphically written into the artefact, leaving few questions unanswered with regard to the reference of this souvenir. The only question left to be uttered is 'what did you

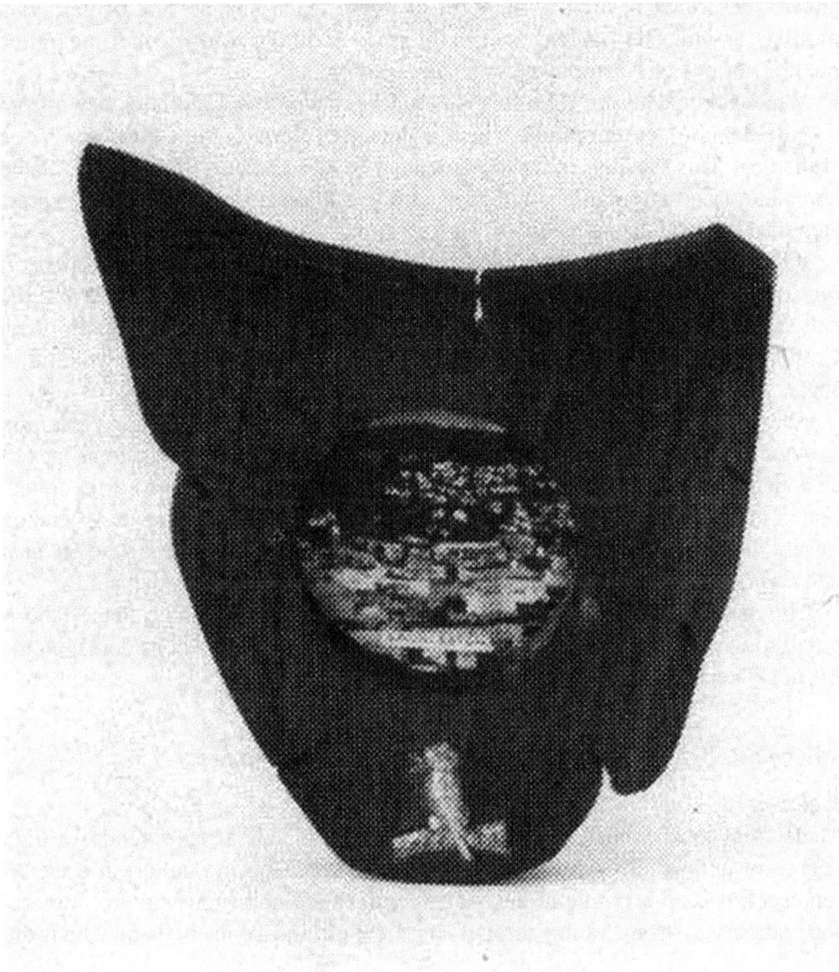

Plate 6.12 R. Shott & Son, *Map of Tasmania Picture Frame with silver plate Kookaburra*, *c.*1925, 11 × 12.5 cm. Collection: Queen Victoria Museum & Art Gallery, Tasmania.

do there?' Today that image may be replaced and is ostensibly there to indicate the framing function of the souvenir. It may be removed and will probably be replaced with a selected holiday snap. This will replace the specificity of the site with evidence of the tourist experience of the site.

The Representative enhancement of the Crafted souvenir is more pronounced in this example, from the R. Shott & Son collection, that highlights further the connection between the Crafted and Representative categories. The silver-plate amendment in this example achieves a different result to the little maps on a matchbox cover and candlestick holders. In this instance the primary site is already described in the overall form of the artefact and the role of the avian motif is to indicate that Tasmania is part of Australia through the integrative qualities of one of Australia's iconic animal symbols.

What can be detected from this is that the primary raw material is hewn from the site the artefact represents, which is enhanced through the skill of the wood craftsman. This, in turn, is further amended by the addition of the silver plated kookaburra and photograph, and they combine to create the resounding expression of this particular souvenir.

In contrasting this souvenir from the R. Shott collection with Smith's *Australian Aspects*, it can be seen, from the graphic summary of Figure 6.19, that the patterns are similar, in that they form a block shape reminiscent of the ideal Crafted souvenir and that the pattern of the former covers a greater volume of space. The block is dominated by the *Iconofetish* and *Invitational* axes.

The *Australian Aspects* souvenir is more subtle in its expression, featuring strong *Relational* attributes and flattening out at the *Medium* axis, due to its lack of an endemic material. The orientation of these patterns also demonstrate the inflection in the expression of each souvenir with *Australian Aspects* seemingly tending toward the ideal Representative category, while the strong rating along the *Medium* and *Invitational* axes demonstrates the *Map of Tasmania's* Sampled qualities.

This nexus is further emphasised in a comparison with many of the Aboriginal souvenirs featured in this project and I want now to consider Mingu's *Lil-lil* (Plate 5.11) in this light.

Mingu, Lil-lil, *Red Gum with pokerwork detail, 70 cm (Plate 5.11)*

Medium: (8)
Made from local timber, the unique lil-lil shape of this artefact retains a high degree of authenticity, as a sample of the environment and culture it seeks to represent. It is an example of the ancient craft of an indigenous culture. It therefore attracts a strong rating through its medium and style, both of which are

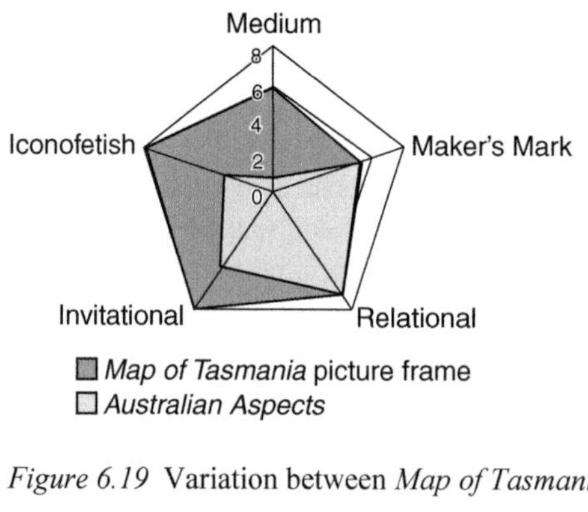

Figure 6.19 Variation between *Map of Tasmania* and *Australian Aspects.*

characteristic of the people and place it seeks to represent. Eight is the highest rating a Crafted souvenir should achieve along this axis, since to score it higher would be to discount the human mediation of the material.

Maker's mark: (7)
The maker's mark is apparent and concise. It includes the artist's name, his town of residence and his specific Aboriginal group. However, it is etched into the narrow side of the artefact and, in that placement, may be equated to the signature on the reverse of the typical Crafted souvenir. But the explicitness of the maker's mark indicates that it is of greater importance, so a rating of seven is accorded this artefact.

Relational: (5)
The lil-lil clearly relates to people and/or place; and, indeed, in the hunting scene burned into the face of the club it shows people in place, even featuring the artefact itself as if to demonstrate its use in the hunting of emu. It therefore attracts a rating of five, in line with the typical Crafted souvenir.

Invitational: (3)
The narrative contained in this souvenir is detailed and largely closed. It features an allegorical scene that instructs the tourist in its use, while the place of representation is also apparent. So there is little that the subsequent viewer needs to ask of the collector. This, in turn, restricts the space for the tourist's own experiential narrative. This club therefore gravitates toward the Representative category and attracts a rating of three.

Iconofetish: (3)
As an Aboriginal tool, this artefact is not as well-known as the boomerang, spear thrower or coolamon. Even as a nula-nula it is obscure and unlikely to be recognised for what it is in the public domain. In this respect it is more likely to be of fetishistic interest and requires some explanation regarding its authenticity. It is in the description of traditional Aboriginal ways that this object is given its iconic value. But even here the scene is not specific to Koori or Aboriginal people and may be read simply as 'returning from the hunt' in any indigenous culture with hunting and gathering traditions. This souvenir therefore attracts a rating of three to reflect the personal-private nature of the narrative.

In this rare souvenir we have an Aboriginal weapon whose original purpose is now largely moribund. In Chapter 5 I have traced the authenticity of this lil-lil to its site of origin through the discussion of an anthropologically authentic artefact (Plate 5.13). It can be seen, therefore, as a genuine souvenir of that site and located in the Crafted category. However, the pokerwork detail depicting the Aboriginal heritage and traditional lifestyle of the maker sees the later example positioned more toward the Representative category.

Similarly, Namatjira's spear thrower (Plate 3.6) comes to rest in the identical location as shown in Figure 6.20. By also comparing the later work of both

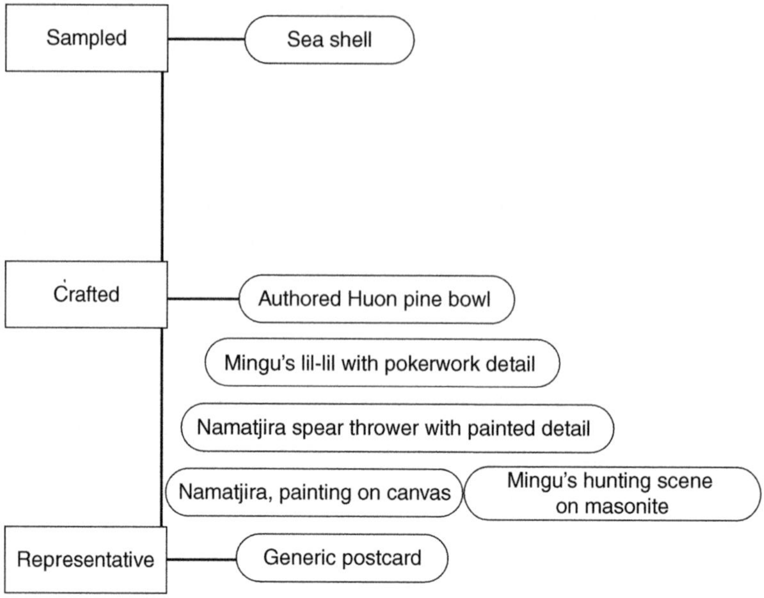

Figure 6.20 Three category axis showing variation between Mingu's lil-lil with pokerwork detail (Plate 5.11), Namatjira's spear thrower with painted detail (Plate 3.6) and Mingu's *Untitled camp scene* on Masonite (Plate 5.15) and any Namatjira painting on canvas.

artists – Mingu's *Untitled camp scene* (Plate 5.15) and any of Namatjira's Western style landscape paintings on canvas – it is possible to see a development that demonstrates how the importance of the Aboriginal tool, the spear thrower and the lil-lil, has given way to the artists' desire to express their culture and environment through the pictorial medium. These works are then seen to be positioned more fully within the Representative category, as shown in Figure 6.20. It can, therefore, be seen that the strength of the artefact, as a souvenir, rests in the artist's full realisation of the potential of his chosen material, in that the timber is of the site, it is mediated to an authentic form and is then enhanced through a pokerwork process. But while pokerwork is a common method of decoration and illustration to Aboriginal people across Australia, I have shown in Chapter 5 that the style of illustration on this nulanula is particular to the Aboriginal people of Southeast Australia. Therefore, if we are to recognise the Dombrovskian style of landscape photography as a particular style developed around the Tasmanian landscape, and locate his work away from the Representative category and towards the Crafted, it makes sense to consider the rudimentary pokerwork images from Mingu in the same way.

What is detectable from the above examples is that an endemic material is advantageous in the artefact's function as a souvenir. But, if an endemic medium is not present, one has to consider whether the style is particular to the site. This is apparent in Mingu's *Untitled camp scene* (Plate 5.15). Here the artist has dispensed with the endemic medium and traditional sculptural form, but has retained the typical figurative drawing style and subject matter found in his lil-lil. Indeed, as I have pointed out previously, in the top left of the image he has actually enhanced the hunting scene with the inclusion of an iconic Aboriginal pose, made popular in kitsch representations of Aboriginal people in the 1970s. The effect of this is summarised in Figure 6.21; it reflects the importance of the traditional medium and form in the lil-lil and the enhancement of the similar scene in the Masonite rendition, through the inclusion of the iconic Aboriginal pose.

If we then explore the aforementioned comparison between Mingu's *Untitled camp scene* and the Dombrovskis postcard, we can see from Figure 6.22 how the Dombrovskis greeting card (Plate 6.3) and Mingu's *Untitled camp scene* trace a similar pattern on the *Medium*, *Maker's mark*, *Invitational* and *Iconofetish* axes, but diverge on the *Relational* axis. This has to do with the reference to place, and people and place, respectively.

Figure 6.21 and 6.22 make a comparison, firstly, between Mingu's two works. Then the Dombrovskis postcard and Mingu's *Untitled camp scene* are illustrated to demonstrate the value of attributes crucial to the Sampled category of souvenirs and

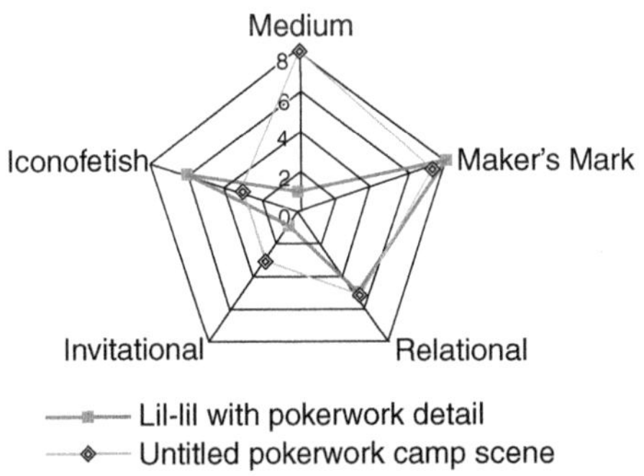

Figure 6.21 Variation between Mingu's pokerwork souvenirs.

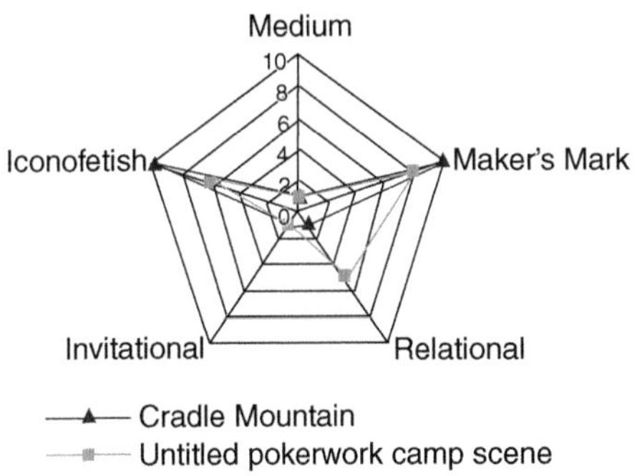

Figure 6.22 Variation between Dombrovskis' *Cradle Mountain* greeting card and Mingu's *Untitled camp scene* on Masonite.

the effect they may have on the Representative group of souvenirs. This relationship is explored further and demonstrated ingeniously in the following postcards.

Conforming largely to the ideal Representative souvenir, the following two postcards – *Windows of Australia*: *Tasmania* (Plate 6.13) and *A Little bit of the Outback* (Plate 6.14) – have shrewdly appropriated fundamental, sampled materials within a Representative type souvenir. The first of these postcards comes from a series titled *Windows of Australia* and refers to Tasmania. It consists of a small cellophane envelope that holds a collection of tiny shell fragments and coloured pebbles. This is sandwiched between two stiff pieces of postcard-size cardboard that serve to frame the fragments. The fragments are not fixed but rattle about in the transparent envelope each time the postcard is handled. They vary in colour, from the pearl of the shells, through to brown, purple and black rock fragments. Close inspection reveals a myriad of natural patterns including striations and regular dots, while some fragments boast a number of different hues and levels of opacity. The reverse of the card bears the printed plan of a postcard.

The second example (Plate 6.14) is titled *A Little bit of the Outback* and is formed largely in the same way as the first. The contents of the cellophane envelope are in this case, as the label on the reverse informs us, 'Australian desert sand, Spinifex and Iron Stone collected near Alice Springs Central Australia'. In this example, two of the three contents are loose and shift every time the card is handled. Only the spinifex is fixed, radiating out from one corner in a skeletal fan pattern. The fixed nature of this component allows the image to operate on the vertical, while the sand and iron stone may be shifted around to

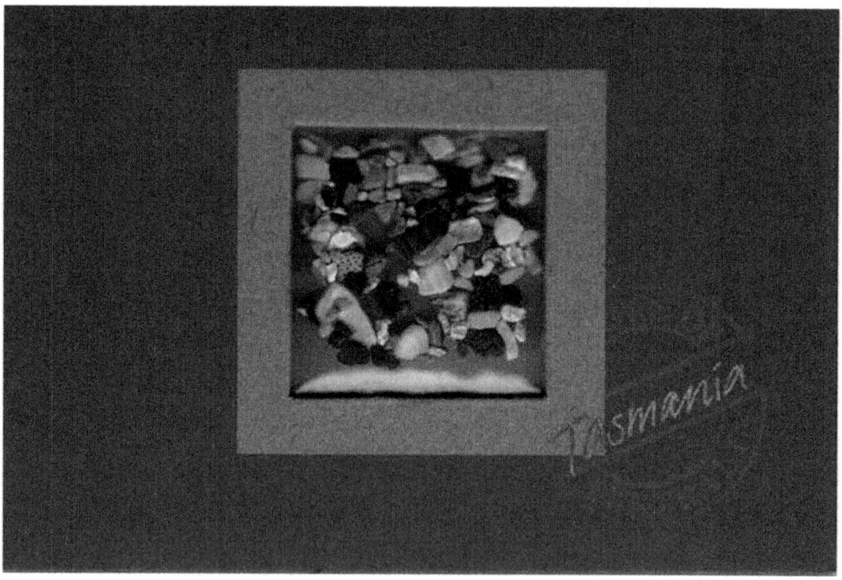

Plate 6.13 Magic Rabbit, *Windows of Australia: Tasmania*, 2002, shell fragments, stone, card and clear plastic, 10.5 × 15 cm. Private collection.

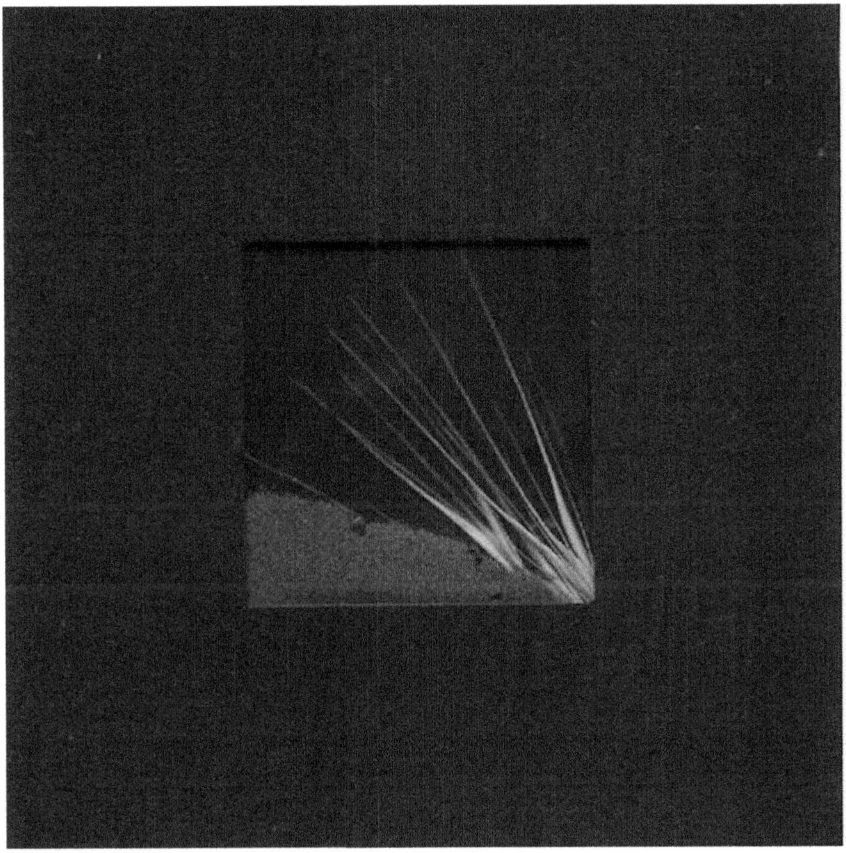

Plate 6.14 Magic Rabbit, *A Little bit of the Outback*, 2002, Australian desert sand, Spinifex and Iron Stone, card and clear plastic, 12 × 12 cm. Private collection.

form a desert plane, hilly dune with boulders, or a number of other landscape formations. This is not possible in the first example, which operates most successfully on the horizontal by referring to the detritus of the beach.

The trick to both postcards rests in the use of sampled fragments, which are objects from the site they represent. These are skilfully brought together in a photographic format and are framed as postcards. In this way the maker has identified the objects that tourists collect as samples from the visited site and has put them together in an invitational manner. Unlike the fixed photographic postcard image, the collector is able to engage in a form of play and to adjust the contents to suit him or herself.

I now want to see how these delightful souvenirs fit within the structure being developed. I will assess both postcards together and rate them in the order of their appearance.

Medium: (8) (6)
If we include the framing materials, such as the cardboard and plastic used to form the postcard, then the medium is clearly mixed and is both of the site and generic. In the first example, *Windows of Australia, Tasmania* (Plate 6.13), it is not crafted but framed, while the second example, *A Little bit of the Outback* (Plate 6.14), with its single fixed component, shows a more developed state of craft. The objects attract a rating of eight and six respectively.

Maker's mark: (3) (3)
This is present but not dominant, as each card is stamped only with the commercial brand. The maker's mark is therefore collective and this is reflected in the rating of three for both examples.

Relational: (1) (1)
Initially the contents of these cards, which are sampled objects, relate to a personal experience and not a particular site. However, we are informed that one is from Tasmania and the other is from the Central Australian Desert, near Alice Springs. In this respect both postcards refer to a place that is, in the images, unpeopled and, therefore, attract a rating of one.

Invitational: (3) (7)
The narrative progression of the Representative group of souvenirs is typically closed and complete, in that they consist of a fixed image that is clearly labelled. However, in this case the first example – *Windows of Australia*: *Tasmania* – is somewhat light in this respect. There is no label other than the generalised title, so the contents are simply fragments of a Tasmanian beach that may be collected by anyone. In this lack of specificity, the narrative content is more open and therefore invites the collector to complete it, in the same way that the fetish object relies upon the collector for its narrative. The content of this postcard draws much from the fetishistic allure of pretty pebbles and sea shells, as fragments of the visited site, which this postcard frames for the collector so that he or she may share the experience of the site. The unfixed form of the fragments also allows the collector to organise the image to some degree. In this respect the invitational quality of this postcard is unusually open and attracts a rating of three. The second example – *A Little bit of the Outback* – however, is more complete in that it informs the viewer of the site near where it was collected. This is achieved through the use of more site-specific materials and the fixed nature of the spinifex sample. Through this stable component and the specificity of the sampled materials, the maker has framed the ensuing tourist narrative and so this postcard is rated at seven, in order to reflect the fixed but pliable photographic format.

Iconofetish: (2) (9)
In the postcard that refers to Tasmania there is no hint of an icon; it contains nothing that could be recognised as being specifically Tasmanian. The objects

contained here are clearly fetish type objects that may be found on many beaches around Australia and, for that matter, the world. The underlying theme of this souvenir is a private experience of a particular but unknown site. This renders the site of this narrative a personal one and thus attracts a rating of two. This takes into account the generalised title, which locates the experience somewhere in Tasmania.

In the second example, there is more of a sense of the iconic in the object. Hundreds and possibly thousands of tourists carry away a phial or sachet of the red sand that marks the Central Australian Desert as unique. This lifts this example away from the fetish narrative, in which meaning is reliant upon the collector, and ties it to a specific site, in the same way that the rich colours of Dombrovskian postcards are synonymous with the Tasmanian landscape. The rating of this postcard is therefore nine and demonstrates how an iconic feature may be sampled and integrated into a Representative souvenir.

I have shown, in this assessment and the graphic summaries of Figures 6.23 and 6.24, how the qualities of these imaginative postcards relate graphically to the ideal Representative souvenir exampled through the unsigned *Views of Tasmania* postcard (Figure 6.8) and the signed Dombrovskian greeting card (Figure 6.22).

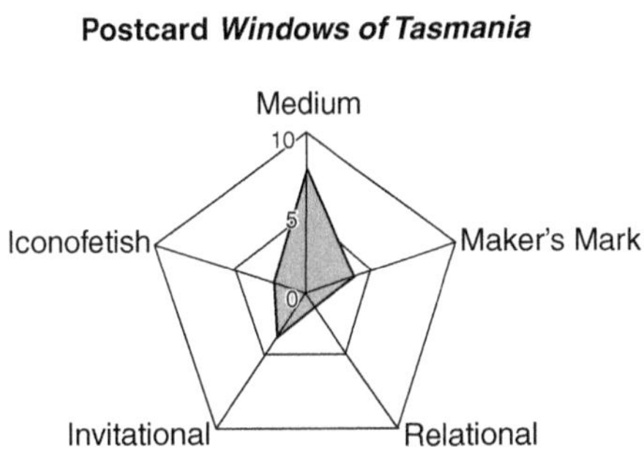

Figure 6.23 Souvenir expression of postcard *Windows of Australia: Tasmania.*

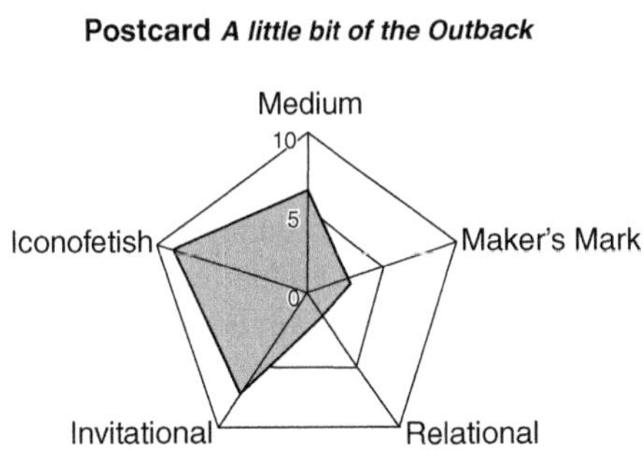

Figure 6.24 Souvenir expression of postcard *A Little bit of the Outback.*

In summarising the patterns described in those graphs, it can be seen, first, how both the generic postcard, *Views of Tasmania* (Figure 6.9) and the authored greeting card, *Cradle Mountain* from Peter Dombrovskis (Figure 6.22) reveal similar patterns of expression but with altered orientation. The pattern described by the souvenir expression of both postcards is also similar to the sea shell example, cited as the stable Sampled souvenir, indicating that all three artefacts offer the same potential as souvenirs but for differing reasons. Where the sea shell's strength exists in its medium and gives rise to the sharp angle typical of Sampled souvenirs, the same acute angle is achieved by the Dombrovskis postcard via the *Maker's mark* axis and in the generic postcard through its relational dexterity.

The same expressive shape in *Windows of Australia: Tasmania* (Figure 6.23) is less well-formed but does show the value of the sampled medium. This postcard seems to orient itself toward the *Medium* and *Invitational* axes, at the expense of a reduced register along the *Invitational* and *Relational* axes, that is commensurate with the ideal Sample souvenir. The register along the *Maker's mark* and *Iconofetish* axes is conventionally low in the Sampled souvenir. The presence of a moderate register along these latter axes causes the *Windows of Australia: Tasmania*, postcard to make some exertions toward the rounded pattern of the Crafted souvenir.

This tendency occurs to a greater degree with the second Magic Rabbit postcard – *A Little bit of the Outback* (Figure 6.24). The pattern described by this souvenir shows that much more is going on than is possible with the fixed image of the generic *Views of Tasmania* or the Dombrovskis postcard. Like many images of Central Australia, this souvenir rests its claim on the red sand that has become so iconic of the site. However, it occurs here in sample form, together with other fragments of the Central Australian Desert. This gives rise to a strong register along the *Medium* and *Iconofetish* axes. It is, however, the invitationality of this souvenir that provides its dominant attribute. This is typical of many Crafted souvenirs and is a feature of the play or interactivity of the artefact. As a device designed for communication, all postcards are fundamentally invitational. But this fundamental feature is massively enhanced through the invitation to order the sampled components and create one's own miniature image of the Central Australian landscape. There is also the attachment of narrative, describing the collector's experience to a material anchor, something which is at the heart of the souvenir's function.

From the above illustrations it can be seen how the attributes of these fundamentally Representative souvenirs are drawn from each category. The central medium is drawn from the Sampled group, while it is configured through the agency of craft into an image reminiscent of a photographic transparency. This clearly relates to Stewart's identification of the relationship between the pressed flower and the photographic souvenir. Furthermore, it demonstrates how some souvenirs, while fundamentally based in one group, may be located closer to another category. This, in turn, influences the tone of souvenir expression in the resultant artefact.

7 Conclusion

The impulse to souvenir, together with the history of souvenirs, stretches back at least as far as recorded history and, most likely, beyond that. Far from being insignificant kitsch items, produced simply to make a profit, souvenirs are complex objects and artefacts. They harbour an array of features and, above all, have the capacity to accept a densely woven narrative, propelled by the impulse to record experience, most often the experience of travel and 'Otherness' or the unrepeatable.

Souvenirs are indeed historical artefacts and, like history, they are not fixed in meaning but are open to interpretation. Some souvenirs remain as personal items displayed on shelves or in cabinets or, at worst, are packed away in boxes in a corner of the attic or garage. If they are fortunate enough to see the light, then their form has the capacity to provoke a story, an oral history of the event, sparked by the sighting of the object as an aide-memoire, a memory jogger. Under such conditions the narrative is far from fixed. It is likely to be often repeated, in the endeavour to recreate the story of the event, but prone to variation, as all oral history is.

How often have the following questions been uttered in reference to some trinket on the mantelpiece: *What's that? Where did you get that? How does it work? What is it made of?* And what images are formed in the mind's eye of the inquirer as they absorb the story of a once in a life time holiday: images of far away places, people and cultures, kept current through a cheap souvenir of dubious aesthetic quality; images that will acquire more fanciful detail with each telling and retelling, and perhaps eventually blur in the narrative of the collector or subsequent collector?

This narrative is, however, expansive and, unlike the conventional closed nature of the fetish, demonstrates its capacity to travel beyond the domestic environment, coming to rest in public museums. Here, with the official recording of its provenance, the narrative becomes more concrete in its status of authority, for here it becomes a part of the communal memory and meaning is fixed in the records of the institution – as we have seen in such instances as the Ashmolean Museum, the *Behind the Mask* exhibition and a number of other souvenired artefacts unearthed at various museums during the course of this research.

Whether it is displayed in the domestic or public environment, the language by which the narrative is composed remains constant and consists of five key components that may be manipulated by the producer and highlighted, in turn, by the consumer.

The object's concrete form, the material from which the souvenir is produced, is its most apparent feature. The importance given to this feature by the producer I have recorded as the *Medium* axis, showing how the features of the raw material are enhanced to engage with the tourist as a marker of the visited site. In assessing this component, it is important to consider the visibility of the raw material and ask oneself is the tourist buying a crafted product or simply a natural sample of the site that has been tamed to fit within the domestic environment.

The level and importance of craft was the next feature analysed. How important is the work of the craftsperson to the object's activity as a souvenir? Does the craftsperson, or at least the craft, feature in the ongoing narrative of the object? To assess this I have surveyed each artefact cited for the thumbprint of the maker, either individual or in the known traditions of the visited site, with individual signatures of traditional practitioners rated as more likely to retain a feature in the ongoing narrative and recently imported crafts less likely.

After establishing the code, or language, of these intriguing objects, their expression has been plotted visually so common patterns can be recognised and, from that, three distinct groups of souvenirs identified: Sampled, Crafted and Representative. It has been shown that a clear distinction exists in the patterns generated by the three souvenir groups, and, of course, that variation exists within each group.

Souvenirs typical of each group have been identified. This showed that the typical Sampled souvenir is strong in its reliance upon the *Medium* and *Invitational* axes and delineated a pattern faithful to those strengths. It registers no expression in terms of *Maker's mark*, as it is devoid of human shaping; it is also, therefore, equally vague in its simple *Relational* component, instead relying heavily on the collector to supply meaning in the ensuing commentary, as recorded in its *Invitational* register. While citing the commonly collected sea shell as the typical Sampled souvenir there is no register along the *Iconofetish* axis, as a sea shell is simply that. Only when it is a specific type of sea shell, collectively recognised by tourists as being of a specific site, will it record movement from fetish to icon along this axis.

A similar form is described by the Representative group of souvenirs – here the orientation is distinctly toward the *Iconofetish* and *Relational* axes. This class of souvenir, in its typical form, records nothing along the *Medium* axis as it does not rely upon an endemic material. It is also, in its typical form, without authorship (or, at best, of corporate faceless authorship) so does not register anything along that axis; the story it has to tell is overtly told through its iconic form of image, therefore reducing the reliance on the collector for meaning.

What is common to these typical forms of both classes of souvenir is their limited expression, which is dominated by two registers: *Iconofetish – Relational* in the case of the Representative group and *Medium – Invitational* in the case of the Sampled. They are, in typical form, both limited to a binary expression.

The Crafted class of souvenir, however, has been shown to be a much more complex artefact, which in its ideal form describes a symmetrical pentagonal pattern from its equal register along all five axes. In this class of souvenir, the pull of each expressive utterance is shown to be equal. The exampled souvenir registers meaning along the *Medium* axis by being produced of an endemic material, such as timber, a timber that is reasonably iconic of the site of collection.The *Maker's mark* is present, but not overt, being a signature on the underside. It has some utility so invites use and relates to the traditions of the visited site, thereby recording an equal rating along the remaining *Relational* and *Iconofetish* registers.

No theory is complete without testing and to do this I have sought anomalous souvenirs and tested them against this structure. This has resulted in a number of even more complex artefacts, that support the overall thesis of the identified five prong code of souvenirs and the establishment of the third Crafted category of souvenir, which without doubt is beneficial to our understanding of the material culture generated from tourism. This comprehension is enhanced through graphic illustrations demonstrating its flexibility to record the language of complex variations.

A number of issues have emerged during the writing of this book. At the beginning of the twenty-first century new, undiscovered sites are rare and those that do emerge are quickly incorporated into a well-organised and highly-developed tourist industry as commodified destinations. Equally, so many souvenirs are now less organic in their development and tend to be created rather like corporate logos. This has the effect of giving the site high visibility in a very competitive environment, which tends to be especially at the expense of site specific souvenir production.

A further important issue arising from this research is its application as a design guide. It can be seen from this research that different classes of souvenir are embedded with narratives that are of different developmental stages, which may now be considered when designing souvenirs for different segments of the tourist industry. For example, a fleeting or shallow engagement with the destination is likely to generate a market for souvenirs with a more complete narrative, such as ones that feature strongly in the Representative category – for example, the *Views of Tasmania* postcard, with its overt representation of sites to be seen in the state. On the other hand, a more sustained and deeper engagement with a destination (during which a small chapter of life history may be developed, along with attendant narrative) would most likely result in a market for more esoteric souvenirs, arising from objects designed with the qualities of the Sampled and Crafted categories in mind.

Above all what I hope has been elaborated in the pages of this book is the complex visual language with which these modest objects, artefacts and works of art reflect the touristic experience.

Notes

1 Introduction

1 Urry (1990: 2), draws our attention to the deviant nature of tourism and the tourist gaze, informing us that:

> [w]hat makes a particular tourist gaze depends upon what it is contrasted with; what the forms of non-tourist experience happen to be.... Such practices involve a notion of a limited breaking with established routines and practices of everyday life and allowing one's senses to engage with a set of stimuli that contrast with the everyday and mundane.

This dislocation from familiar routines results in what Urry (1990: 10) refers to as a 'licence for permissive and playful "non serious" behaviour and the encouragement of a relatively unconstrained "communitas" or social togetherness'. I will show, later, how the souvenir both assists in producing this social cohesion among tourists and reflects it.

2 Urry (1990: 40) cites a 1980s example explaining how 'coral from around tourist islands like Barbados is dying because of the pumping of raw sewage into the sea from beachside hotels and because locals remove both plants and fish from the coral to sell to tourists'. More recently, in Tasmania, the popularity of certain wilderness sites has demanded the development of management plans that prescribe modes of engagement designed to minimise the impact of visitor traffic.

3 See Smith, V. (1977: 4–5).

4 Here Smith, V. (ibid.) cites the effect of tourism on a Tongan community, where the introduction of a cash economy, through tourism, led to the abandonment of subsistence agriculture and a resultant decline in local food production.

5 Greenwood (1977: 129–131), is deeply worried about the impact of the tourist gaze and its propensity to highlight economic 'cleavages within the (host) community', and takes the view that 'onlookers often alter the meaning of the activities being carried on by local people'. He goes on to say: 'Under these circumstances local culture is ... being expropriated, and local people ... exploited'.

6 Greenwood's gaze may well be focused on the impact that tourism has on the host-to-host relationship and in that his concerns are worthy. But he seems incapable of considering the long term benefits that tourism brings, such as the exchange of knowledge and promotion of understanding.

7 Torgovnick (1990: 78) first notes Michel Leiris' recognition of similarities between a museum and a whorehouse. Citing the jumble of late nineteenth century ethnographic displays, she points to the way ethnographic artefacts are displayed at the end of the twentieth century, writing:

> Today museums and galleries of what we have agreed to call primitive art resemble jewellery stores.... Dramatic spotlights isolate the objects from each

other and from us.... Walls are modernist white ... the walls ground the objects against a solid neutral background, conducive to the contemplation of form.

8 The relationship between the souvenir and the work of art is confused further through the expanded meaning of the term 'Gallery', applied as it is today to souvenir and craft outlets with variable goods.
9 Smith, V. (1977: 4), terms this surplus value 'double pricing' and suggests that it is the result of the economic disruption that tourism brings, writing that 'the tourist is often trapped into paying the asked for price but carries a bitter aftertaste that he's been had'.
10 See Levi-Strauss (1958).

2 The European collection of 'Other' cultures: a historical structure from which to assess tourist art and souvenirs

1

> The collection presented to the University of Oxford by Elias Ashmole (1617–1692) was in origin already half a century old by this time, having been founded by John Tradescant (died 1638) and displayed to the public (for a fee), first by him and later by his son John (1608–1662) in their dwelling house at Lambeth, widely known as 'The Ark'. The contents were universal in scope, with man-made and natural specimens from every corner of the known world.
> (The Historical Development of the Ashmolean)

2 Turner and Ash, (1976: 29) offer a concise definition of the Grand Tour as the way in which:

> [t]he new world pays its respects to the old.... Its development follows a shift in the focus of culture and of economic and political power. The wealthy and educated of states whose position of dominance in the world is relatively new, visits countries that have passed their peak of prestige and creativity but are still venerated for historic and cultural reasons. Thus Romans visited Greece and the Eastern Mediterranean; the English, from the sixteenth century onwards visited Italy and in this century Americans 'do' Europe.

3 It should also be acknowledged, at this point, that the exchange of material culture in Australia was taking place well before European colonisation. Indigenous nations have, for hundreds of years, traded raw materials (such as ochre, and pearl shells, tools, weapons and other goods) across tribal boundaries.

3 Souvenirs and the anthropological gaze: the study and reception of souvenirs over the last half century

1 I have omitted Graburn's category of the 'Popular arts' as it has little relevance in the context of this study.
2 Due to the complexities of gaining the permission of identifiable people, it is not possible to reproduce the following images in this text: *Tasman Snider Carving A Boomerang Outside His Home In Mantaka Watched By Leroy Diamond And Fleur Hobson*, and *John Dixon Decorating a Boomerang For Sale at La Perouse.* To view the images within the context of this chapter, the reader is directed to my earlier publication, Hume (2009).

4 The souvenir and the fetish

1 Rojek (1997: 53) explains:

> In theory one might speak of an index of representations; that is a range of signs, images and symbols which make the sight familiar to us in ordinary culture. The

> process of indexing refers the set of visual, textual and symbolic representations to the original object. It is important to recognise that representational culture is not a uniform entity. Rather one might speak of files of representation. A file of representation refers to the medium and conventions associated with signifying a sight.

The author then cites examples from literature, television, and cinema that are brought together to formulate the intended tourists' preconception of the site. It is important to note at this point that Rojek's thesis is concerned with the 'social constructions of tourist sights', as its title suggests. His essay is a convincing study of why tourists visit well-known destinations and as such is concerned with events that occur prior to the collection of souvenirs and in many ways prior to the actual holiday. However, the structures set out in his paper are germane to this ensuing analysis of souvenirs.

2 Freud (1962: 154) writes:

> It is not true that, after the child has made his observation of the woman, he has preserved unaltered his belief that women have a phallus. He has retained that belief, but he has also given it up. In the conflict between the weight of the unwelcome perception and the force of his counter wish, a compromise has been reached, as is only possible under the dominance of the unconscious laws of thought – the primary processes. Yes, in his mind the woman *has* got a penis ... but this penis is no longer the same as it was before. Something has taken its place, has been appointed its substitute ... and now inherits the interest.... But this interest suffers an extraordinary increase as well, because horror of castration has set up a memorial to itself in the creation of the substitute.

3 Freud (1962: 74–75) writes:

> [T]he system of doctrines and promises which on the one hand explains to him the riddles of this world with enviable completeness, on the other, assures him that a careful Providence will watch over his life and will compensate him in a future existence for any frustrations here.

Then addressing the measures of placation, Freud returns to the mechanism of substitution that underlies his formulation of the fetish, writing: 'There are perhaps three such measures: powerful deflections, which cause us to make light of our misery; substitutive satisfactions, which diminish it; and intoxicating substances, which make us insensitive to it' (ibid.).

4 The belief was that the further down the evolutionary ladder you travelled, then the least developed the rational conscious mind was. Therefore, without the routine of a developed society in the western sense – that is, highly differentiated – the more primitive, animal-like and lethargic the people were, and the less likely such cultures were to have developed the freedom to produce art in the Western sense. Phillips and Steiner (1999: 7) summarise this Victorian imperialist discourse as follows:

> Art assumed the prominence within their larger project precisely because it constituted, for Westerners, the ultimate measure of human achievement. The presence or absence of 'true art,' defined as free creation unfettered by functional requirement, could be used as a kind of litmus test of the level of civilisation a group of people had supposedly achieved.

5 Torgovnick (1990: 197) writes:

> The analysand would work down through various 'primitive' states of mind to share 'civilised' outputs of the powerful doctor.... In 'Freud's corner' the arrangement of objects fits the traditional Western paradigms on the primitive, which assume that primitive is prior to the civilized and can be subordinated by it.

6 Torgovnick (1990: 205) directs our attention to this relationship between the female and nature as primitive environment and subject in the work of Freud. She informs us that 'In Freud's work the feminine often functions as the primitive does ... as when he compares the female psyche to a "dark continent" with himself as the intrepid explorer Stanley.'

7 I am thinking here of the Jungian archetypes so ably discussed in Jung (1972); Neumann (1963) and Michael Fried's (1990) art historical study of Gustave Courbet's *The Origins of the World* and other grotto paintings.

8 See Fried (1990).

9 Many communities that fall under the gaze of the tourist present a museumified emplacement to the tourist that is significantly different to their own domestic reality. This is most evident in the costumes donned by workers in tourist enterprises, demonstrations of hunting skills and ceremonial displays. It is a direct development from the perceived, ahistorical structure of the primitive society. MacCannell (1976: 91) refers to this as 'Staged Authenticity' and focuses his study on the modern, western mode of production that is falling increasingly under the tourist gaze, writing that, 'Modernity is quite literally turning industrial structure inside out as these workaday, "real life", "authentic" details are woven into the fabric of modern solidarity alongside the other attractions'. The subject is different but the principle is the same. In my research I have, as noted earlier, viewed a number of demonstrations of wood-turning and other old western crafts, and spear throwing performances; both are, I suspect, preserved and kept visible by the demands of the tourist gaze.

10 There are numerous and varied descriptions of proto museums that range from small windowless rooms to entire buildings and grounds. These varied descriptions take account of the development and expansion of such collections (see Pearce (1995); Impey (1997); Torgovnick (1990); and Alexander (1979) for detailed descriptions of the *Wunderkammer*). Their contents ranged from small works of art, such as miniatures and sculptures, to botanical and zoological samples and often included what were then considered freaks of nature.

11 Relph (1976: 149) proposes that it takes a matter of days for the tourist to feel at home in a strange place.

12 Pietz (1993: 130) claims 'that Marx appealed to the language of magic and theology in general, and fetishism in particular, as a way of evoking materialist imaginary proper to a communist mode of apprehending capitalist reality'.

13 It is fitting to invoke Blake's notion of the sublime in regard to tourism as both present notions of innocence and experience. For Blake, particularly in his *Songs of Innocence and of Experience* (first published 1794), they are constant states through which the human subject travels back and forth. Similarly, the tourist seeks new sites and experiences that will likewise provoke a sense of transcendence (see Curran (1973) and Hirsch (1964)).

14 On this type of exchange, Marx (1951: 178) writes: 'Only labour which is directly transformed into capital is productive'. And later, in considering the productivity of the independent producer, he asks:

> What then is the position of the independent handicraftsmen or peasants who employ no worker and therefore do not produce as capitalists? ... they are commodity producers and I buy the commodity from them.... In this relationship they meet me as sellers of commodities, not as sellers of labour.... Their productive system does not fall under the capitalist mode of production.
>
> (Ibid.: 191)

That is not to say that there is no surplus value generated by the independent craftsperson. For Marx recognises that 'their position makes it possible for them to appropriate their own surplus labour' (ibid.:192). That is, they work during their own leisure time.

15 Other equally revealing contributions to this field include: Nicks (1999); Bol (1999); Phillips (1999); Phillips and Steiner (1999); Traugott (1999); Lippard (1999a); and Feddersen and Woody (1999).

5 Contexts of display: tourist art in recent museogallery exhibitions

1 I refer here to the boomerang as a redundant hunting tool, displaced by the rifle, while recognising the continuing importance of the boomerang in Aboriginal ceremony.
2 See Jones (1996) for an overview of the boomerang's use in contemporary Australia; headings include 'Military and Patriotic Emblems', 'Momentos and Souvenirs' and 'Boomerangs in Advertising'.
3 Central Desert Aboriginal dot painting emerged relatively recently as a commodifiable art form during the mid-1970s. Prior to the introduction of canvas and an increased range of colours through the agency of school teacher Geoffrey Bardon at Papunya in 1971, dot painting mainly occurred as ephemeral works in a restricted palette on the desert floor. See Bardon (2000: 208–211) for further detail.
4 See Steiner (1999) for further elaboration.
5 This exhibition was part of the first 'Ten Days on the Island' festival, Tasmania's international cultural festival and, as such, the exhibition extended its role in the tourist narrative. Much of the factual information about this exhibition was gathered in conversation with the exhibition's curator, Patricia Sabine, formerly Director of the Tasmanian Museum and Art Gallery.
6 Collection of The Australian Museum, Sydney, Australia. For further information see www.amonline.net.au/anthropology/collections/asia_africa_americas02.html
7 This information was included in the wall text that accompanied the exhibit at the Tasmanian Museum and Art Gallery.
8 For further detail, see Sayers (1994) and Cooper *et al.* (1981).
9 The spelling 'Koori' sometimes appears as 'Koorie'. Nula-nula also apears in various forms, sometimes without the hyphen and sometime as 'nulla nulla'. In the spelling of all Aboriginal words I have referred to Kleinert and Neale (2000) for guidance.
10 See Sayers (1994: 13) who writes that 'Drawing for Barak, was one of the things that helped keep his traditional culture alive, not only for him but for those around him'.
11 See Chapter 4, Figures 4.1 and 4.2.
12 The source for this was a personal conversation with the then curator, P. Sabine.
13 There are a number of recent case studies dealing with this, notably Kasfir's report on the pressures imposed by tourism that led to the miniaturisation of the Samburu hunting spear (Kasfir 1999). Of course, the viability of souvenir weapons in full and reduced scale has come under further scrutiny following the 9/11 terrorist attacks.
14 See Turner and Ash (1976: 19–29); MacCannell (1976: 43); Urry (1990: 4–9); and Shields (1991) who all document the development of contemporary tourism out of pre-modern pilgrimages and associated rituals.

6 The language of souvenirs: three discrete groups – the Sampled, Crafted and Representative

1 Pearce (1995); see also Chapter 5 for commentary.
2 Graburn (1976: 4); see also Chapter 3 for commentary.
3 Within the context of this project I shall refer to these souvenirs as 'Settler' souvenirs.
4 Other photographers focusing on the Tasmanian wilderness as their primary subject, in the Dombrovskian style, include Rob Blakers, Chris Bell and others. All produce high definition, deep colour wilderness images in a range of formats, from fine art prints to glossy, coffee table texts and postcards.

5 It may, however, be argued that the reverse of all postcards provides a space for the tourist's narrative. But this space is negligible and is normally filled with the message that the sender is at the site and arrived safely, all of which can be ascertained from a glance at the image on the front. The use of the postcard for this purpose is, moreover, one of correspondence and not for the purpose of enhancing the collector's knowledge of the visited site. It is as a small poster or readymade photograph that the postcard operates as a souvenir.

6 See Chapter 4 for commentary on Steiner's (1999) notion of typicality and seriality in tourist art production.

7 See Chapter 4.

8 While the incidents of contraband coral jewellery being offered to tourists in Australia seem to be very small, the manufacture and sale of black coral souvenirs is reported more widely (see European Commission, *Environment – Wildlife souvenirs guide*; and Bischoff (2001)).

9 See Chapter 2.

10 Levi-Strauss (1979) uses this triangular graphic to demonstrate degrees of cultural development. He shows how raw food is unmediated by culture, while boiled food is reliant upon the development of a flameproof vessel to contain the food and liquid. Smoked food rests in the middle, governed by the use of fire, which Levi-Strauss sees as both natural and cultural. This triangular figuration allows the plotting of variously produced objects and the metaphor matches and describes the level of cultural intervention that has taken place in these essentially Sampled souvenirs. See also Leach (1974).

11 Stewart (1984: 138) disagrees on this point and states that Representative souvenirs appeal more to children because as they have no life history they need to purchase it. This is a very odd statement in an otherwise sound, albeit limited, study of souvenirs. Children are not only without the purchasing power of most adults but are also in possession of a more naturally inquiring mind, that leads them to a primordial engagement with the site, which assists in developing their analytical skills.

12 For further commentary see Urry (1990: 5–17); Shields (1991); and MacCannell (1992).

13 See Chapters 3 and 5.

14 See, for example, Neumann (1963) on Jungian archetypes, in which the tree forms the visual representation of many primordial worlds.

15 See Chapter 4.

16 Hamilton (1984: 8) tells how in 1925 some 70 different wood souvenirs were produced by the Shott family business in Launceston, mostly from Blackwood, but also other minor species timbers, including Tasmanian Tree Fern. She concludes that 'Little has been recorded about these early practitioners and their craft and yet they should be considered the founders of the current renaissance in the use of Tasmania's distinctive timbers'.

17 See Chapter 3.

18 See Chapter 3 on the uniform size of bark paintings requested by missionary settlement art dealers.

19 See Tozer and Fox (2000: 640–641).

20 Isaacs (1992: 46–53) records that 'the late sixties and early seventies' was an important period of development for punu, it 'created an awareness in the state and federal funding bodies concerned with Aboriginal art and craft, that the Pitjantjatjara and Yankunytjatjara communities had a unique genre of craftwork for exhibition and sale'. Today punu is exhibited and sold in every major Australian city and in 2000 exquisite examples of punu from Ernabella were displayed at SOFA Chicago.

21 See Chapter 3.

22 See Chapter 3.

23 See Chapter 2.

24 See Chapter 4.
25 See Chapter 4.
26 Most of the information pertaining to this example was gained in personal conversation with a number of timber craftsmen, while carrying out field work in Far North Queensland.
27 See Chapter 2 in which I have cited Impey's (1977) reference to the Roman appreciation of porcelain china, and Chapter 3 in which I have referred to the distinctive style of Hopi pottery through the writing of Traugott (1999).

Bibliography

Alexander, E. (1979) *Museums in Motion: An Introduction to the History and Functions of Museums*, Nashville: AltaMira Press.

Appleton, J. (1978) *The Experience of Landscape*, London: John Wiley & Sons.

Apter, E. (1993) 'Introduction', in E. Apter and W. Pietz (eds) *Fetishism as Cultural Discourse*, Ithaca and London: Cornell University Press.

Bardon, G. (2000) 'The Papunya Tula Movement', in S. Kleinert and M. Neale (gen. eds) R. Bancroft (cultural ed.) *The Oxford Companion to Aboriginal Art and Culture*, Melbourne: Oxford University Press.

Barnard, A. (2002) 'Hunting-and-gathering society: an eighteenth-century Scottish invention', paper presented at 9th Conference on Hunters and Gatherers, Edinburgh, Scotland.

Batkin, J. (1999) 'Tourism Is Overrated: Pueblo Pottery and the Early Curio Trade 1880–1910', in R. B. Phillips and C. B. Steiner (eds) *Unpacking Culture – Art and Commodity in Colonial and Postcolonial Worlds*, Berkeley: University of California Press.

Baudrillard, J. (1998) *The Consumer society: myths and structures*, London: Sage.

Ben-Amos, P. (1976) 'On Being an Ebony Carver in Benin', in N. Graburn (ed.) *Ethnic and Tourist Arts: Cultural Expressions from the Fourth World*, Berkeley: University of California Press.

Benjamin, W. (1969) 'The Work of Art in the age of Mechanical Reproduction', in H. Arendt (ed.), *Illuminations*, New York: Schocken.

Bermingham, A. (1986) *Landscape and Ideology*, Berkeley: University of California Press.

Berndt, R. (1964) *Australian Aboriginal Art*, Australia: Ure Smith.

Bischoff, B. (2001) 'Reefs in Crisis' American Museum of Natural History. Available online at www.amnh.org/explore/resource-collections/biodiversity-crisis/reefs-in-crisis (accessed 24 June 2012).

Black, R. (1964) *Old and New Aboriginal Art*, Australia: Angus and Robertson.

Bol, M. (1999) 'Defining Lakota Tourist Art, 1880–1915', in R. B. Phillips and C. B. Steiner (eds) *Unpacking Culture – Art and Commodity in Colonial and Postcolonial Worlds*, Berkeley: University of California Press.

Broch, H. (1979) 'Notes On The Problem Of Kitsch', in G. Dorfles (ed.) *Kitsch: The world of bad taste*, New York: Bell Publishing.

Brody, J. J. (1976) 'The Creative Consumer: Survival, Revival, and Invention in Southwest Indian Arts', in N. Graburn (ed.) *Ethnic and Tourist Arts: Cultural Expressions from the Fourth World*, Berkeley: University of California Press.

Brokensha, P. (1987) *The Pitjantjatjara and their Crafts*, Australia: Aboriginal Arts Board.

Clifford, J. (1994) *The Predicament of Culture: twentieth century ethnography, literature and art*, Cambridge: Harvard University Press.

Cooper, C. (1981) *Aboriginal Australia*, Sydney: Australian Gallery Directors Council.

Crawshaw, C. and Urry, J. (1997) 'Tourism and the Photographic Eye', in C. Rojek and J. Urry (eds) *Touring Cultures: Transformations of Travel and Theory*, London: Routledge.

Curran, S. (ed.) (1973) *Blake's sublime allegory: essays on the four Zoas, Milton, Jerusalem*, Madison: University of Wisconsin Press.

European Commission: Environment – Wildlife souvenirs guide. Available at http://ec.europa.eu/environment/cites/info_souvenirs_en.htm (accessed 13 November 2012).

Feddersen, J. and Woody, E. (1999) 'The Story as Primary Source: Educating the Gaze', in W. Jackson Rushing III (ed.) *Native American Art in the Twentieth Century*, London: Routledge.

Franklin, A. (2010) 'Aboriginalia: Souvenir Wares and the 'Aboriginalization' of Australian Identity', *Tourist Studies*, 10 (3): 195–208.

Freud, S. (1962) *Civilisation and its discontents*, New York: WW. Norton.

Fried, M. (1990) *Courbet's Realism*, Chicago: University of Chicago Press.

Geisz, L. (1979) 'Kitsch-man as tourist', in G Dorfles (ed.) *Kitsch: The world of bad taste*, New York: Bell Publishing.

Graburn, N. (ed.) (1976) *Ethnic and Tourist Arts: Cultural Expressions from the Fourth World*, Berkeley: University of California Press.

Graburn, N. (1977) 'Tourism the Sacred Journey', in V. Smith (ed.) *Hosts and Guests: The Anthropology of Tourism*, Philadelphia: University of Pennsylvania Press.

Greenwood, D. (1977) 'Culture by the Pound: An Anthropological Perspective on Tourism as Cultural Commodification', in V. Smith (ed.) *Hosts and Guests: The Anthropology of Tourism*, Philadelphia: University of Pennsylvania Press.

Hamilton, R. (1984) 'Pioneers In 20th Century Tasmanian Wood Souvenirs', *Tasmanian Wood,* No. 9, May–June.

Hart, C. W. M. and Piling, A. R. (1960) *The Tiwi of North Australia*, New York: Holt Rinehart & Winston.

Heathcote, C. (2001) 'When science meets art: Humbolt, von Guerard and the Australian Wilderness', *Australian Art Monthly*, Nov. #145.

Hinnerson-Berglund, M. (2002) 'GLACIER ICE AND ROCK CRYSTAL: the material and ritual landscape of the Palaeo-Inuit in the Nuuk Fjord in Greenland', paper presented at 9th Conference on Hunters and Gatherers, Edinburgh, Scotland.

Hirsch, E. D. (1964) *Innocence and experience: an introduction to Blake*, New Haven: Yale University Press.

Hume, D. L. (2009) 'The development of tourist art and souvenirs – the arc of the boomerang: from hunting, fighting and ceremony to tourist souvenir', *International Journal of Tourism Research*, Volume 11, Issue 1: 55–70.

Impey, O. (1977) *Chinoiserie: The impact of Oriental Styles on Western Art and Decoration*, New York: Charles Scribner's Sons.

Inglis, S. R. (1999) 'Master, Machine and Meaning: Printed Images in Twentieth – Century India', in R. B. Phillips and C. B. Steiner (eds) *Unpacking Culture – Art and Commodity in Colonial and Postcolonial Worlds*, Berkeley: University of California Press.

Isaacs, J. (1992) *Desert Crafts: Anangu Maruku pu<u>n</u>u*, Sydney: Doubleday.

Jackson Rushing III, W. (ed.) (1999) *Native American Art in the Twentieth Century.* London: Routledge.

Jampijin, R. (1988) 'Boomerang Making At Yaruman', in P. Taylor (ed.) *After 200 Years: Photographic Essays of Aboriginal and Islander Australia Today*, Canberra: Aboriginal Studies Press.

Johannes, C. (1992) *W.C. Piguenit 1836–1914 Retrospective*, Australia: Tasmanian Museum and Art Gallery.

Jones, P. (1996) *Boomerang: Behind an Australian Icon*, Berkeley: Ten Speed Press.

Jung, C. G. (1972) *Four archetypes: mother, rebirth, spirit, trickster*, R. F. C. Hull (trans.), London: Routledge and K. Paul.

Kasfir, S. L. (1999) 'Samburu Souvenirs: Representations of a Land in Amber', in R. B. Phillips and C. B. Steiner (eds) *Unpacking Culture – Art and Commodity in Colonial and Postcolonial Worlds*, Berkeley: University of California Press.

Keringke Arts Centre (1999) *Keringke: Contemporary Eastern Arrente Art*, Alice Springs: Jukurrpa Books.

Kleinert, S. and Neale, M. (gen. eds) Bancroft, R. (cultural ed.) (2000) *The Oxford Companion to Aboriginal Art and Culture*, Melbourne: Oxford University Press.

Krauss, R. (1986) *The Originality of the Avant Garde and Other Modernist Myths.* Cambridge: MIT Press.

Lathrap, D. W. (1976) 'Shipibo Tourist Art', in N. Graburn (ed.) *Ethnic and Tourist Arts: Cultural Expressions from the Fourth World*, Berkeley: University of California Press.

Leach, E. (1974) *Levi-Strauss*, London: Fontana/Collins.

Lee, M. (1999) 'Tourism and Taste Cultures: Collecting Native Art in Alaska at the Turn of the Twentieth Century', in R. B. Phillips, and C. B. Steiner (eds) *Unpacking Culture – Art and Commodity in Colonial and Postcolonial Worlds*, Berkeley: University of California Press.

Levi-Strauss, C. (1958) *Structural Anthropology Volume 1*, New York and London: Basic Books.

Levi-Strauss, C. (1979) *The Raw and the Cooked*, New York: Octagon Books.

Lippard, L. (1999a) 'Independent Identities', in W Jackson Rushing III (ed.) *Native American Art in the Twentieth Century*, London: Routledge.

Lippard, L. (1999b) *On The Beaten Track*, New York: New Press.

Lurry, C. (1997) 'The Objects of Travel', in C. Rojek and J. Urry (eds) *Touring Cultures: Transformations of Travel and Theory*, London: Routledge.

MacCannell, D. (1976) *The Tourist: A New Theory of the Leisure Class*, U.S: Macmillan.

MacCannell, D. (1992) *Empty Meeting Grounds*, London and New York: Routledge.

MacGregor, A. (ed.) (1985) *Tradescent Rarities*, U.K: Oxford University Press.

Maduro, R. (1976) 'The Brahmin Painters of Nathdwara, Rajasthan', in N. Graburn (ed.) *Ethnic and Tourist Arts: Cultural Expressions from the Fourth World*, Berkeley: University of California Press.

Marx, K. (1951) *Theories of Surplus Value*, London: Lawrence & Wishart.

Marx, K. (1954) *Capital: A Critique of Political Economy Vol. 1*, London: Lawrence & Wishart.

Mason, K. (2000) 'Made from memory' in conversation with S. Jenkins, in *Keeping Culture: Aboriginal Art to Keeping Places and Cultural Centres*, Canberra: National Gallery of Australia.

Maughan, J. (1986) *The Dreamtime Today: A Survey of Contemporary Aboriginal Arts and Crafts*, Adelaide: Flinders University of South Australia.

Megaw, J. V. S. (1986) 'The Dreamtime Yesterday and Today', in *The Dreamtime*

Today: A Survey of Contemporary Aboriginal Arts and Crafts, Adelaide: Flinders University of South Australia.

Morphy, H. (1991) *Ancestral Connections: Art and an Aboriginal System of Knowledge*, Chicago: University of Chicago Press.

Morphy, H. (1998) *Aboriginal Art*, London: Phaidon.

Mulvey, L. (1996) *Fetishism and Curiosity,* Bloomington: BFI Publishing Indiana University Press.

Nash, D. (1977) 'Tourism as a form of Imperialism', in V. Smith (ed.) *Hosts and Guests: The Anthropology of Tourism*, Philadelphia: University of Pennsylvania Press.

Neale, M. (2000) 'Renegotiating Tradition: Before visibility', in S. Kleinert and M. Neale (gen. eds) R. Bancroft (cultural ed.) *The Oxford Companion to Aboriginal Art and Culture*, Melbourne: Oxford University Press.

Neumann, E. (1963) *The great mother: an analysis of the archetype*, R. Manheim (trans.), Princeton, NJ: Princeton University Press.

Nicks, T. (1999) 'Indian Villages and Entertainments: Setting the Stage for Tourist Souvenir Sales', in R. B. Phillips and C. B. Steiner (eds) *Unpacking Culture – Art and Commodity in Colonial and Postcolonial Worlds*, Berkeley: University of California Press.

Nochlin, L. (1986) 'Courbet's *L'Origin du monde*: The Origin without an Original', *October.* vol. 37, Summer.

Ousby, I. (2002) *The Englishman's England: Taste, Travel and the Rise of Tourism*, London: Pimlico.

Panofsky, E. (1972) *Studies in Iconology*, New York: Harper & Row.

Pearce, S. (ed.) (1991) *Museum Studies in Material Culture*, Washington DC: Smithsonian Institution Press.

Pearce, S. (1995) *On Collecting: An investigation into collecting in the European tradition*, London: Routledge.

Pearce, W. (1988) 'Boomerang factory at Robinvale', in P. Taylor (ed.) *After 200 Years: Photographic Essays of Aboriginal and Islander Australia Today*, Canberra: Aboriginal Studies Press.

Phillips, R. (1999) 'Nuns, Ladies and 'The Queen of the Huron': Appropriating the Savage in Nineteenth-Century Huron Tourist Art', in R. B. Phillips and C. B. Steiner (eds) *Unpacking Culture – Art and Commodity in Colonial and Postcolonial Worlds*, Berkeley: University of California Press.

Phillips, R. B. and Steiner, C. B. (1999) 'Art, Authenticity, and the Baggage of Cultural Encounter', in R. B. Phillips and C. B. Steiner (eds) *Unpacking Culture – Art and Commodity in Colonial and Postcolonial Worlds*, Berkeley: University of California Press.

Pietz, W. (1993) 'Fetishism and Materialism: The Limits of Theory in Marx', in E. Apter and W. Pietz (eds) *Fetishism as Cultural Discourse*, Ithaca and London: Cornell University Press.

Potter, K. (1999) 'James Houston, Armchair Tourism, and the Marketing of Inuit Art', in W. Jackson Rushing III (ed.) *Native American Art in the Twentieth Century*, London: Routledge.

Relph, E. (1976) *Place and Placelessness.* London: Pion.

Richards, G. (2011) 'CREATIVITY AND TOURISM: The State of the Art', *Annals of Tourism Research*, Vol. 38, No. 4: 1225–1253.

Rojek, C. (1997) 'Indexing, Dragging and the Social Construction of Tourist Sights', in C. Rojek and J. Urry (eds) *Touring Cultures: Transformations of Travel and Theory*, London: Routledge.

Rose, S. (2000) Artist's statement included on the reverse of the artwork.

Sayers, A. (1994) *Aboriginal Artists of the Nineteenth Century*, Melbourne: Oxford University Press.

Shields, R. (1991) *Places on the Margin: alternative geographies of modernity*, London: Routledge.

Snider, T. (1988) 'Tasman Snider Carving A Boomerang Outside His Home In Mantaka Watched By Leroy Diamond And Fleur Hobson', in P. Taylor (ed.) *After 200 Years: Photographic Essays of Aboriginal and Islander Australia Today*, Canberra: Aboriginal Studies Press.

Smith, B. (1992) *Imagining the Pacific: In the Wake of Cook's Voyages*, Australia: Melbourne University Press.

Smith, V. (1977) 'Introduction', in V. Smith (ed.) *Hosts and Guests: The Anthropology of Tourism*, Philadelphia: University of Pennsylvania Press.

SOFA Chicago. Available online at www.sofaexpo.com (accessed 20 November 2003).

Soper, K. (1995) *What is Nature*, Malden, MA: Blackwell.

Steiner, C. B. (1999) 'Authenticity, Repetition and the Aesthetics of Seriality: The Work of Tourist Art in the Age of Mechanical Reproduction', in R. B. Phillips and C. B. Steiner (eds) *Unpacking Culture – Art and Commodity in Colonial and Postcolonial Worlds*, Berkeley: University of California Press.

Sternberg, J. (1972) *Kitsch*, London: Academy Editions.

Stewart, S. (1984) *On Longing*, Baltimore: Johns Hopkins University Press.

Strain, E. (1996) 'Exotic Bodies, Distant Landscapes: Touristic Viewing and Popularised Anthropology in the Nineteenth Century', in *Wide Angle*, 18.2, Ohio: Ohio University School of Film.

The Dreamtime Today: A Survey of Contemporary Aboriginal Arts and Crafts (1986) Kintore Gallery 10–28 September 1986, Adelaide: Flinders University South Australia.

The Historical Development of the Ashmolean. Available online at www.ashmol.ox.ac.uk/ash/faqs/q003/html (accessed 17 June 2003).

Taylor, P. (ed.) (1988) *After 200 Years: Photographic Essays of Aboriginal and Islander Australia Today*, Canberra: Aboriginal Studies Press.

Torgovnick, M. (1990) *Gone Primitive, Savage Intellects, Modern Lives*, Chicago and London: University of Chicago Press.

Townsend-Gault, C. (1999) 'Hot Dogs, a Ball Gown, Adobe and Words', in W. Jackson Rushing III (ed.) *Native American Art in the Twentieth Century*, London: Routledge.

Tozer, K. and Fox, S. (2000) 'Maruku Arts and Crafts', in S. Kleinert and M. Neale (gen. eds) R. Bancroft (Cultural Ed.) *The Oxford Companion to Aboriginal Art and Culture*, Melbourne: Oxford University Press.

Traugott, J. (1999) 'Fewkes and Nampeyo. Clarifying a Myth-Understanding', in W. Jackson Rushing III (ed.) *Native American Art in the Twentieth Century*, London: Routledge.

Tuckson, J. A. (1964) 'Introduction', in R. Berndt *Australian Aboriginal Art*, Australia: Ure Smith.

Turner, L. and Ash, J. (1976) *The Golden Hordes*, New York: St. Martins Press.

Urry, J. (1990) *The Tourist Gaze: Leisure and Travel in Contemporary Societies*, London: Sage Publications.

Williams, N. (1976) 'Australian Aboriginal Art at Yirrkala', in N. Graburn (ed.) *Ethnic and Tourist Arts: Cultural Expressions from the Fourth World*, Berkeley: University of California Press.

Index

Page numbers in *italics* denote tables, those in **bold** denote figures.